POOL DARK REIGN

WRITER: **DANIEL WAY** • PENCILS: **PACO MEDINA**

INKS: **JUAN VLASCO** WITH **SANDU FLOREA**

COLORS: **MARTE GRACIA** WITH **RAÚL TREVIÑO**

LETTERS: **VIRTUAL CALLIGRAPHY'S CORY PETIT**

COVER ARTIST: **JASON PEARSON**

ASSISTANT EDITOR: **JODY LEHEUP**

EDITOR: **AXEL ALONSO**

COLLECTION EDITOR: **CORY LEVINE**

ASSISTANT EDITOR: **SARAH BRUNSTAD**

ASSOCIATE MANAGING EDITOR: **ALEX STARBUCK**

EDITORS, SPECIAL PROJECTS: **JENNIFER GRÜNWALD** & **MARK D. BEAZLEY**

SENIOR EDITOR, SPECIAL PROJECTS: **JEFF YOUNGQUIST**

SVP PRINT, SALES & MARKETING: **DAVID GABRIEL**

BOOK DESIGN: **RODOLFO MURAGUCHI**

EDITOR IN CHIEF: **AXEL ALONSO**

CHIEF CREATIVE OFFICER: **JOE QUESADA**

PUBLISHER: **DAN BUCKLEY**

EXECUTIVE PRODUCER: **ALAN FINE**

PREVIOUSLY:

RECENTLY, DEADPOOL INFILTRATED A LEGION OF THE INVADING SKRULL ARMY IN AN ATTEMPT TO GATHER VITAL SKRULL BIO-DATA FOR NICK FURY. THE GOOD NEWS: HE BEAT THE CRAP OUT OF THE SKRULLS AND GOT THE DATA! THE BAD NEWS: THE TRANSMISSION WAS INTERCEPTED — BY NONE OTHER THAN NORMAN OSBORN — AND NEVER GOT TO NICK! WHAT DOES OSBORN INTEND TO DO WITH THAT DATA? NO DOUBT, THE WORLD WILL FIND OUT SOON ENOUGH…

IN THE MEANTIME, DEADPOOL IS ON HIS WAY HOME FROM A RECENT ASSIGNMENT IN EASTERN EUROPE WHEN HE IS MYSTERIOUSLY ATTACKED BY THE SAVAGE MAN-FISH, TIGER SHARK!

S0-AHX-566

6

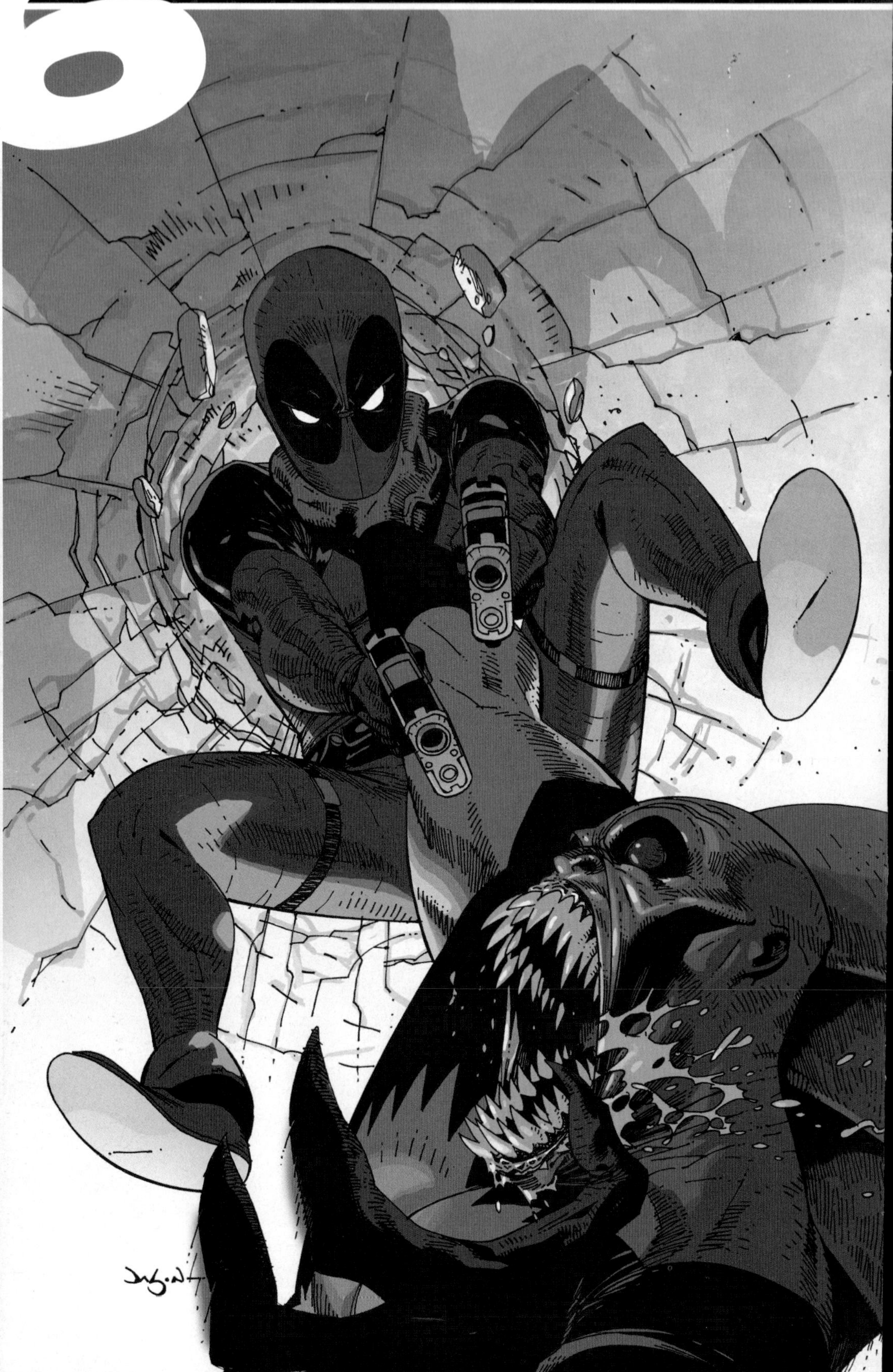

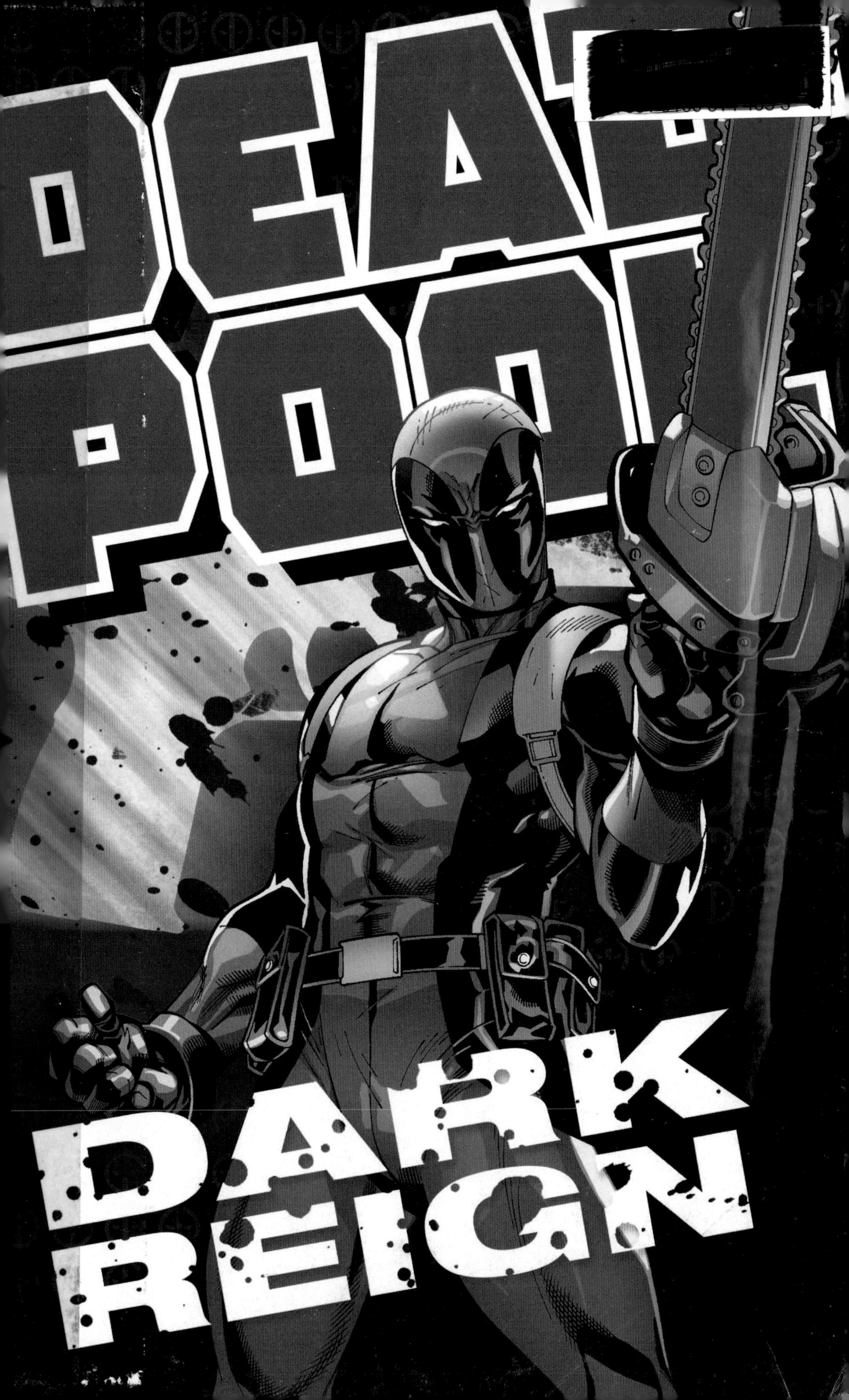
[redacted]
DARK
REIGN

DEADPOOL VOL. 2: DARK REIGN. Contains material originally published in magazine form as DEADPOOL #6-7 and #10-12. Sixth printing 2014. ISBN# 978-0-7851-3274-5. Published by MARVEL WORLDWIDE, a subsidiary of MARVEL ENTERTAINMENT, LLC. OFFICE OF PUBLICATION: 135 West 50th Street, New York, NY 10020. Copyright © 2009 Marvel Characters, Inc. All rights reserved. All characters featured in this and the distinctive names and likenesses thereof, and all related indicia are trademarks of Marvel Characters, Inc. No similarity between any of the names, characters, persons, and/or institutions in this mag with those of any living or dead person or institution is intended, and any such similarity which may exist is purely coincidental. **Printed in the U.S.A.** ALAN FINE, EVP - Office of the President, Marvel Worldwid and EVP & CMO Marvel Characters B.V.; DAN BUCKLEY, Publisher & President - Print, Animation & Digital Divisions; JOE QUESADA, Chief Creative Officer; TOM BREVOORT, SVP of Publishing; DAVID BOGART, S Operations & Procurement, Publishing; C.B. CEBULSKI, SVP of Creator & Content Development; DAVID GABRIEL, SVP Print, Sales & Marketing; JIM O'KEEFE, VP of Operations & Logistics; DAN CARR, Executive Di of Publishing Technology; SUSAN CRESPI, Editorial Operations Manager; ALEX MORALES, Publishing Operations Manager; STAN LEE, Chairman Emeritus. For information regarding advertising in Marvel Comics Marvel.com, please contact Niza Disla, Director of Marvel Partnerships, at ndisla@marvel.com. For Marvel subscription inquiries, please call 800-217-9158. **Manufactured between 10/22/2014 and 11/24/20** **R.R. DONNELLEY, INC., SALEM, VA, USA.**

10 9 8 7 6

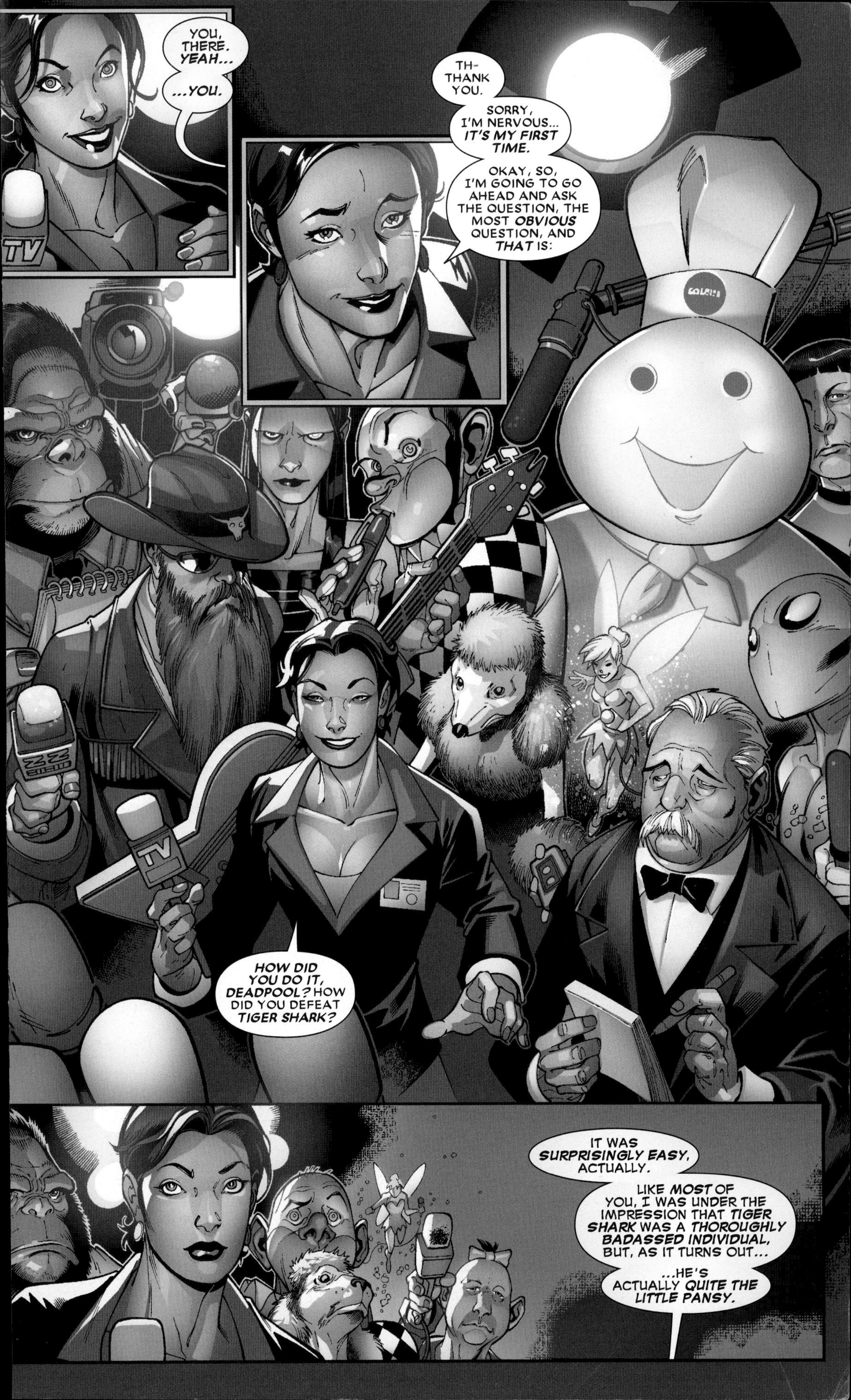
YOU, THERE. YEAH...
...YOU.
TH-THANK YOU.
SORRY, I'M NERVOUS... IT'S MY FIRST TIME.
OKAY, SO, I'M GOING TO GO AHEAD AND ASK THE QUESTION, THE MOST OBVIOUS QUESTION, AND THAT IS:
HOW DID YOU DO IT, DEADPOOL? HOW DID YOU DEFEAT TIGER SHARK?
IT WAS SURPRISINGLY EASY, ACTUALLY.
LIKE MOST OF YOU, I WAS UNDER THE IMPRESSION THAT TIGER SHARK WAS A THOROUGHLY BADASSED INDIVIDUAL, BUT, AS IT TURNS OUT...
...HE'S ACTUALLY QUITE THE LITTLE PANSY.

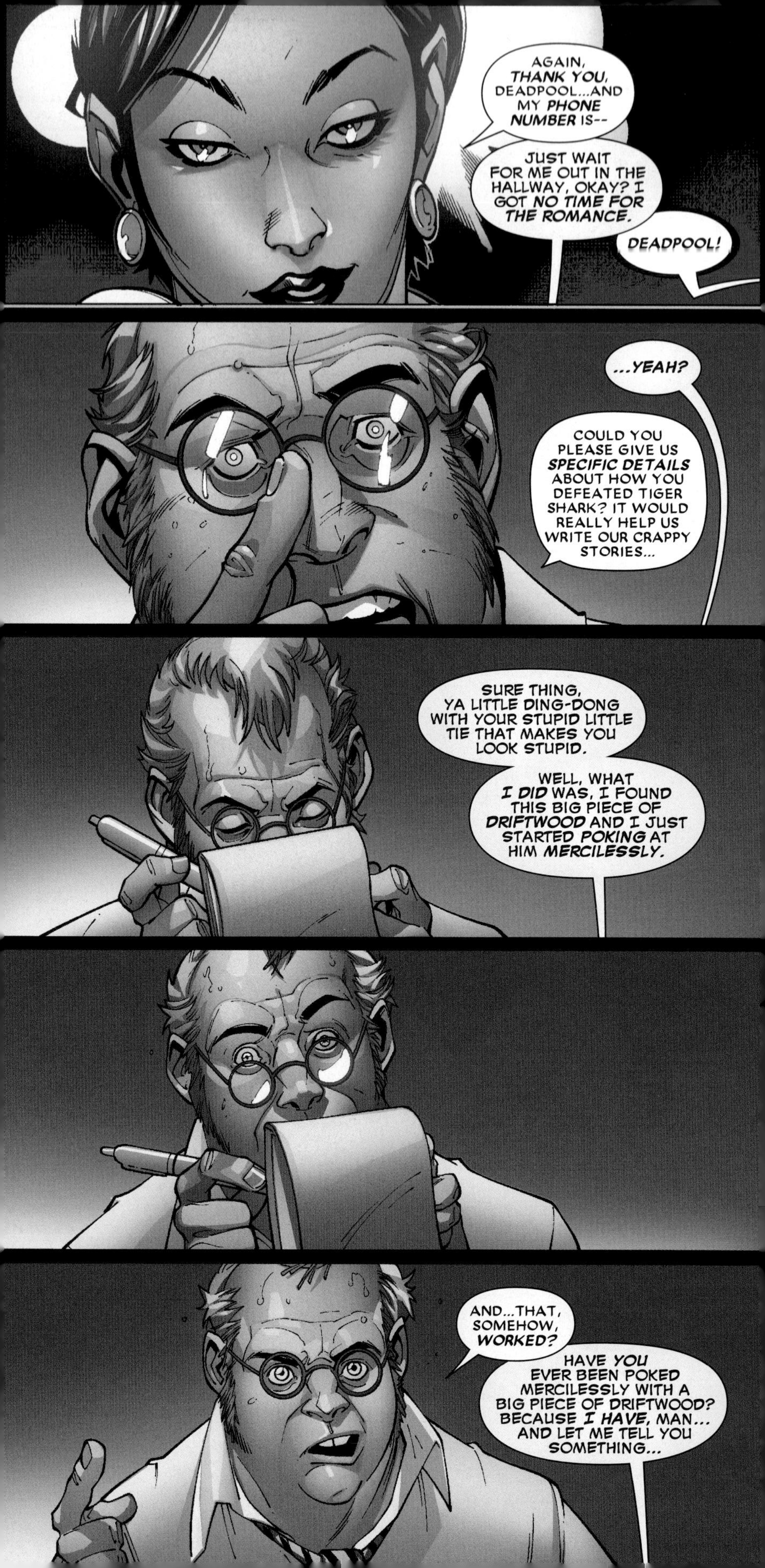
AGAIN, THANK YOU, DEADPOOL...AND MY PHONE NUMBER IS--
JUST WAIT FOR ME OUT IN THE HALLWAY, OKAY? I GOT NO TIME FOR THE ROMANCE.
DEADPOOL!
...YEAH?
COULD YOU PLEASE GIVE US SPECIFIC DETAILS ABOUT HOW YOU DEFEATED TIGER SHARK? IT WOULD REALLY HELP US WRITE OUR CRAPPY STORIES...
SURE THING, YA LITTLE DING-DONG WITH YOUR STUPID LITTLE TIE THAT MAKES YOU LOOK STUPID.
WELL, WHAT I DID WAS, I FOUND THIS BIG PIECE OF DRIFTWOOD AND I JUST STARTED POKING AT HIM MERCILESSLY.
AND...THAT, SOMEHOW, WORKED?
HAVE YOU EVER BEEN POKED MERCILESSLY WITH A BIG PIECE OF DRIFTWOOD? BECAUSE I HAVE, MAN... AND LET ME TELL YOU SOMETHING...

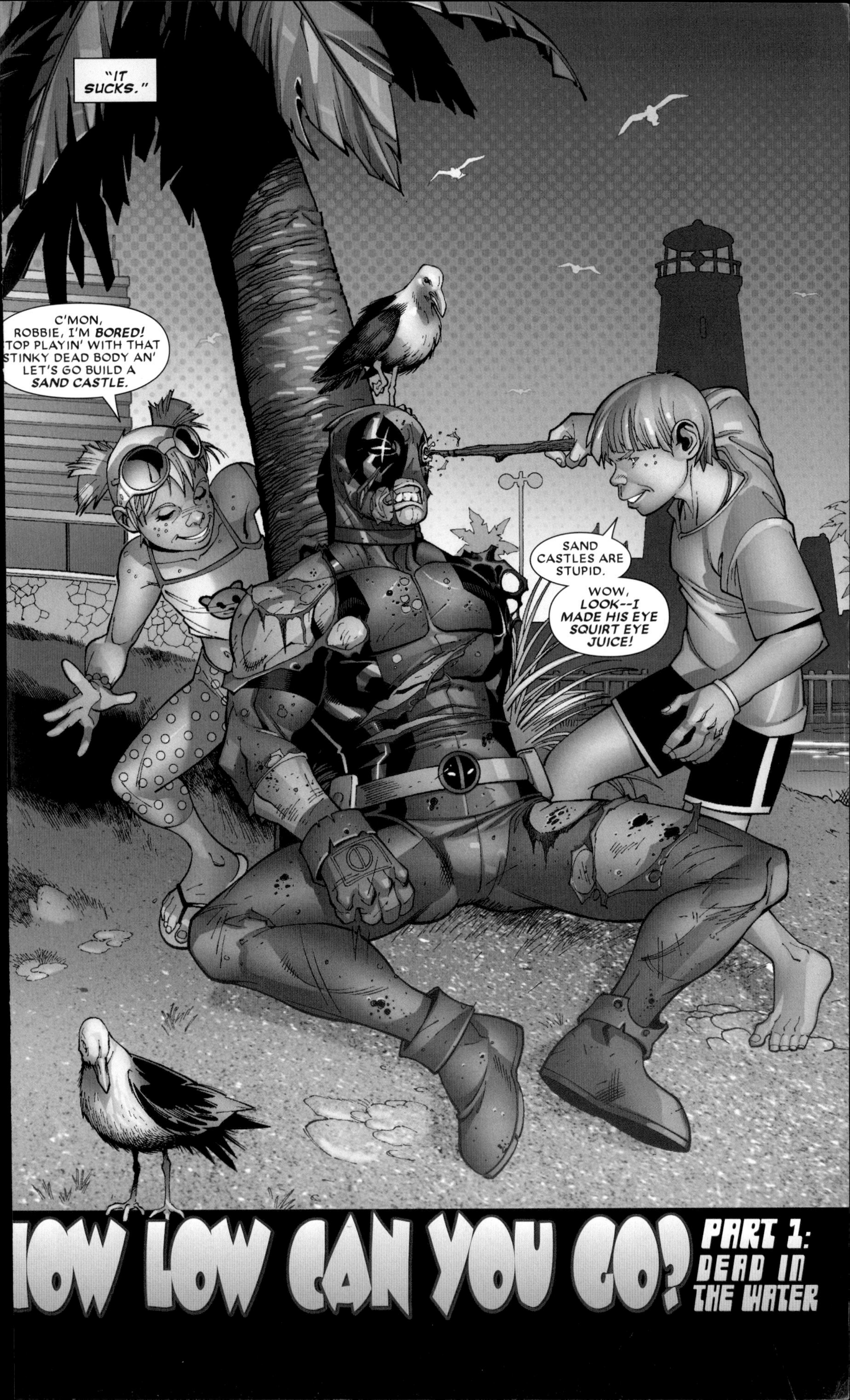

"IT SUCKS."
C'MON, ROBBIE, I'M BORED! TOP PLAYIN' WITH THAT TINKY DEAD BODY AN' LET'S GO BUILD A SAND CASTLE.
SAND CASTLES ARE STUPID.
WOW, LOOK--I MADE HIS EYE SQUIRT EYE JUICE!
IOW LOW CAN YOU GO?
PART 1: DEAD IN THE WATER

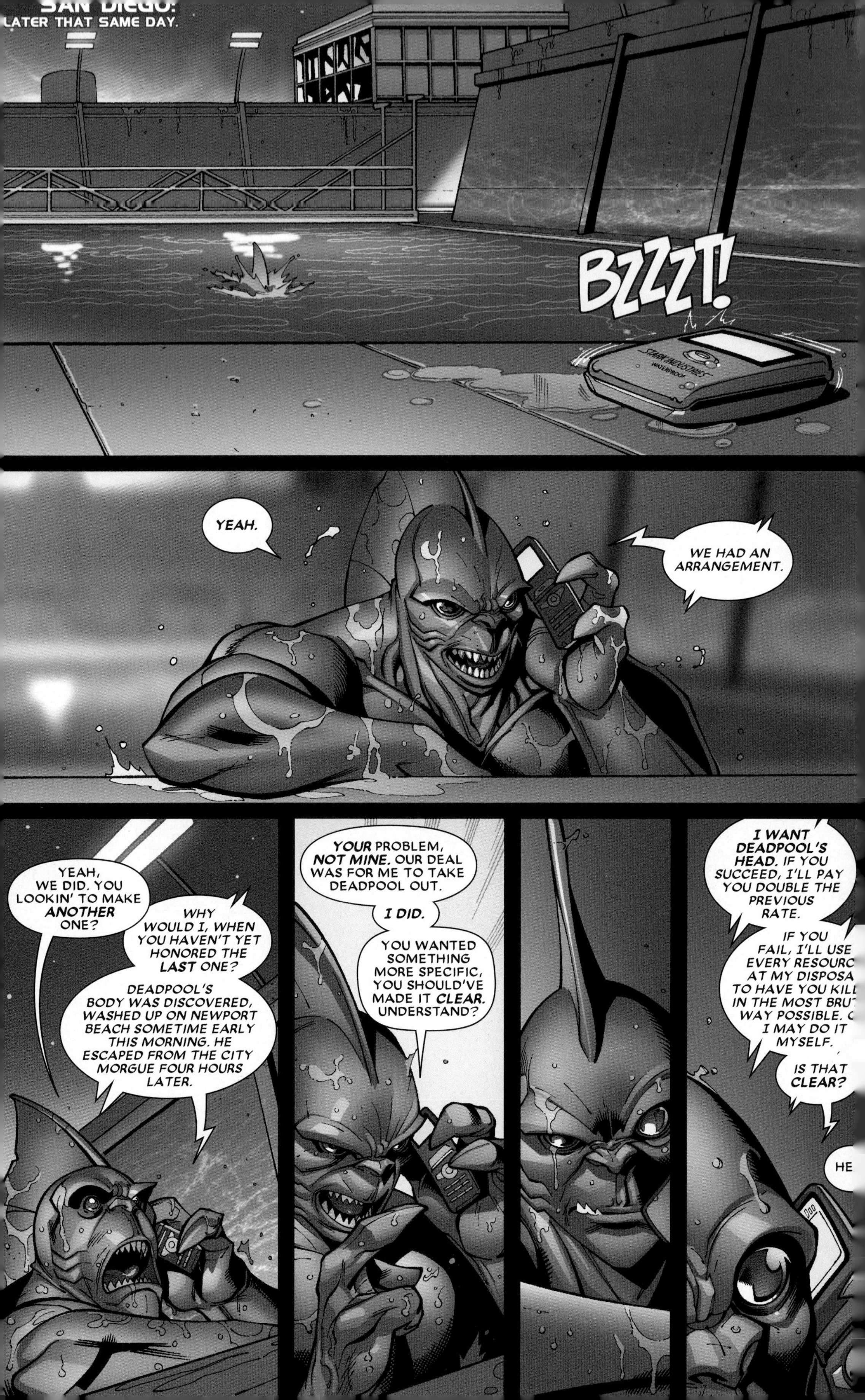

SAN DIEGO:
LATER THAT SAME DAY.
BZZZT!
STARK INDUSTRIES
WATERPROOF
YEAH.
WE HAD AN ARRANGEMENT.
YEAH, WE DID. YOU LOOKIN' TO MAKE ANOTHER ONE?
WHY WOULD I, WHEN YOU HAVEN'T YET HONORED THE LAST ONE?
DEADPOOL'S BODY WAS DISCOVERED, WASHED UP ON NEWPORT BEACH SOMETIME EARLY THIS MORNING. HE ESCAPED FROM THE CITY MORGUE FOUR HOURS LATER.
YOUR PROBLEM, NOT MINE. OUR DEAL WAS FOR ME TO TAKE DEADPOOL OUT.
I DID.
YOU WANTED SOMETHING MORE SPECIFIC, YOU SHOULD'VE MADE IT CLEAR. UNDERSTAND?
I WANT DEADPOOL'S HEAD. IF YOU SUCCEED, I'LL PAY YOU DOUBLE THE PREVIOUS RATE.
IF YOU FAIL, I'LL USE EVERY RESOURC AT MY DISPOSA TO HAVE YOU KILL IN THE MOST BRUT WAY POSSIBLE. I MAY DO IT MYSELF.
IS THAT CLEAR?
HE

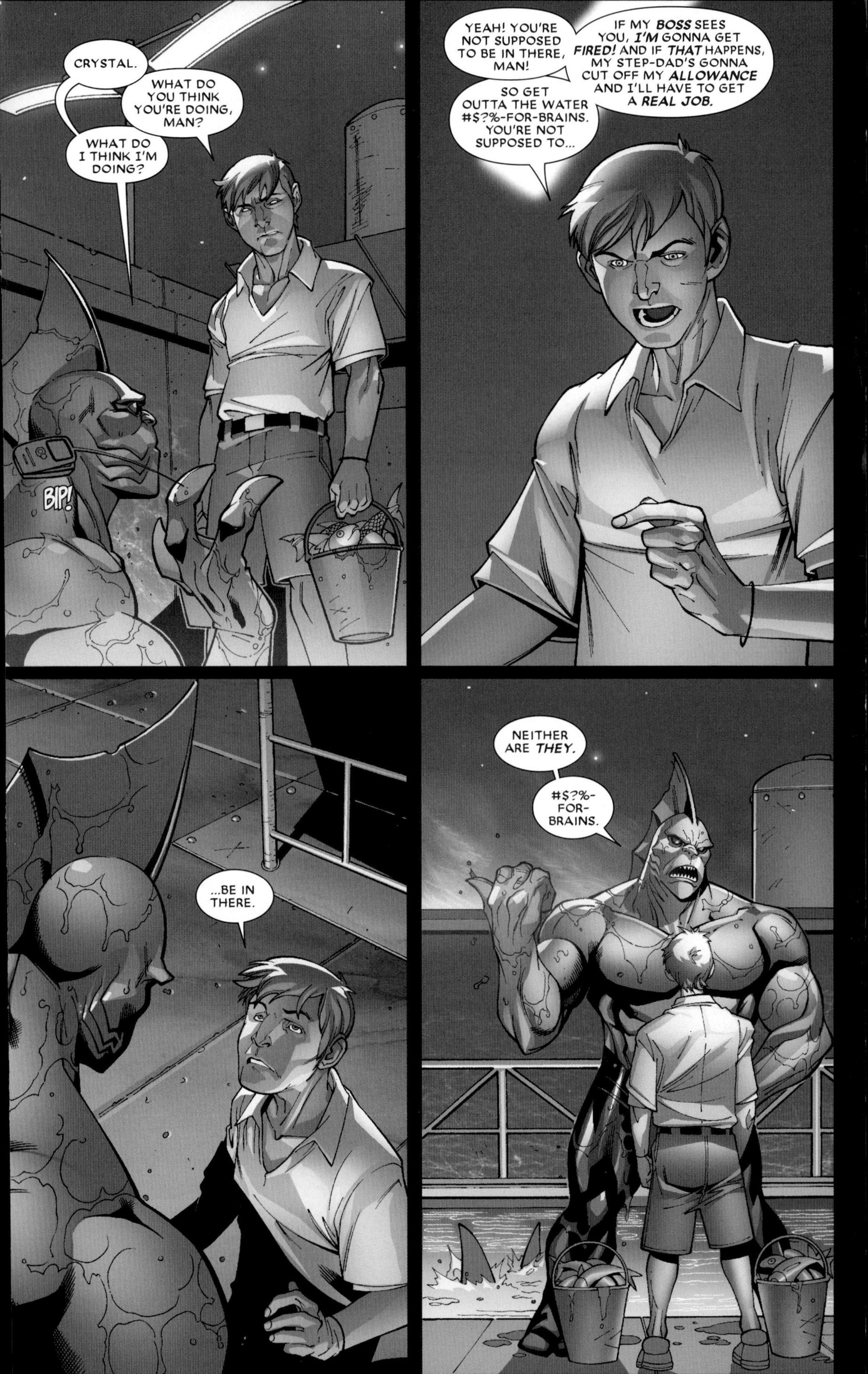
CRYSTAL.
WHAT DO YOU THINK YOU'RE DOING, MAN?
WHAT DO I THINK I'M DOING?
BIP!
YEAH! YOU'RE NOT SUPPOSED TO BE IN THERE, MAN!
IF MY BOSS SEES YOU, I'M GONNA GET FIRED! AND IF THAT HAPPENS, MY STEP-DAD'S GONNA CUT OFF MY ALLOWANCE AND I'LL HAVE TO GET A REAL JOB.
SO GET OUTTA THE WATER #$?%-FOR-BRAINS. YOU'RE NOT SUPPOSED TO...
...BE IN THERE.
NEITHER ARE THEY.
#$?%-FOR-BRAINS.

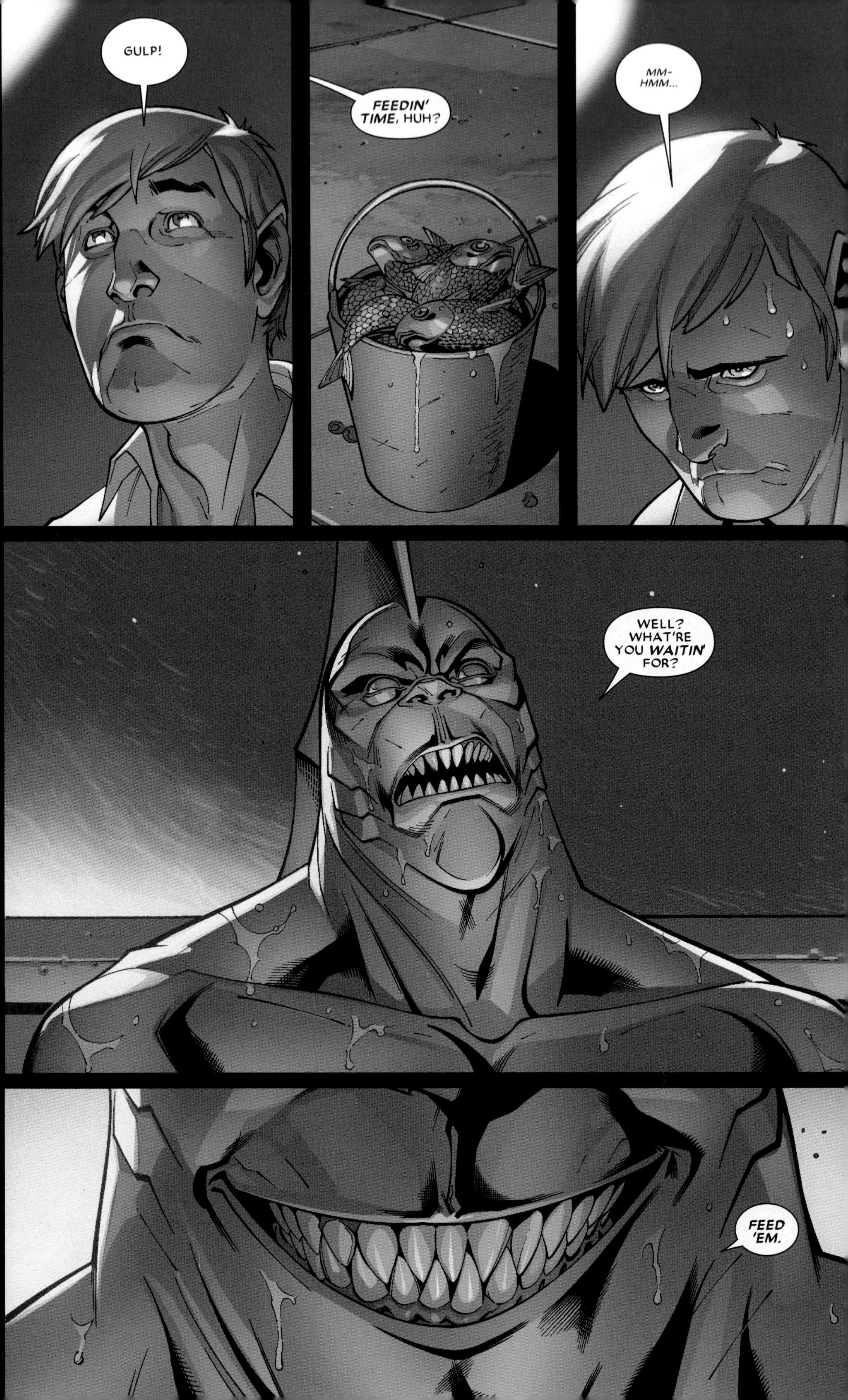
GULP!
FEEDIN' TIME, HUH?
MM-HMM...
WELL? WHAT'RE YOU WAITIN' FOR?
FEED 'EM.

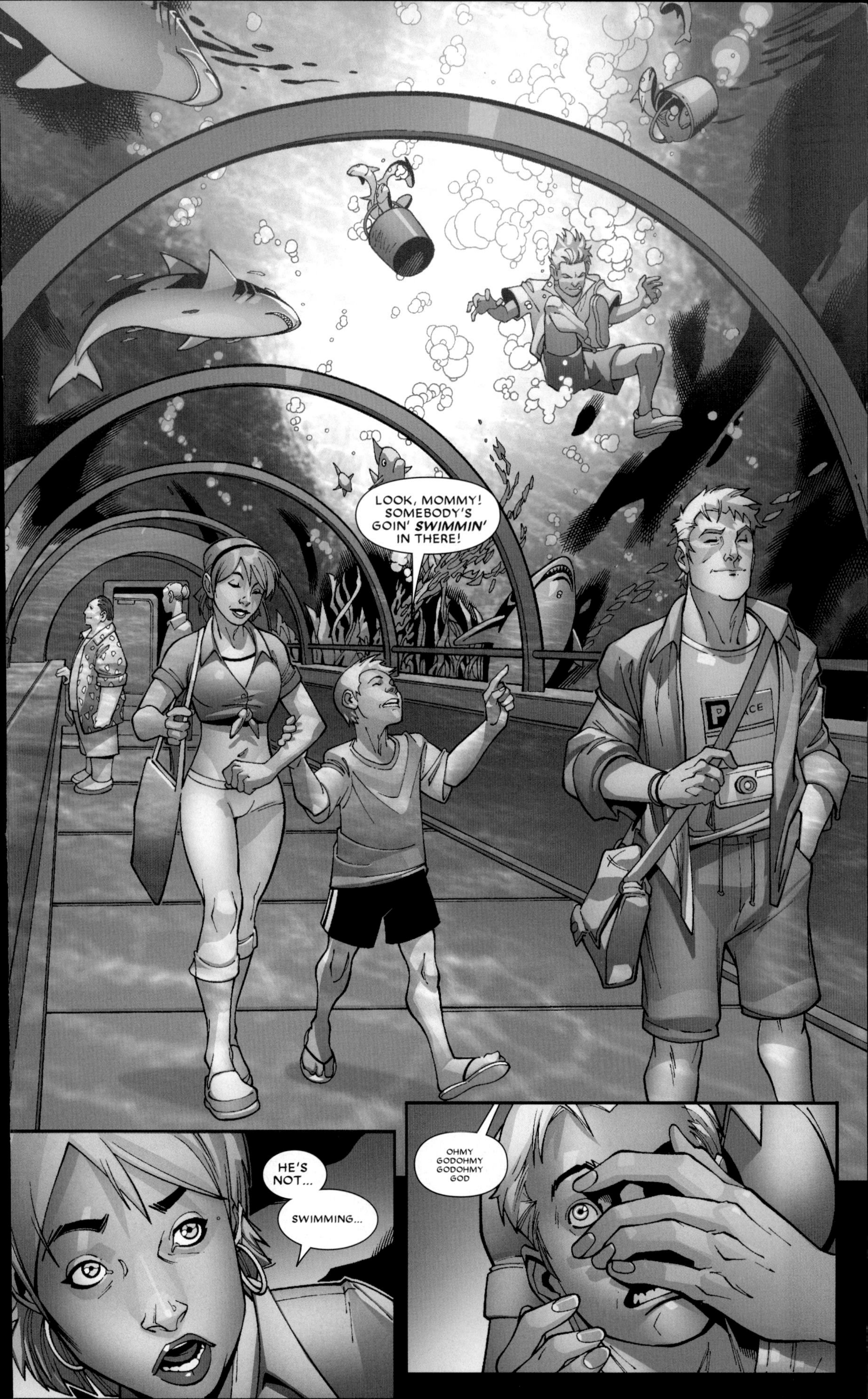
LOOK, MOMMY! SOMEBODY'S GOIN' SWIMMIN' IN THERE!
HE'S NOT...
SWIMMING...
OHMY GODOHMY GODOHMY GOD

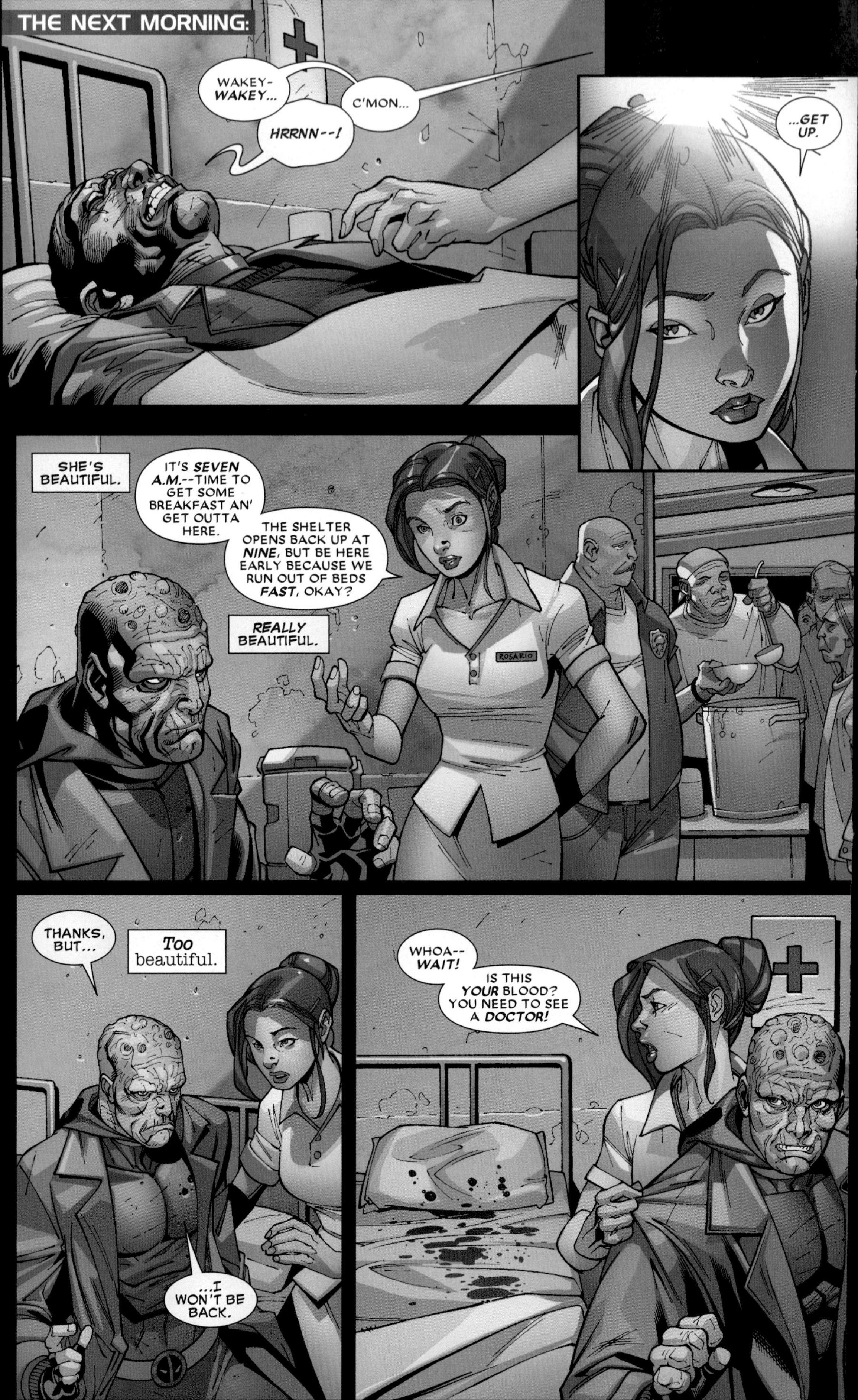
THE NEXT MORNING:
WAKEY-WAKEY...
C'MON...
HRRNN--!
...GET UP.
SHE'S BEAUTIFUL.
IT'S SEVEN A.M.--TIME TO GET SOME BREAKFAST AN' GET OUTTA HERE.
THE SHELTER OPENS BACK UP AT NINE, BUT BE HERE EARLY BECAUSE WE RUN OUT OF BEDS FAST, OKAY?
REALLY BEAUTIFUL.
ROSARIO
THANKS, BUT...
Too beautiful.
...I WON'T BE BACK.
WHOA--WAIT!
IS THIS YOUR BLOOD? YOU NEED TO SEE A DOCTOR!

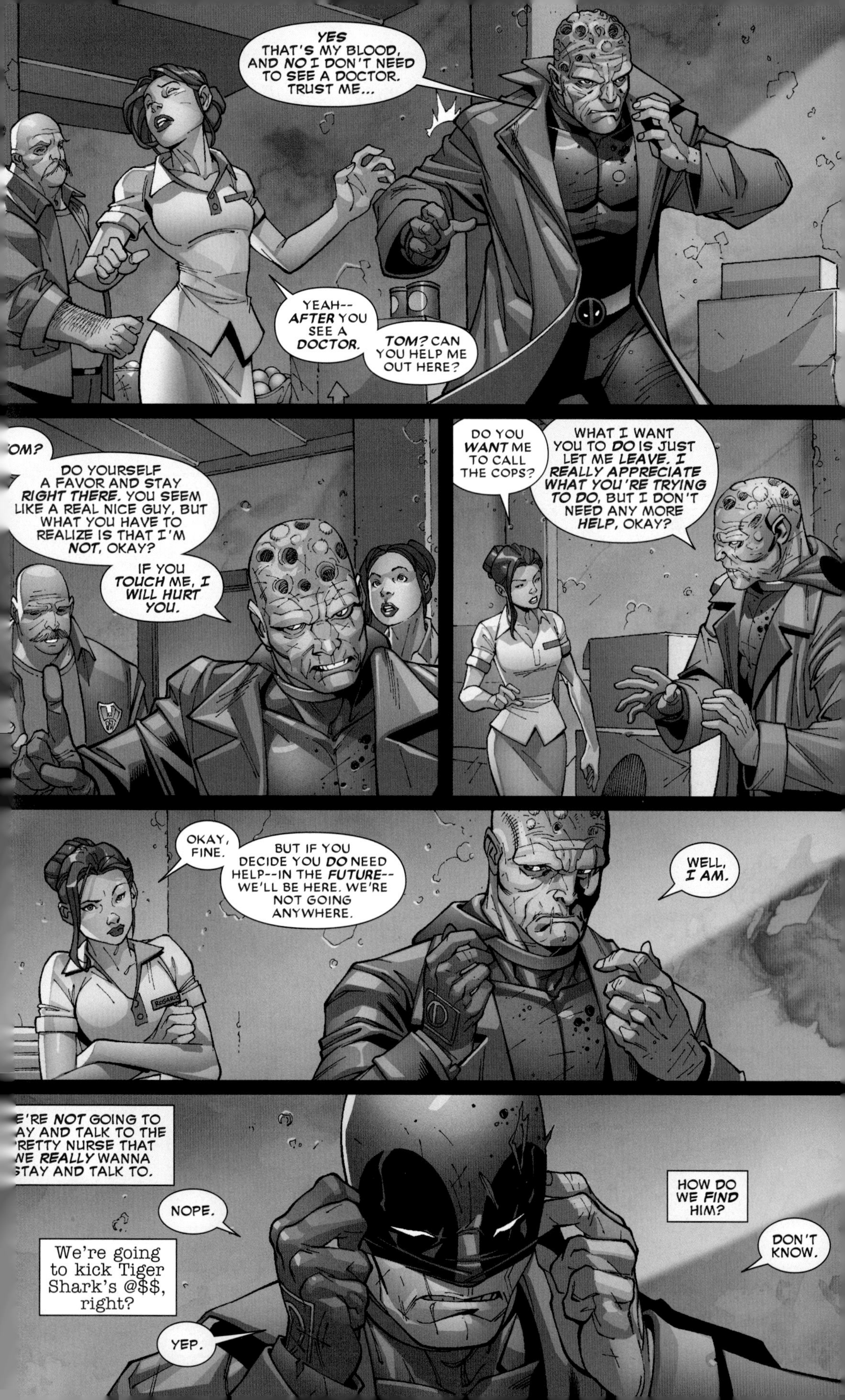
YES THAT'S MY BLOOD, AND NO I DON'T NEED TO SEE A DOCTOR. TRUST ME...
YEAH-- AFTER YOU SEE A DOCTOR.
TOM? CAN YOU HELP ME OUT HERE?
OM?
DO YOURSELF A FAVOR AND STAY RIGHT THERE. YOU SEEM LIKE A REAL NICE GUY, BUT WHAT YOU HAVE TO REALIZE IS THAT I'M NOT, OKAY?
IF YOU TOUCH ME, I WILL HURT YOU.
DO YOU WANT ME TO CALL THE COPS?
WHAT I WANT YOU TO DO IS JUST LET ME LEAVE. I REALLY APPRECIATE WHAT YOU'RE TRYING TO DO, BUT I DON'T NEED ANY MORE HELP, OKAY?
OKAY, FINE.
BUT IF YOU DECIDE YOU DO NEED HELP--IN THE FUTURE-- WE'LL BE HERE. WE'RE NOT GOING ANYWHERE.
WELL, I AM.
E'RE NOT GOING TO AY AND TALK TO THE RETTY NURSE THAT WE REALLY WANNA STAY AND TALK TO.
NOPE.
We're going to kick Tiger Shark's @$$, right?
YEP.
HOW DO WE FIND HIM?
DON'T KNOW.

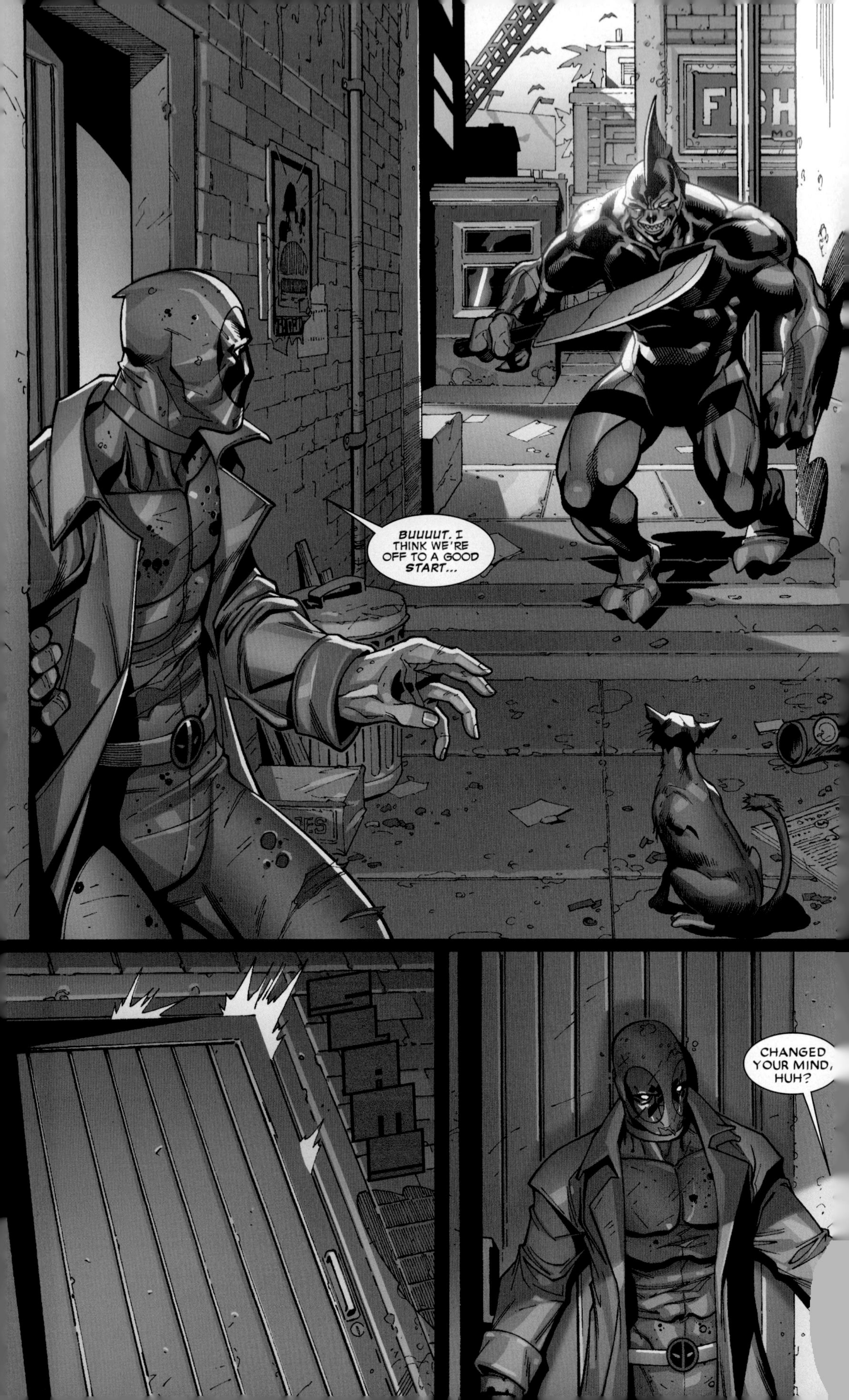
BUUUUT. I THINK WE'RE OFF TO A GOOD START...
CHANGED YOUR MIND, HUH?

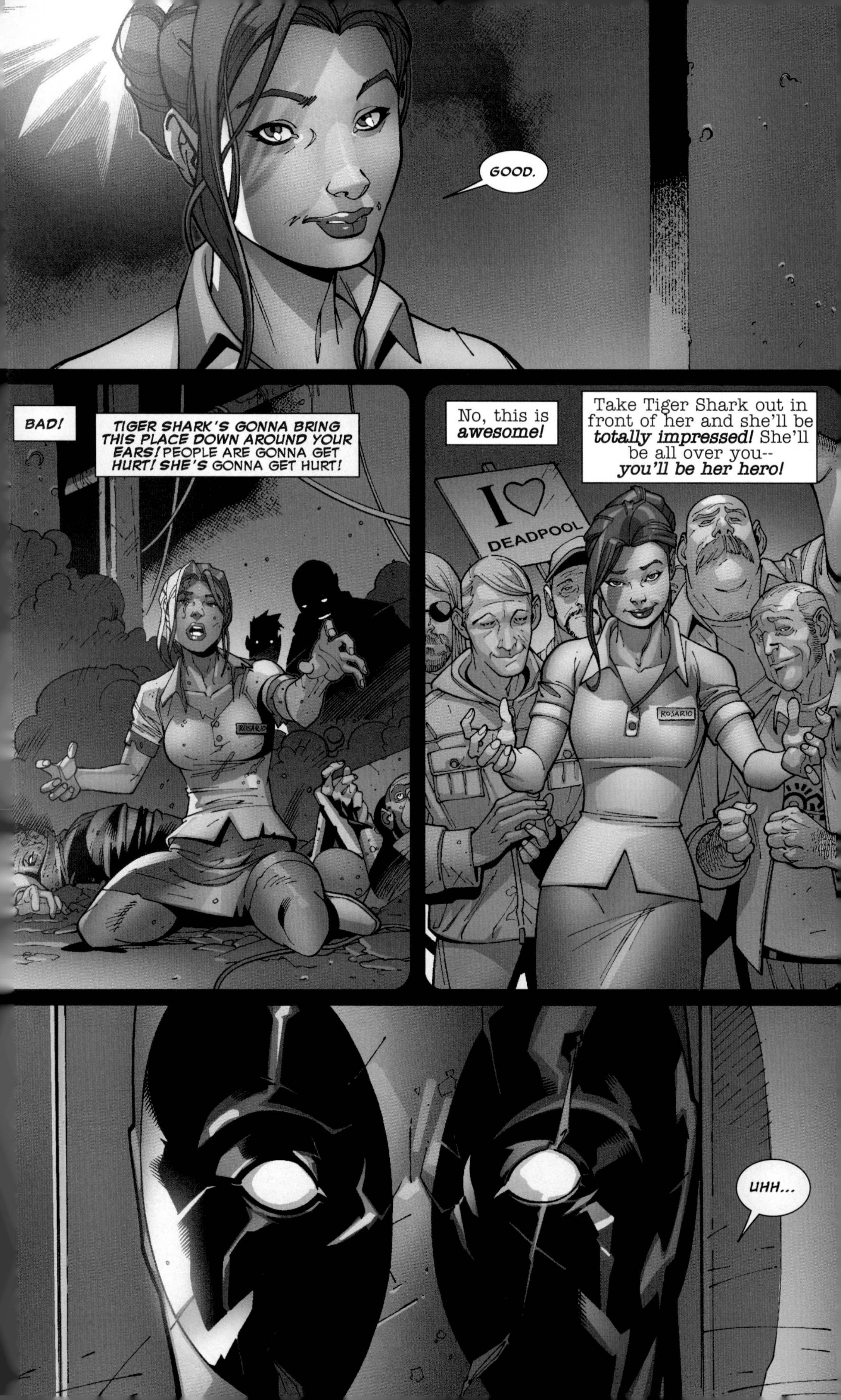
GOOD.
BAD!
TIGER SHARK'S GONNA BRING THIS PLACE DOWN AROUND YOUR EARS! PEOPLE ARE GONNA GET HURT! SHE'S GONNA GET HURT!
No, this is awesome!
Take Tiger Shark out in front of her and she'll be totally impressed! She'll be all over you-- you'll be her hero!
I ♡ DEADPOOL
ROSARIO
UHH...

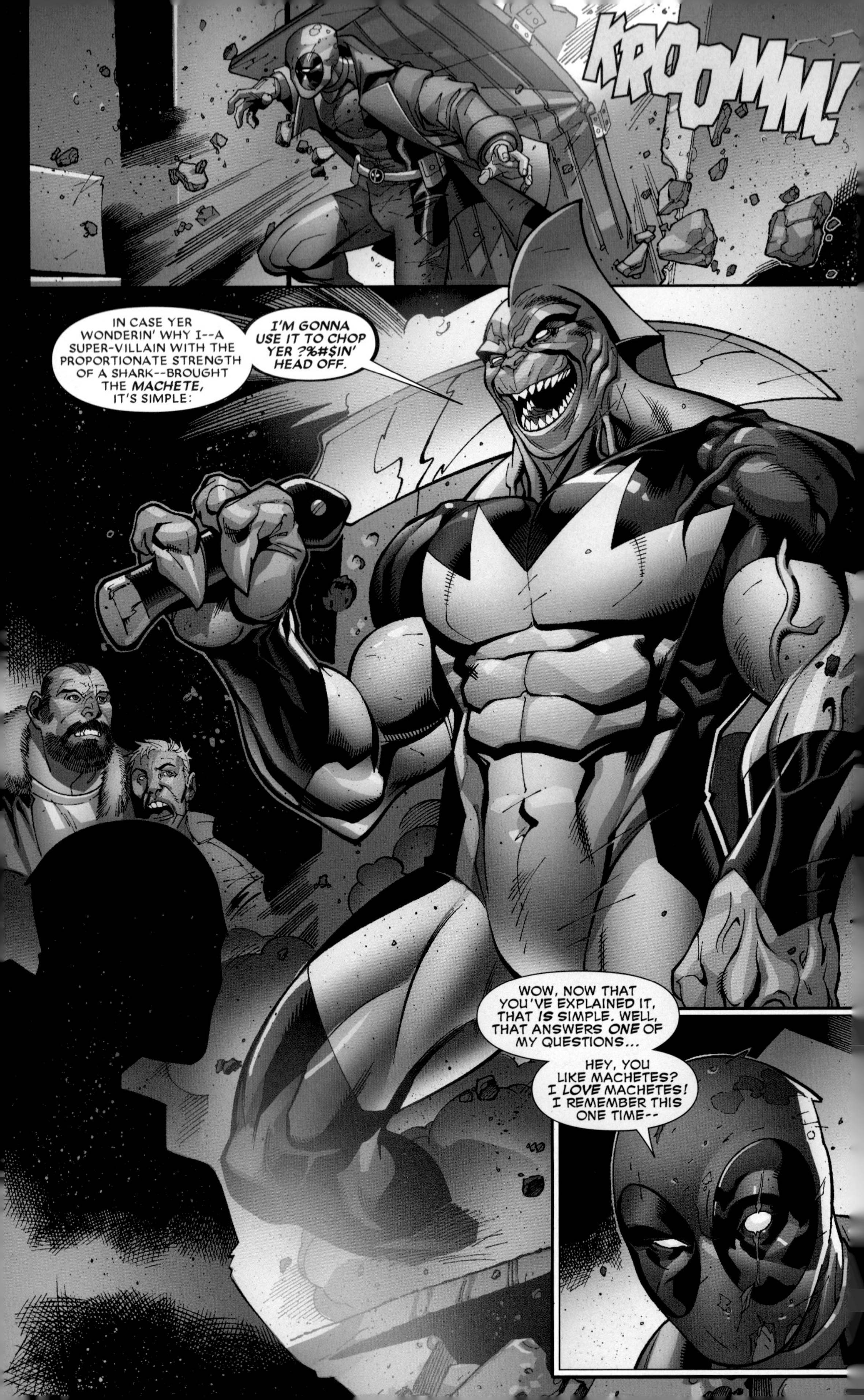
KROOMM!
IN CASE YER WONDERIN' WHY I--A SUPER-VILLAIN WITH THE PROPORTIONATE STRENGTH OF A SHARK--BROUGHT THE MACHETE, IT'S SIMPLE:
I'M GONNA USE IT TO CHOP YER ?%#$IN' HEAD OFF.
WOW, NOW THAT YOU'VE EXPLAINED IT, THAT IS SIMPLE. WELL, THAT ANSWERS ONE OF MY QUESTIONS...
HEY, YOU LIKE MACHETES? I LOVE MACHETES! I REMEMBER THIS ONE TIME--

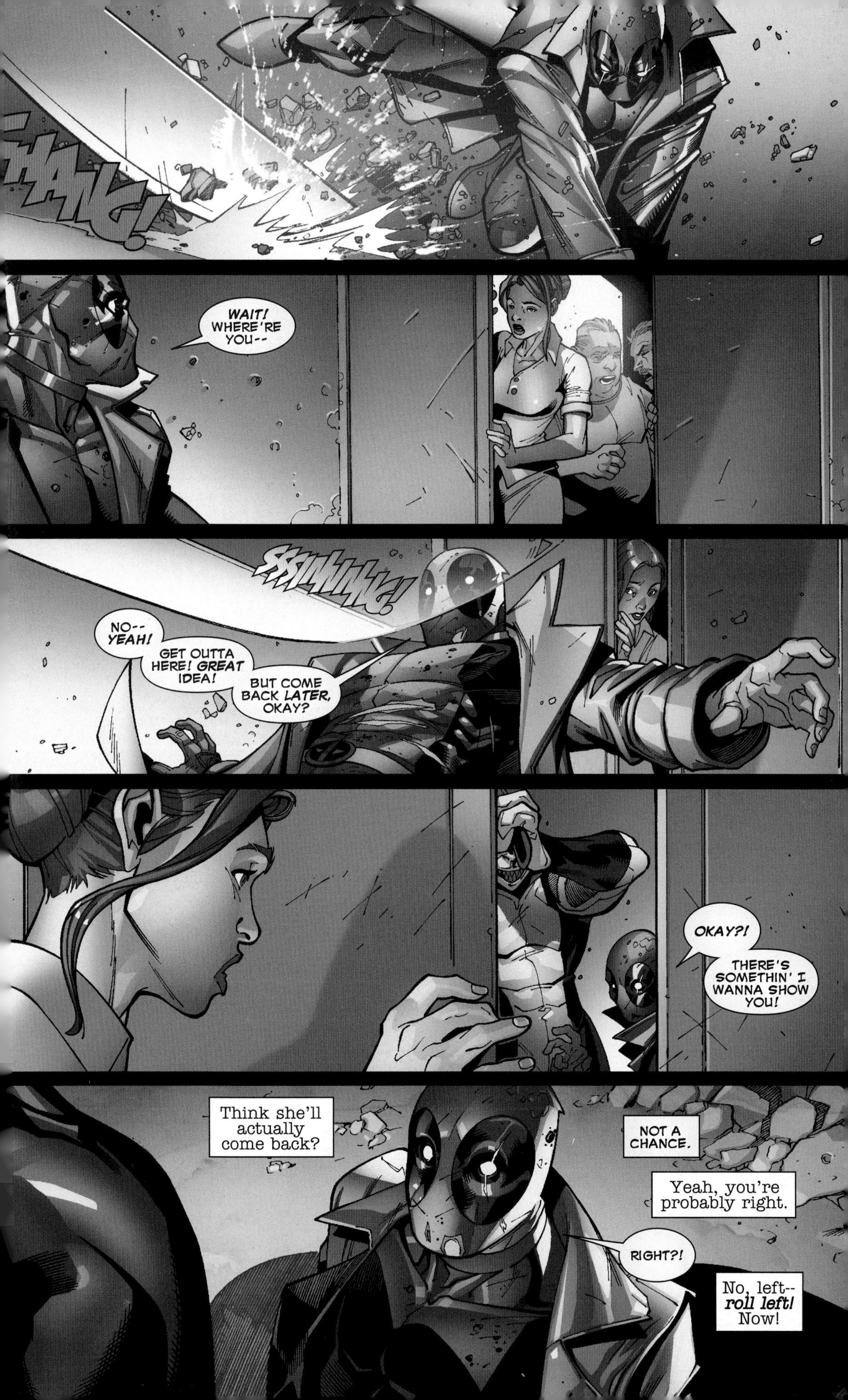
SHANG!
WAIT! WHERE'RE YOU--
SSSHWING!
NO-- YEAH!
GET OUTTA HERE! GREAT IDEA!
BUT COME BACK LATER, OKAY?
OKAY?!
THERE'S SOMETHIN' I WANNA SHOW YOU!
Think she'll actually come back?
NOT A CHANCE.
Yeah, you're probably right.
RIGHT?!
No, left-- roll left! Now!

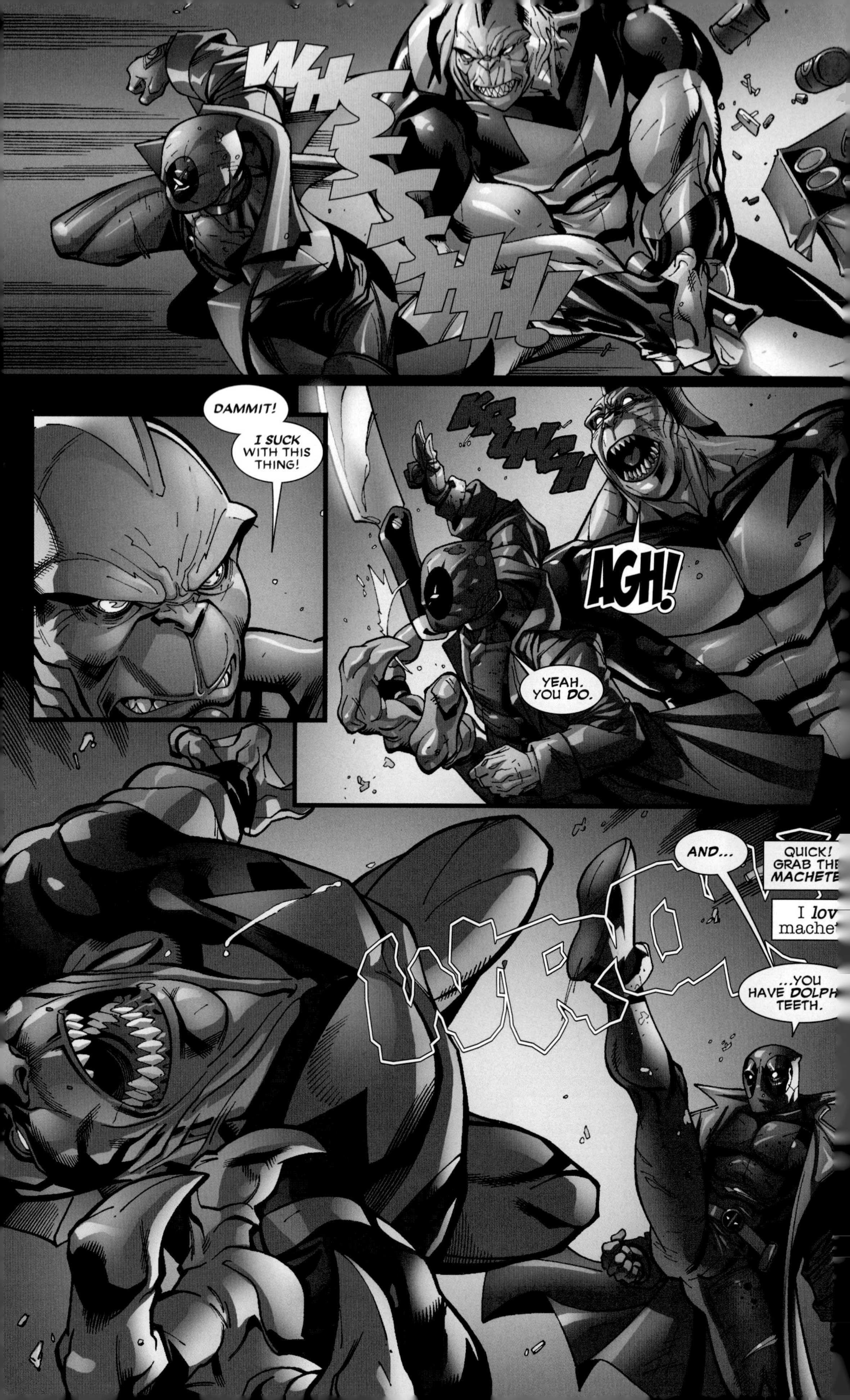
DAMMIT!
I SUCK WITH THIS THING!
KRUNCH
AGH!
YEAH. YOU DO.
AND...
QUICK! GRAB THE MACHETE
I lov machet
...YOU HAVE DOLPH TEETH.

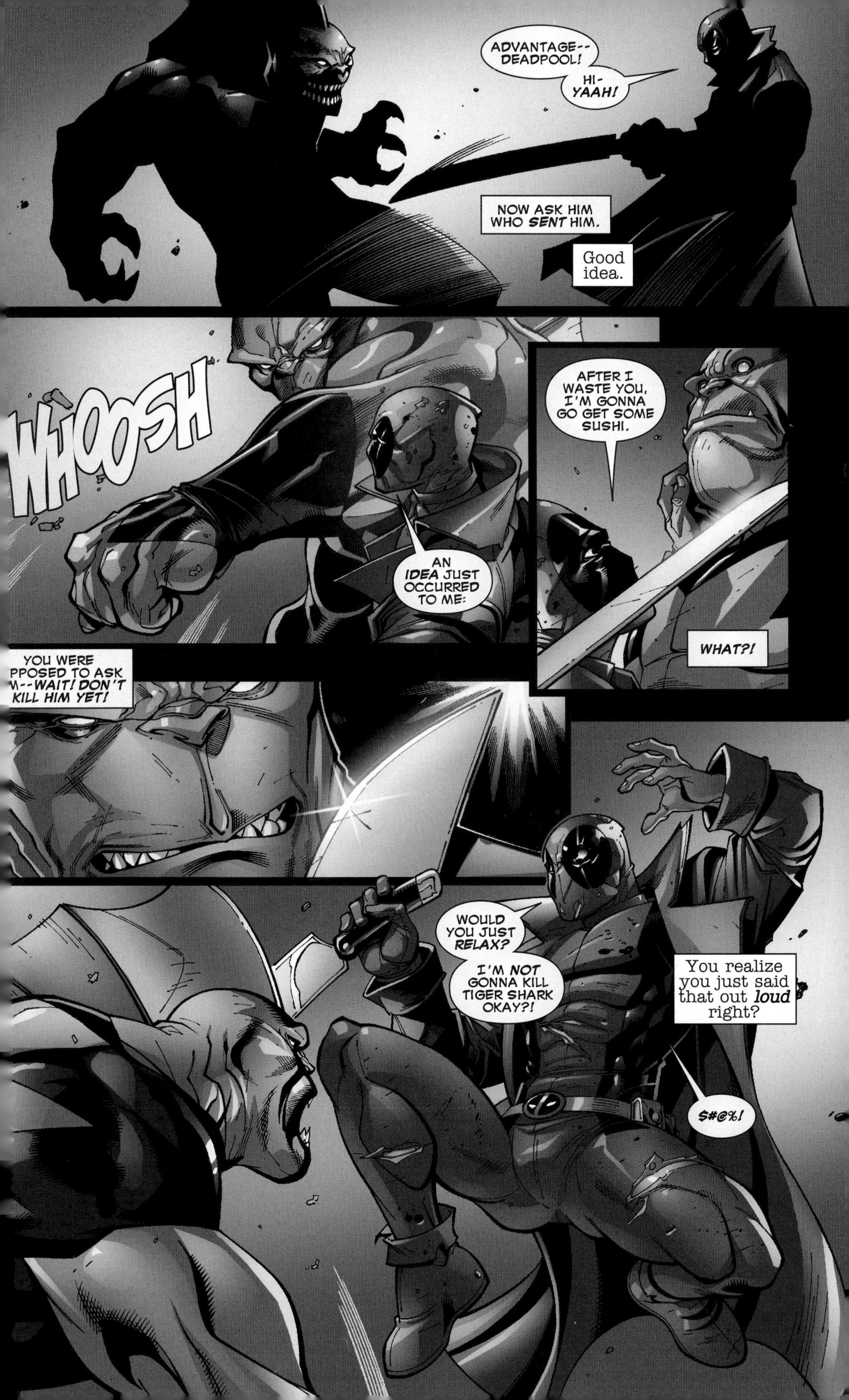
ADVANTAGE--DEADPOOL!
HI-YAAH!
NOW ASK HIM WHO SENT HIM.
Good idea.
WHOOSH
AN IDEA JUST OCCURRED TO ME:
AFTER I WASTE YOU, I'M GONNA GO GET SOME SUSHI.
WHAT?!
YOU WERE PPOSED TO ASK M--WAIT! DON'T KILL HIM YET!
WOULD YOU JUST RELAX?
I'M NOT GONNA KILL TIGER SHARK OKAY?!
You realize you just said that out loud right?
$#@%!

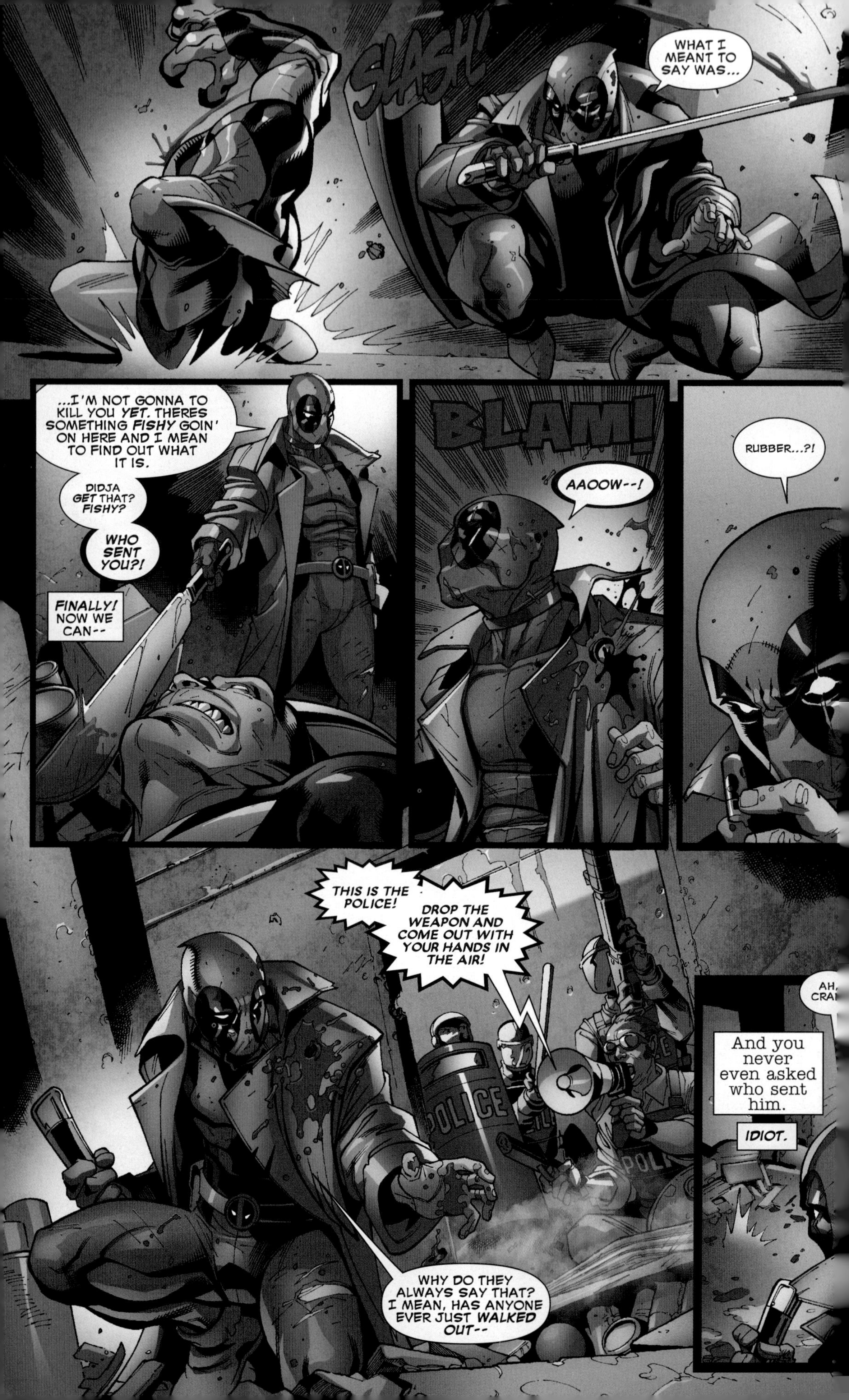
SLASH!
WHAT I MEANT TO SAY WAS...
...I'M NOT GONNA TO KILL YOU YET. THERES SOMETHING FISHY GOIN' ON HERE AND I MEAN TO FIND OUT WHAT IT IS.
DIDJA GET THAT? FISHY?
WHO SENT YOU?!
FINALLY! NOW WE CAN--
BLAM!
AAOOW--!
RUBBER...?!
THIS IS THE POLICE!
DROP THE WEAPON AND COME OUT WITH YOUR HANDS IN THE AIR!
POLICE
WHY DO THEY ALWAYS SAY THAT? I MEAN, HAS ANYONE EVER JUST WALKED OUT--
And you never even asked who sent him.
IDIOT.

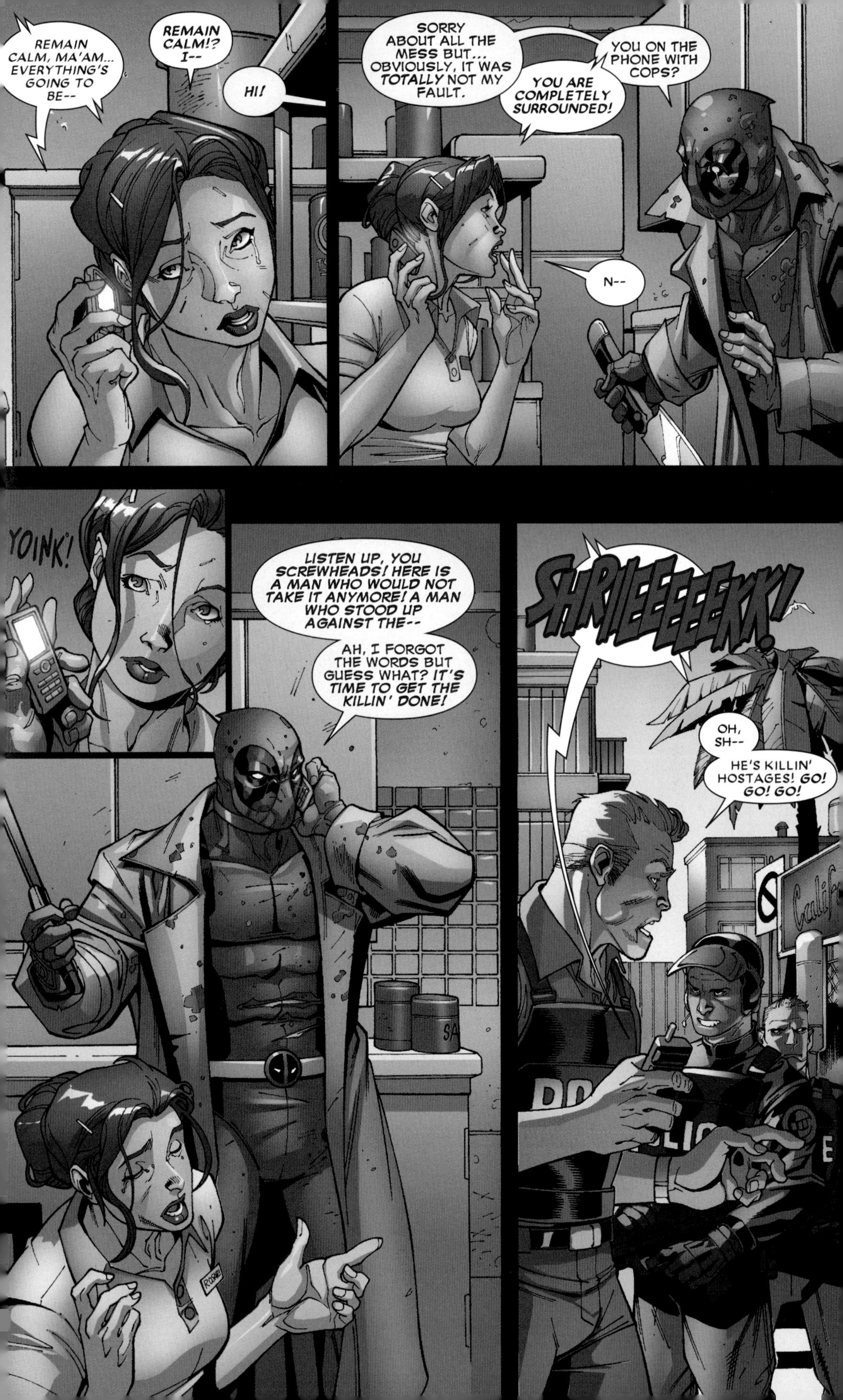
REMAIN CALM, MA'AM... EVERYTHING'S GOING TO BE--
REMAIN CALM!? I--
HI!
SORRY ABOUT ALL THE MESS BUT... OBVIOUSLY, IT WAS TOTALLY NOT MY FAULT.
YOU ON THE PHONE WITH COPS?
YOU ARE COMPLETELY SURROUNDED!
N--
YOINK!
LISTEN UP, YOU SCREWHEADS! HERE IS A MAN WHO WOULD NOT TAKE IT ANYMORE! A MAN WHO STOOD UP AGAINST THE--
AH, I FORGOT THE WORDS BUT GUESS WHAT? IT'S TIME TO GET THE KILLIN' DONE!
SHRIEEEEEEKK!
OH, SH--
HE'S KILLIN' HOSTAGES! GO! GO! GO!

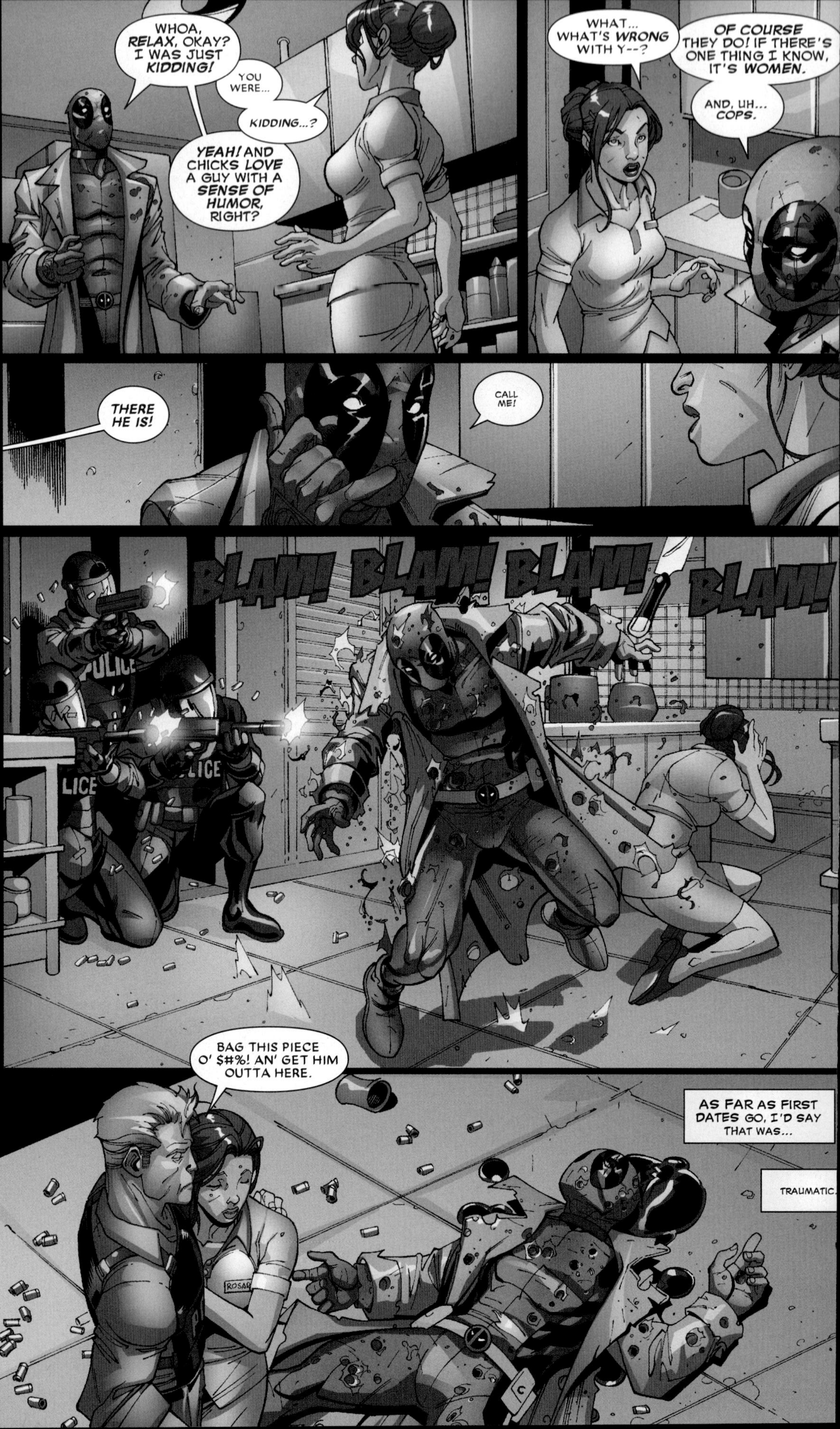

WHOA, RELAX, OKAY? I WAS JUST KIDDING!
YOU WERE...
KIDDING...?
YEAH! AND CHICKS LOVE A GUY WITH A SENSE OF HUMOR, RIGHT?
WHAT... WHAT'S WRONG WITH Y--?
OF COURSE THEY DO! IF THERE'S ONE THING I KNOW, IT'S WOMEN.
AND, UH... COPS.
THERE HE IS!
CALL ME!
BLAM! BLAM! BLAM! BLAM!
POLICE
BAG THIS PIECE O' $#%! AN' GET HIM OUTTA HERE.
AS FAR AS FIRST DATES GO, I'D SAY THAT WAS...
TRAUMATIC.

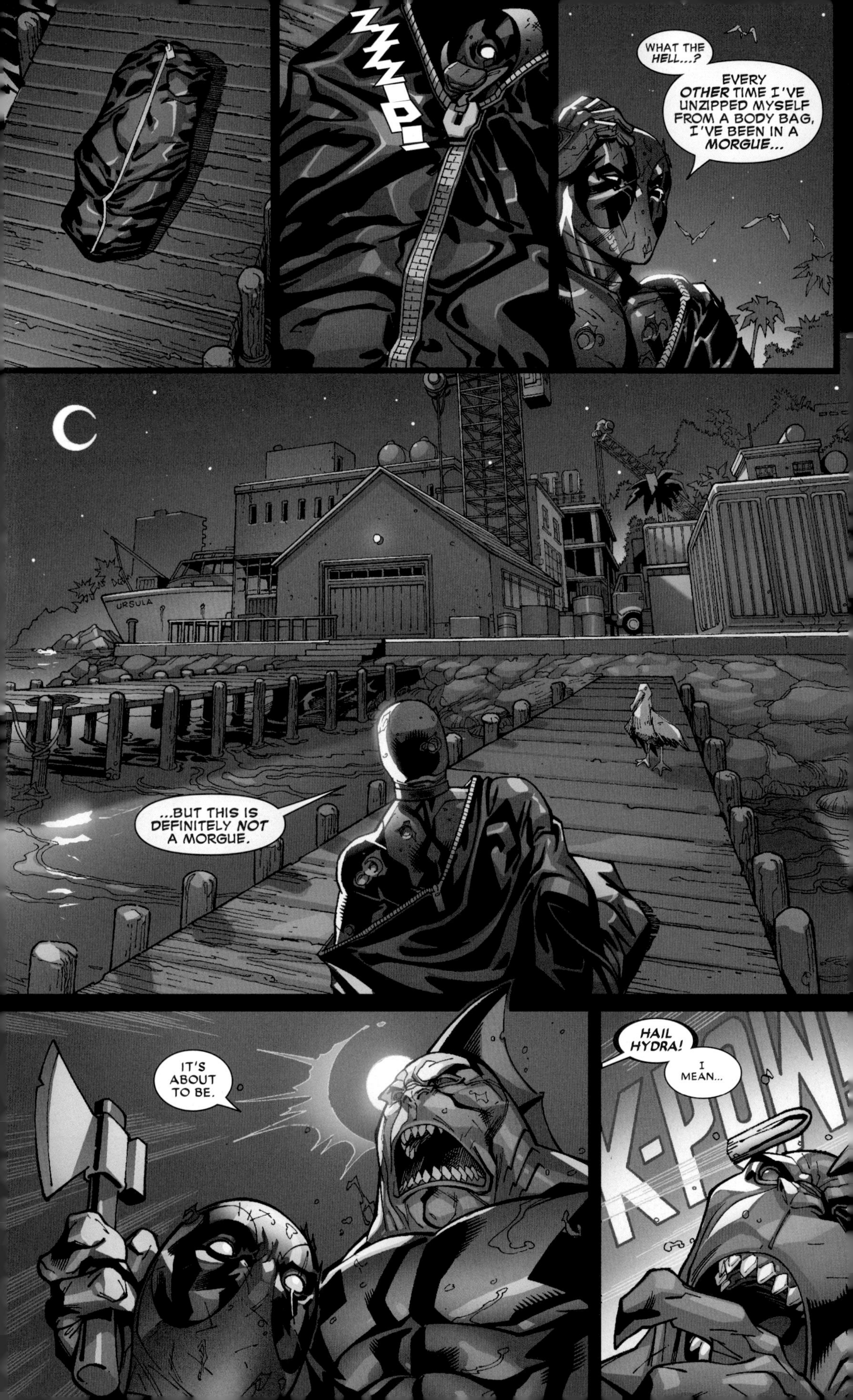
ZZZIP!
WHAT THE HELL...?
EVERY OTHER TIME I'VE UNZIPPED MYSELF FROM A BODY BAG, I'VE BEEN IN A MORGUE...
URSULA
...BUT THIS IS DEFINITELY NOT A MORGUE.
IT'S ABOUT TO BE.
HAIL HYDRA!
I MEAN...

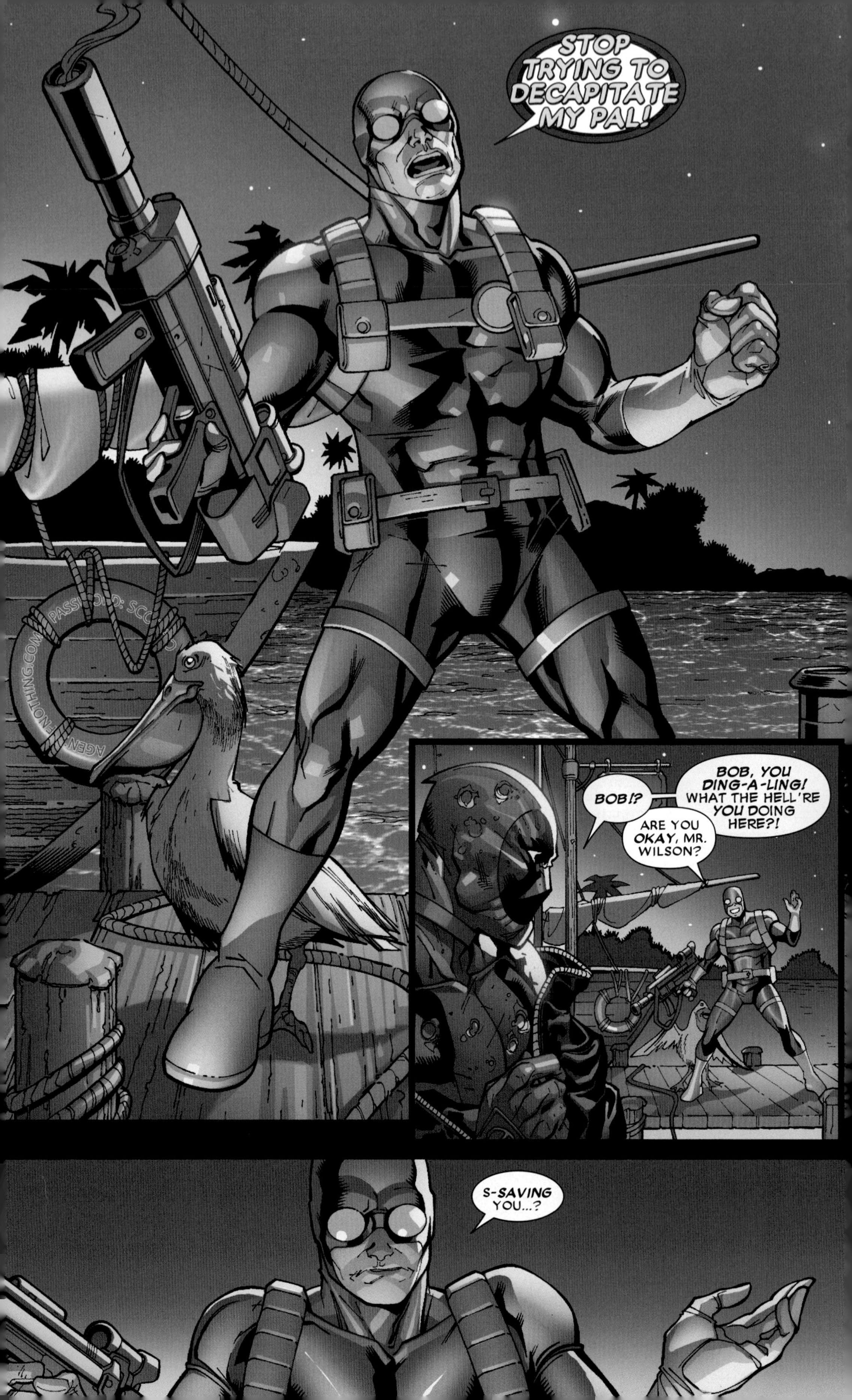
STOP TRYING TO DECAPITATE MY PAL!
BOB!?
BOB, YOU DING-A-LING! WHAT THE HELL'RE YOU DOING HERE?!
ARE YOU OKAY, MR. WILSON?
S-SAVING YOU...?

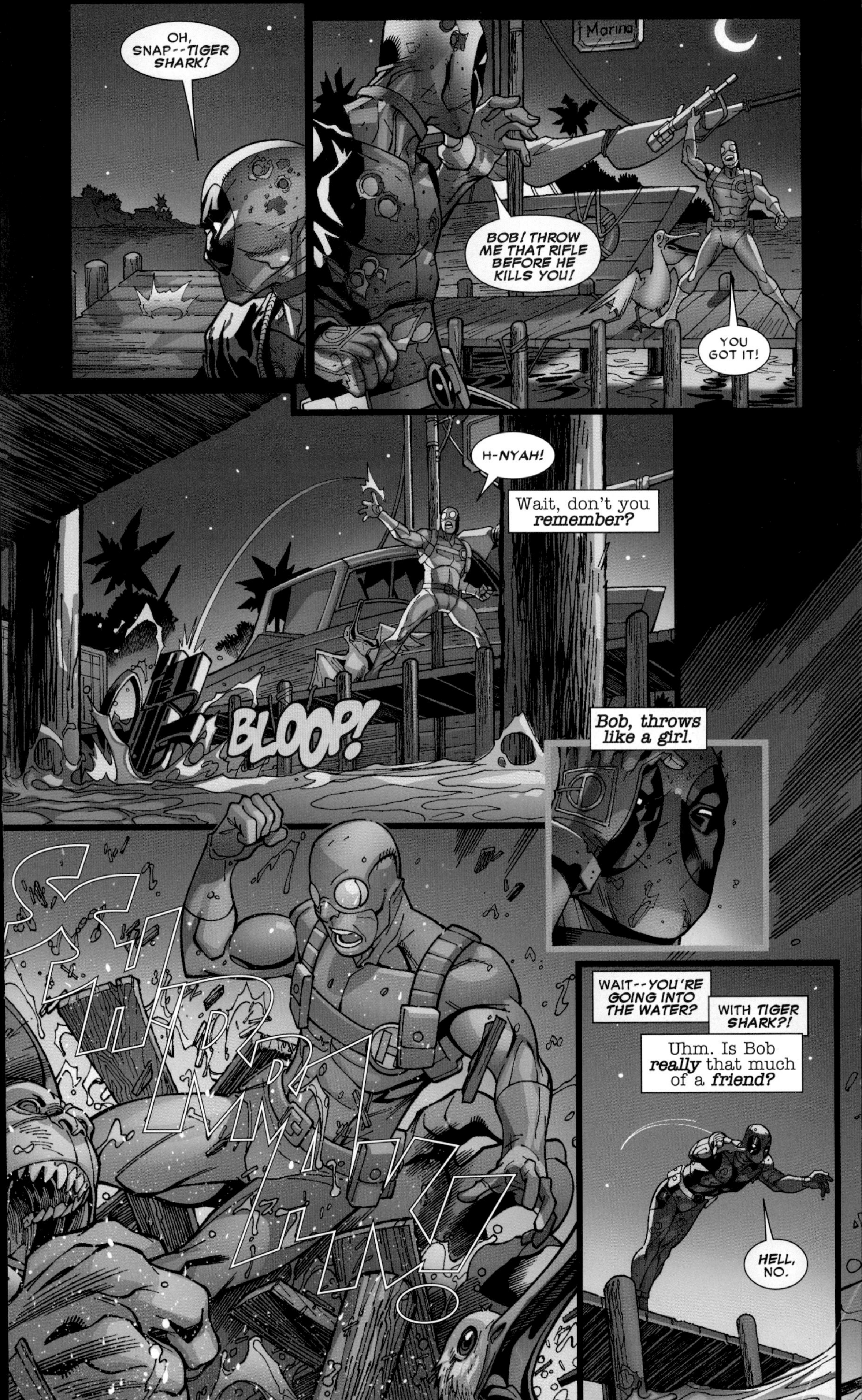

OH, SNAP--TIGER SHARK!
Marina
BOB! THROW ME THAT RIFLE BEFORE HE KILLS YOU!
YOU GOT IT!
H-NYAH!
Wait, don't you remember?
BLOOP!
Bob, throws like a girl.
WAIT--YOU'RE GOING INTO THE WATER?
WITH TIGER SHARK?!
Uhm. Is Bob really that much of a friend?
HELL, NO.

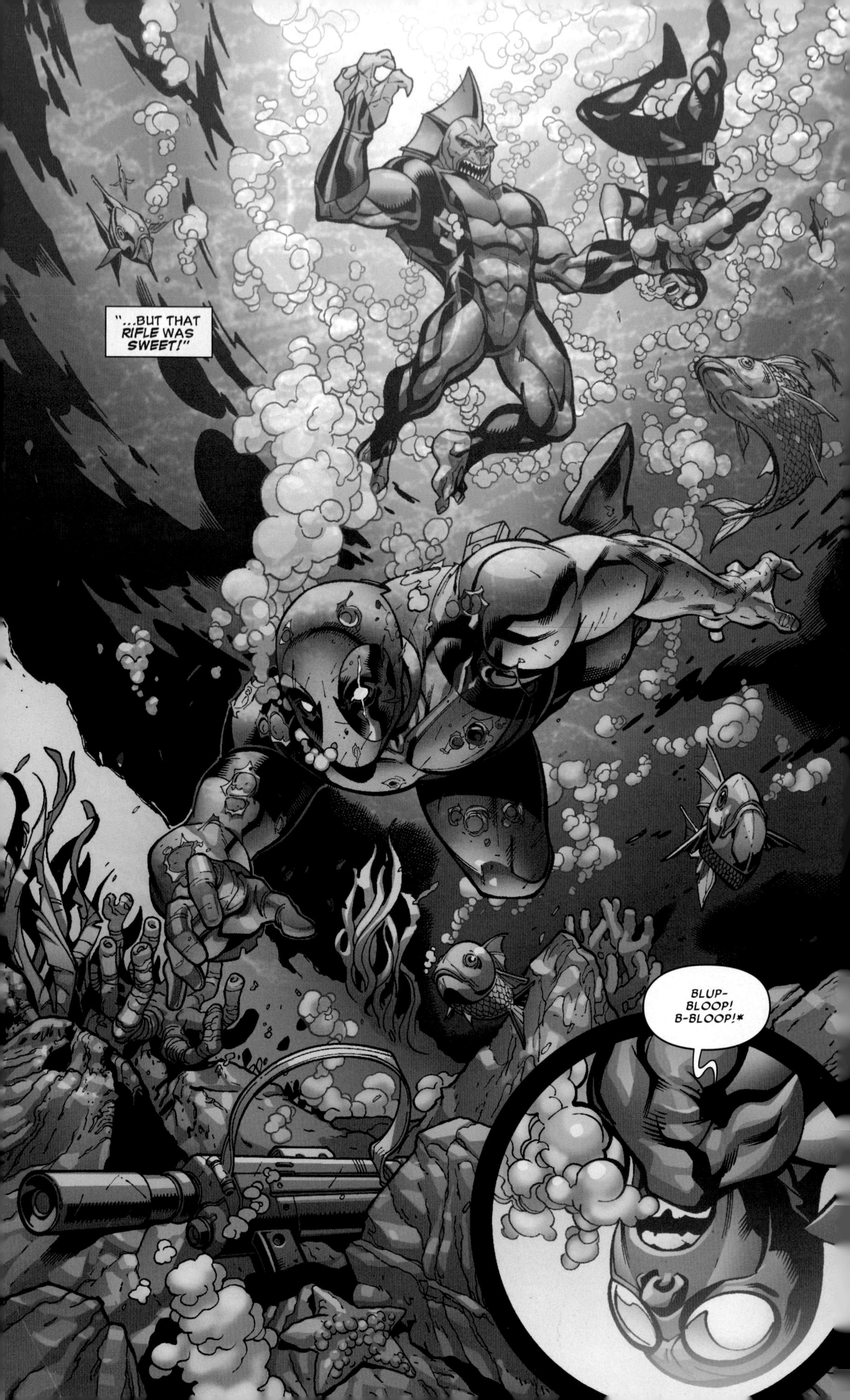
"...BUT THAT RIFLE WAS SWEET!"
BLUP-BLOOP! B-BLOOP!*

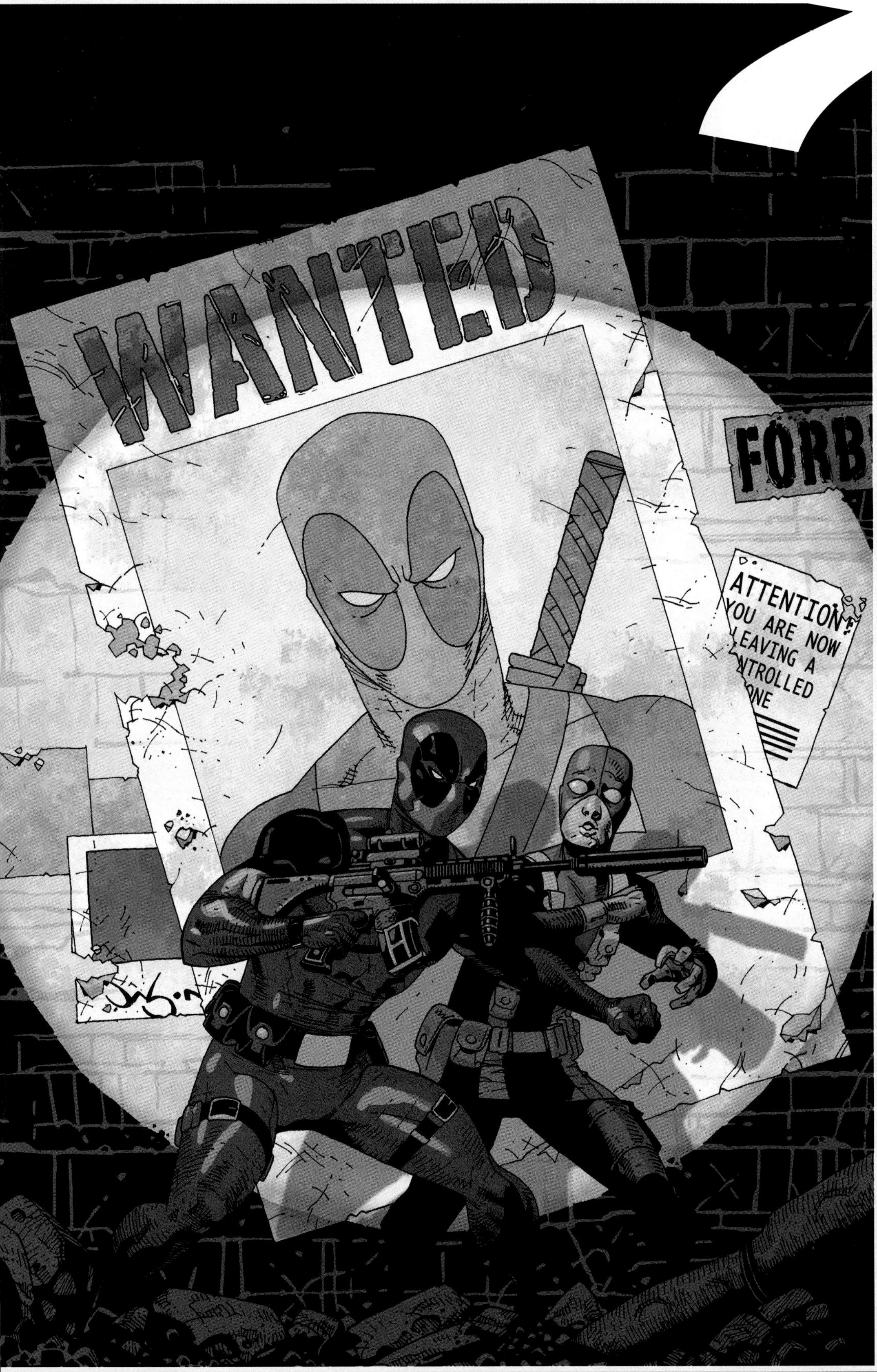

WANTED
FORB
ATTENTION
YOU ARE NOW
LEAVING A
NTROLLED
ONE

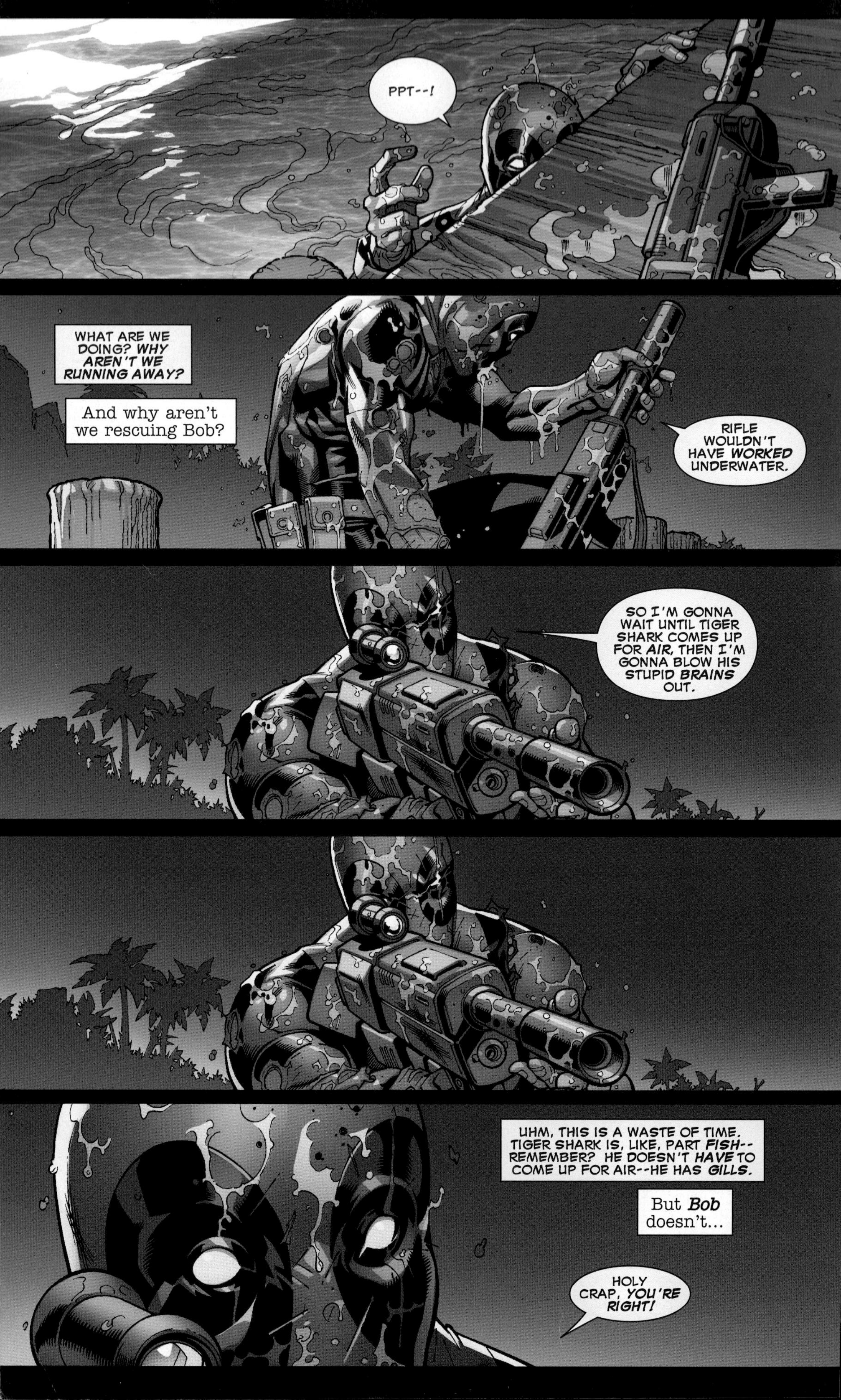
PPT--!
WHAT ARE WE DOING? WHY AREN'T WE RUNNING AWAY?
And why aren't we rescuing Bob?
RIFLE WOULDN'T HAVE WORKED UNDERWATER.
SO I'M GONNA WAIT UNTIL TIGER SHARK COMES UP FOR AIR, THEN I'M GONNA BLOW HIS STUPID BRAINS OUT.
UHM, THIS IS A WASTE OF TIME. TIGER SHARK IS, LIKE, PART FISH--REMEMBER? HE DOESN'T HAVE TO COME UP FOR AIR--HE HAS GILLS.
But Bob doesn't...
HOLY CRAP, YOU'RE RIGHT!

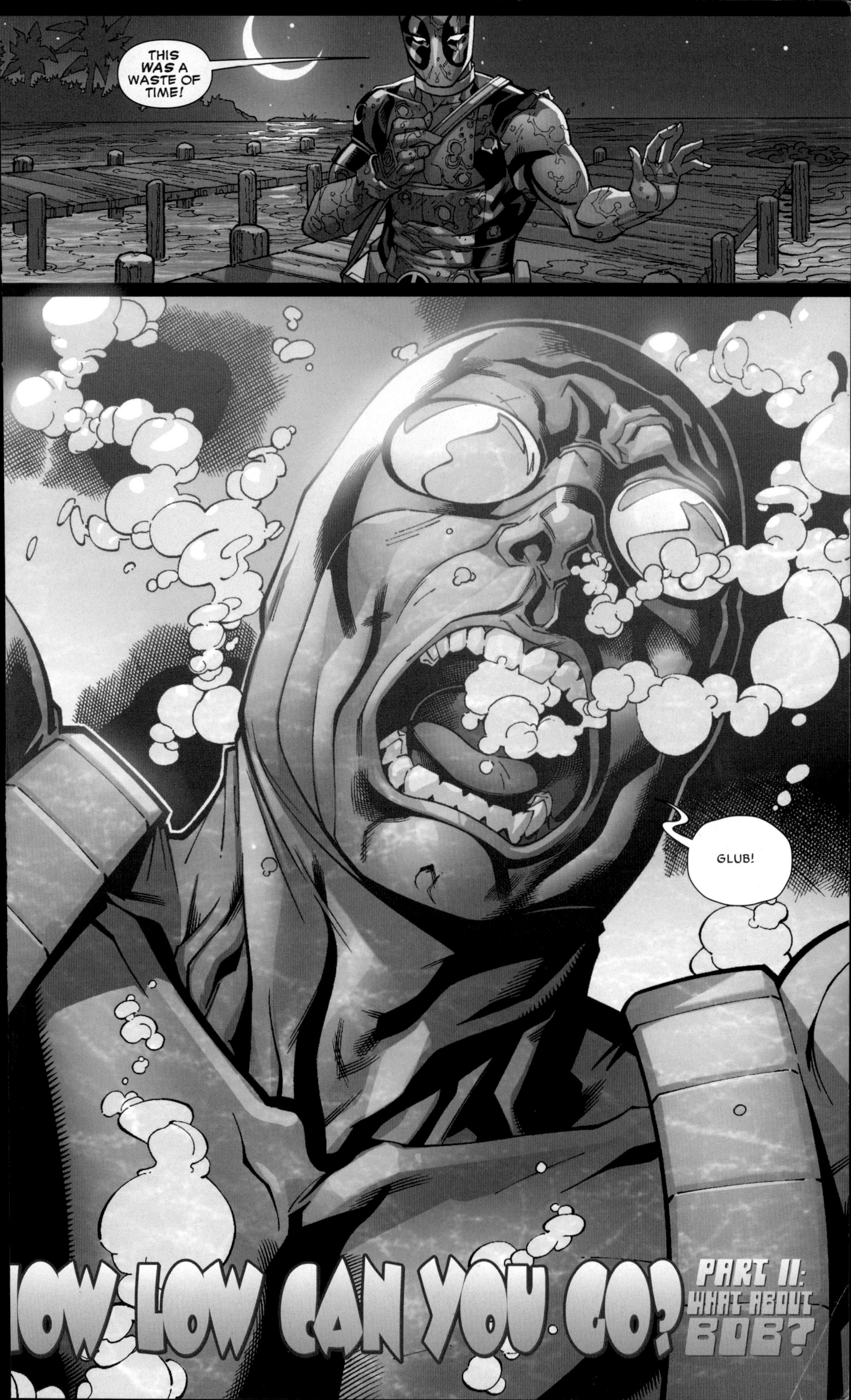
THIS WAS A WASTE OF TIME!
GLUB!
HOW LOW CAN YOU GO?
PART II: WHAT ABOUT BOB?

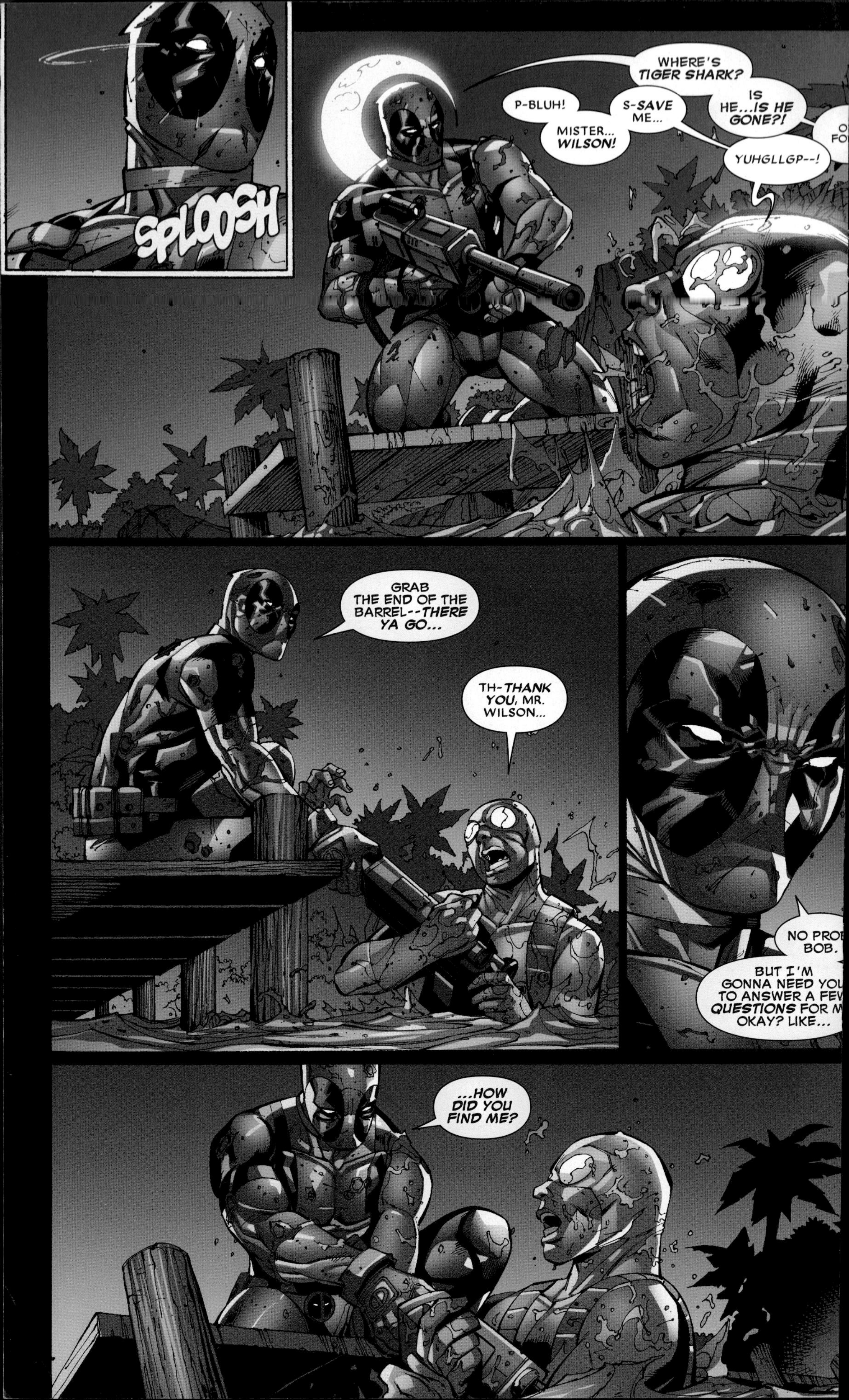

SPLOOSH
P-BLUH!
MISTER... WILSON!
S-SAVE ME...
WHERE'S TIGER SHARK?
IS HE...IS HE GONE?!
YUHGLLGP--!
GRAB THE END OF THE BARREL--THERE YA GO...
TH-THANK YOU, MR. WILSON...
NO PROB
BOB.
BUT I'M GONNA NEED YOU TO ANSWER A FEW QUESTIONS FOR M
OKAY? LIKE...
...HOW DID YOU FIND ME?

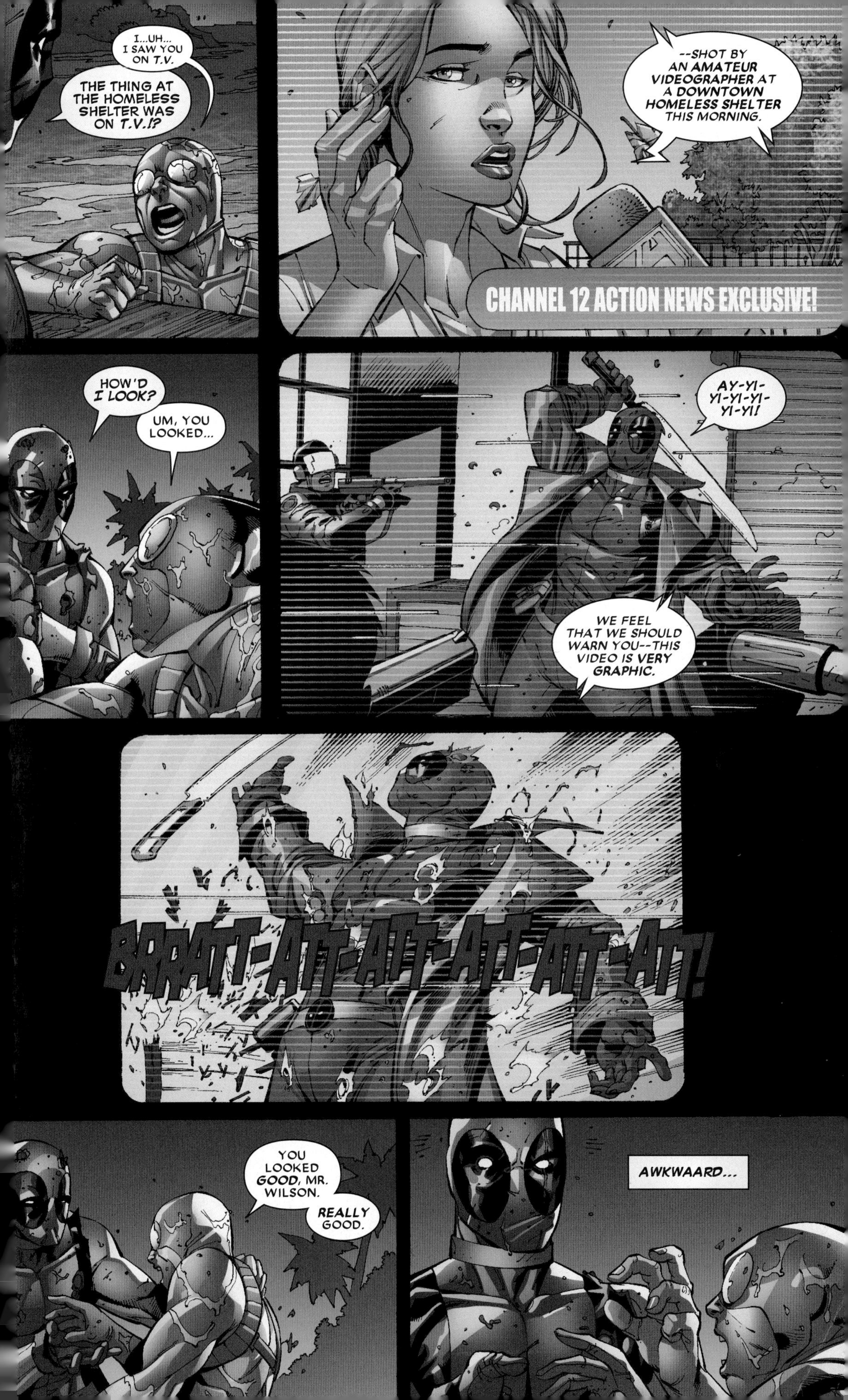
I...UH... I SAW YOU ON T.V.
THE THING AT THE HOMELESS SHELTER WAS ON T.V.!?
--SHOT BY AN AMATEUR VIDEOGRAPHER AT A DOWNTOWN HOMELESS SHELTER THIS MORNING.
CHANNEL 12 ACTION NEWS EXCLUSIVE!
HOW'D I LOOK?
UM, YOU LOOKED...
AY-YI-YI-YI-YI-YI-YI!
WE FEEL THAT WE SHOULD WARN YOU--THIS VIDEO IS VERY GRAPHIC.
BRRATT-ATT-ATT-ATT-ATT-ATT!
YOU LOOKED GOOD, MR. WILSON.
REALLY GOOD.
AWKWAARD...

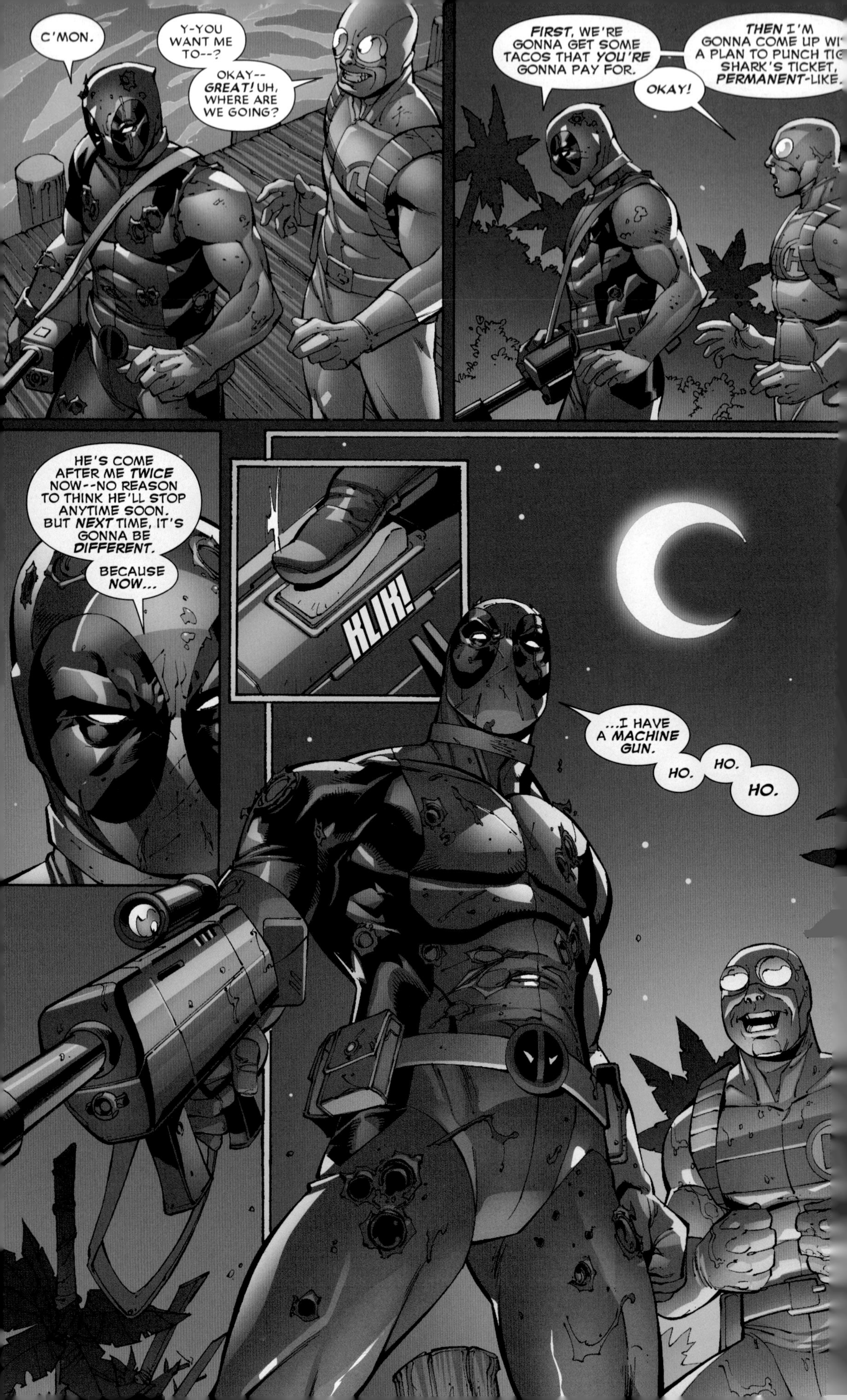

C'MON.
Y-YOU WANT ME TO--?
OKAY-- GREAT! UH, WHERE ARE WE GOING?
FIRST, WE'RE GONNA GET SOME TACOS THAT YOU'RE GONNA PAY FOR.
OKAY!
THEN I'M GONNA COME UP WI A PLAN TO PUNCH TIG SHARK'S TICKET, PERMANENT-LIKE.
HE'S COME AFTER ME TWICE NOW--NO REASON TO THINK HE'LL STOP ANYTIME SOON. BUT NEXT TIME, IT'S GONNA BE DIFFERENT.
BECAUSE NOW...
KLIK!
...I HAVE A MACHINE GUN.
HO.
HO.
HO.

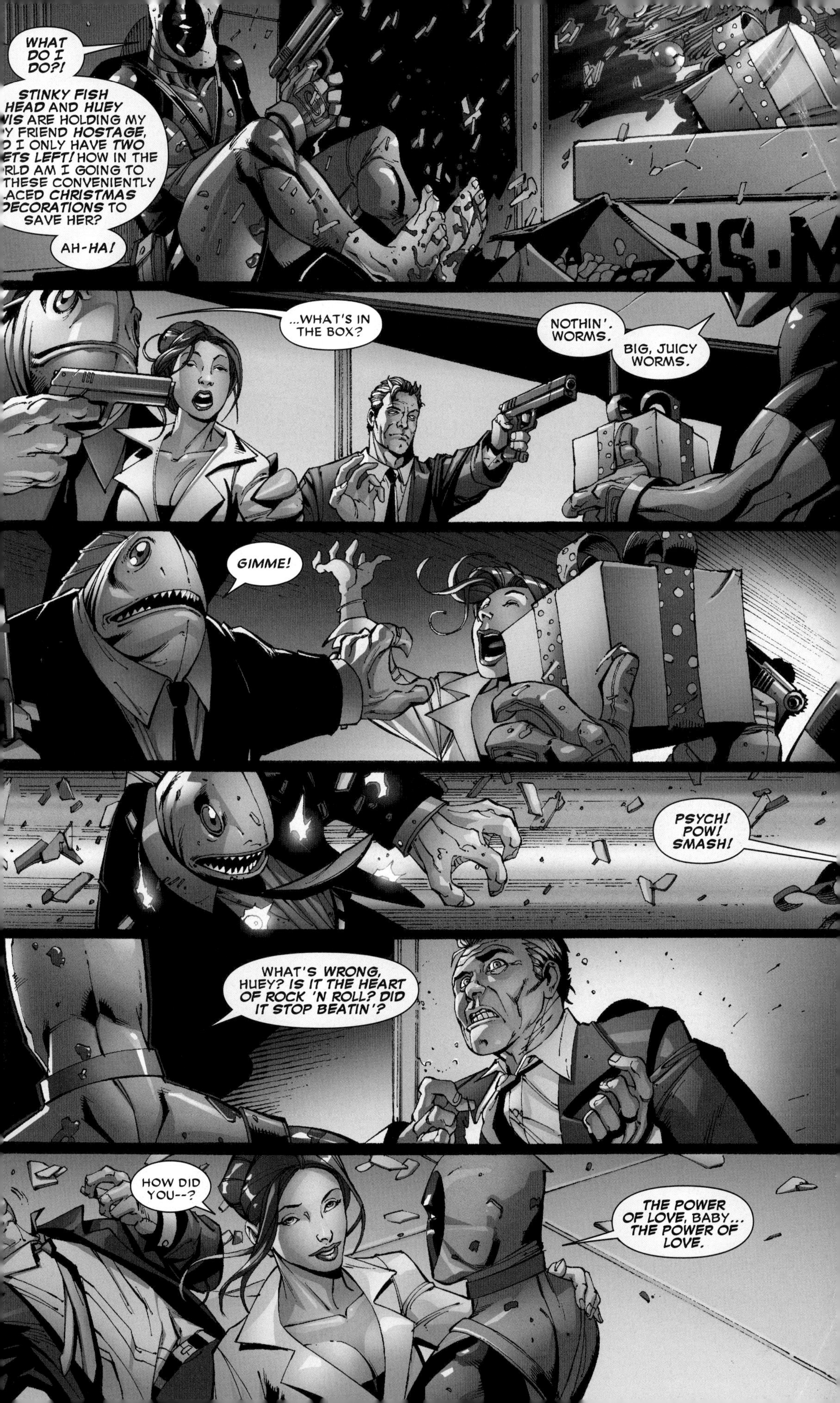

WHAT DO I DO?!
STINKY FISH HEAD AND HUEY WIS ARE HOLDING MY Y FRIEND HOSTAGE, D I ONLY HAVE TWO ETS LEFT! HOW IN THE RLD AM I GOING TO THESE CONVENIENTLY ACED CHRISTMAS DECORATIONS TO SAVE HER?
AH-HA!
...WHAT'S IN THE BOX?
NOTHIN'. WORMS.
BIG, JUICY WORMS.
GIMME!
PSYCH! POW! SMASH!
WHAT'S WRONG, HUEY? IS IT THE HEART OF ROCK 'N ROLL? DID IT STOP BEATIN'?
HOW DID YOU--?
THE POWER OF LOVE, BABY... THE POWER OF LOVE.

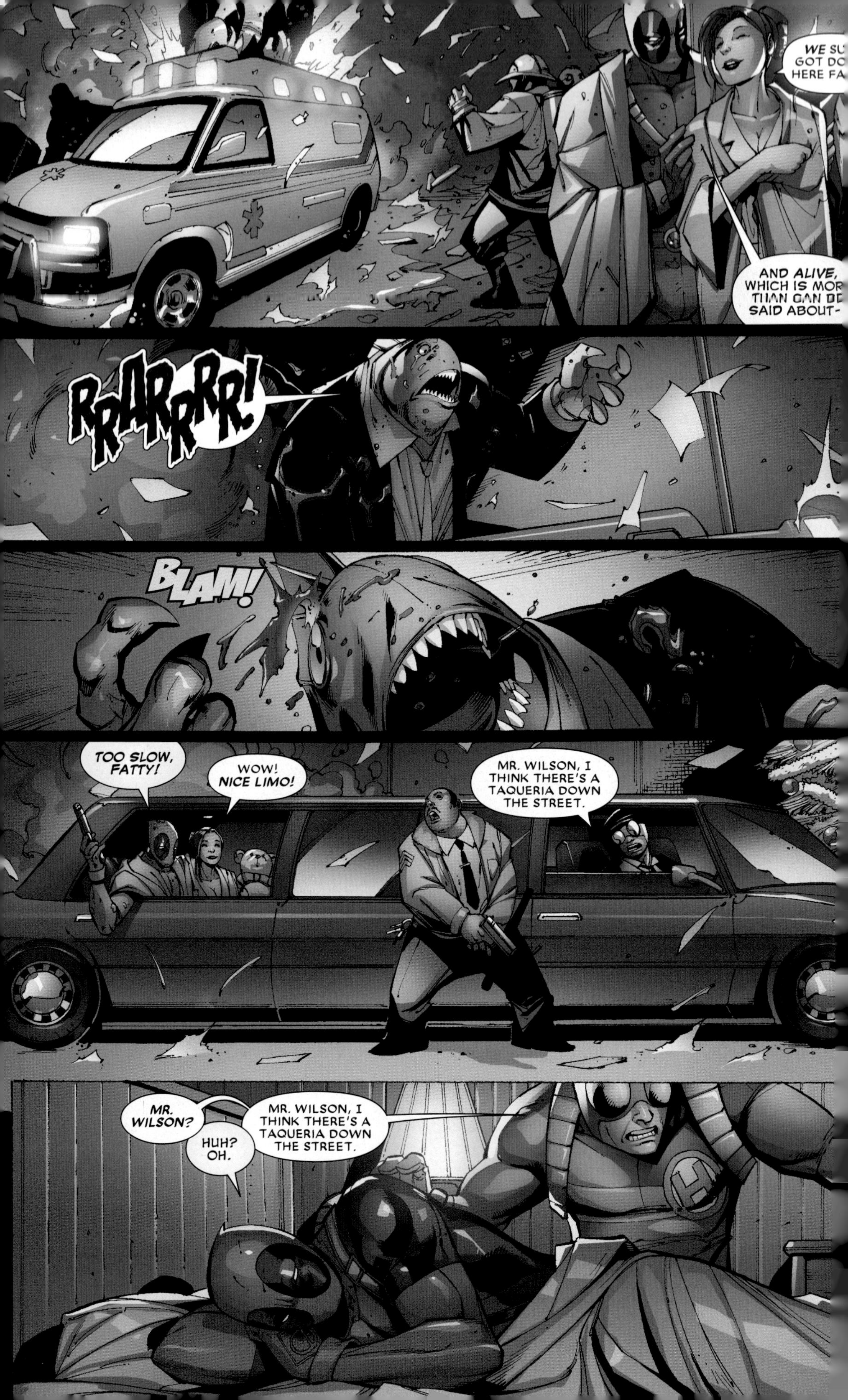
WE SU
GOT DO
HERE FA
AND ALIVE, WHICH IS MOR THAN CAN B SAID ABOUT-
RRAARRRR!
BLAM!
TOO SLOW, FATTY!
WOW! NICE LIMO!
MR. WILSON, I THINK THERE'S A TAQUERIA DOWN THE STREET.
MR. WILSON?
HUH? OH.
MR. WILSON, I THINK THERE'S A TAQUERIA DOWN THE STREET.

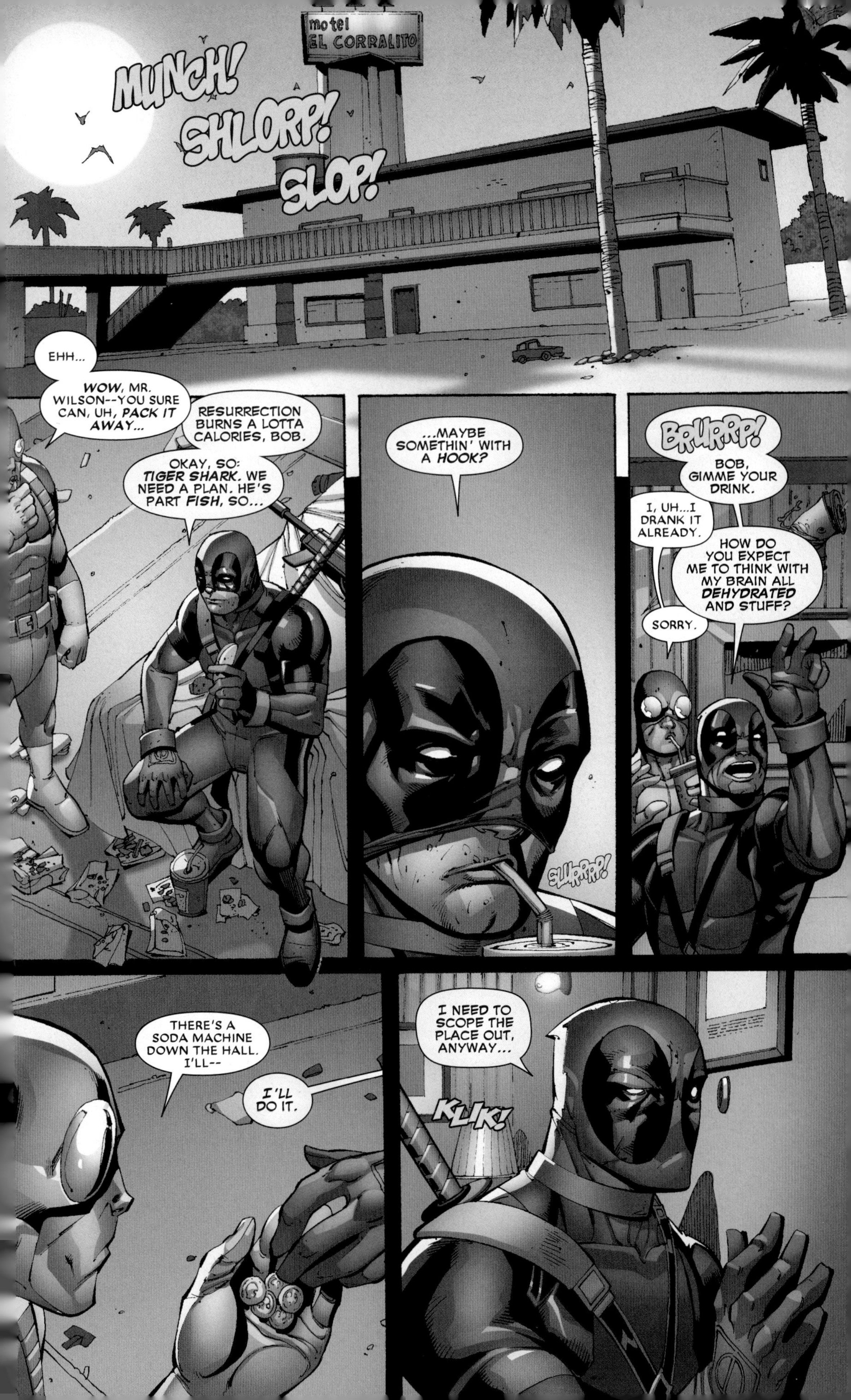
motel
EL CORRALITO
MUNCH!
SHLORP!
SLOP!
EHH...
WOW, MR. WILSON--YOU SURE CAN, UH, PACK IT AWAY...
RESURRECTION BURNS A LOTTA CALORIES, BOB.
OKAY, SO: TIGER SHARK. WE NEED A PLAN. HE'S PART FISH, SO...
...MAYBE SOMETHIN' WITH A HOOK?
SLURRRP!
BRURRP!
BOB, GIMME YOUR DRINK.
I, UH...I DRANK IT ALREADY.
HOW DO YOU EXPECT ME TO THINK WITH MY BRAIN ALL DEHYDRATED AND STUFF?
SORRY.
THERE'S A SODA MACHINE DOWN THE HALL. I'LL--
I'LL DO IT.
I NEED TO SCOPE THE PLACE OUT, ANYWAY...
KLIK!

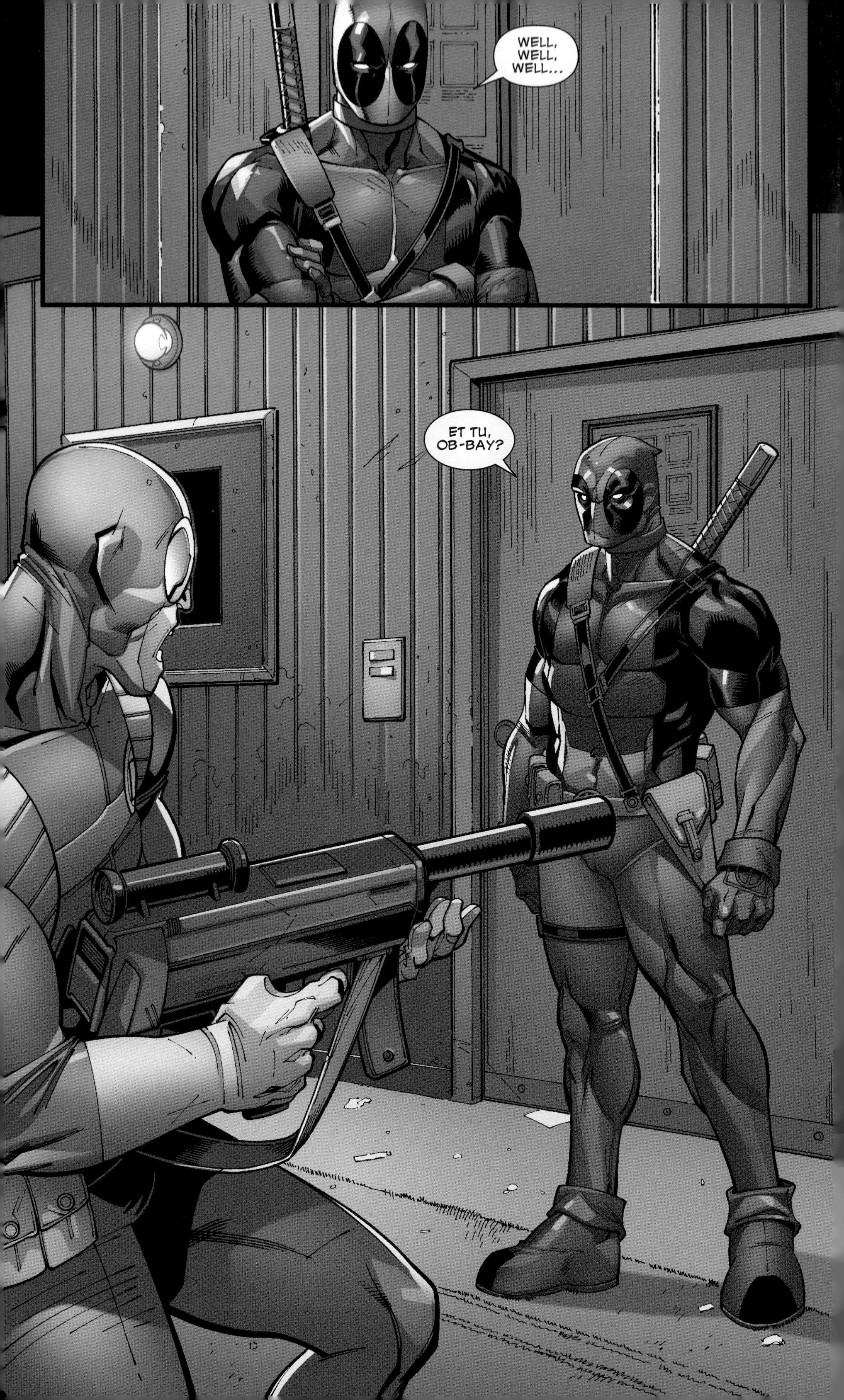
WELL, WELL, WELL...
ET TU, OB-BAY?

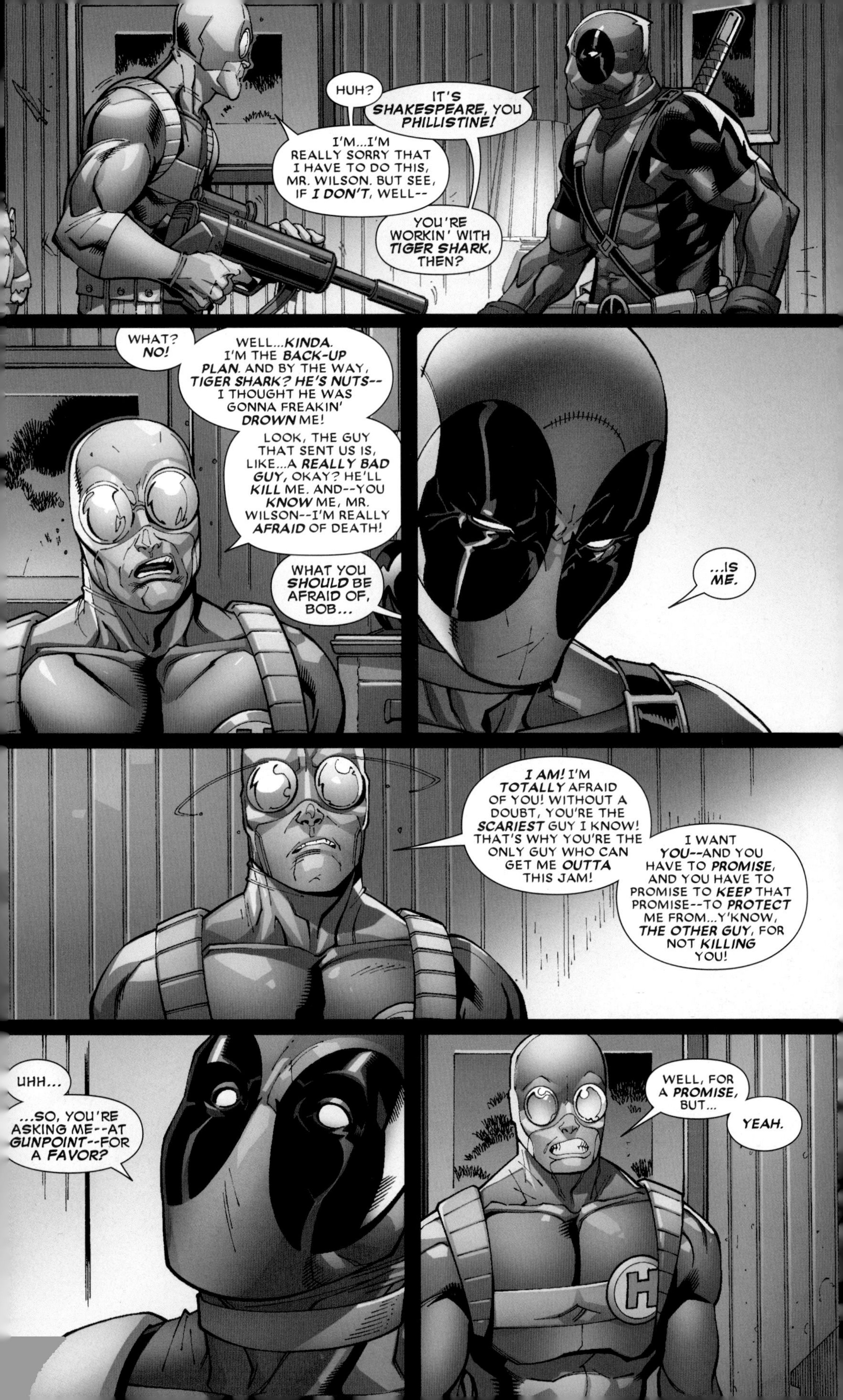
HUH?
IT'S SHAKESPEARE, YOU PHILLISTINE!
I'M...I'M REALLY SORRY THAT I HAVE TO DO THIS, MR. WILSON. BUT SEE, IF I DON'T, WELL--
YOU'RE WORKIN' WITH TIGER SHARK, THEN?
WHAT? NO!
WELL...KINDA. I'M THE BACK-UP PLAN. AND BY THE WAY, TIGER SHARK? HE'S NUTS-- I THOUGHT HE WAS GONNA FREAKIN' DROWN ME!
LOOK, THE GUY THAT SENT US IS, LIKE...A REALLY BAD GUY, OKAY? HE'LL KILL ME. AND--YOU KNOW ME, MR. WILSON--I'M REALLY AFRAID OF DEATH!
WHAT YOU SHOULD BE AFRAID OF, BOB...
...IS ME.
I AM! I'M TOTALLY AFRAID OF YOU! WITHOUT A DOUBT, YOU'RE THE SCARIEST GUY I KNOW! THAT'S WHY YOU'RE THE ONLY GUY WHO CAN GET ME OUTTA THIS JAM!
I WANT YOU--AND YOU HAVE TO PROMISE, AND YOU HAVE TO PROMISE TO KEEP THAT PROMISE--TO PROTECT ME FROM...Y'KNOW, THE OTHER GUY, FOR NOT KILLING YOU!
UHH...
...SO, YOU'RE ASKING ME--AT GUNPOINT--FOR A FAVOR?
WELL, FOR A PROMISE, BUT...
YEAH.

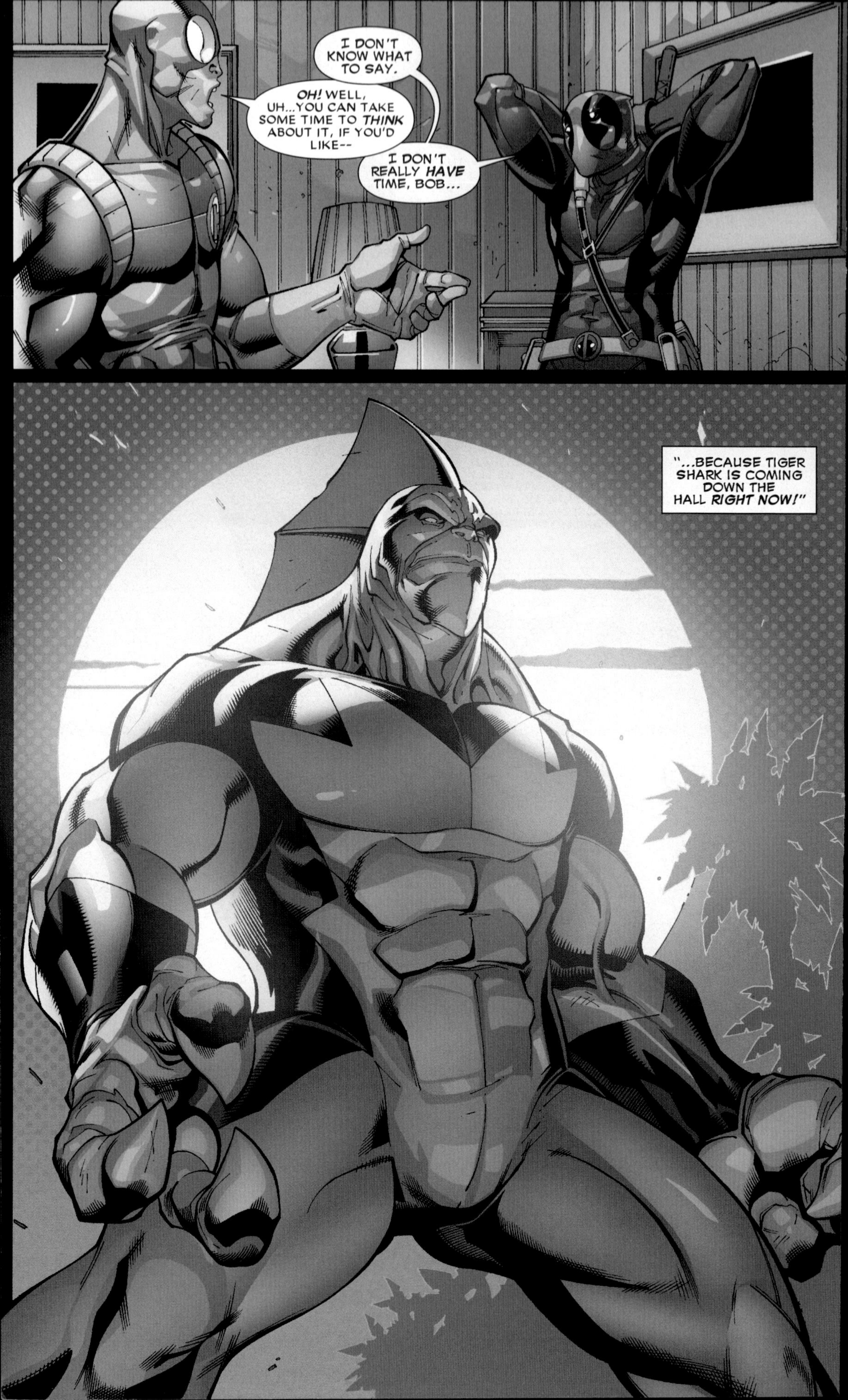
I DON'T KNOW WHAT TO SAY.
OH! WELL, UH...YOU CAN TAKE SOME TIME TO THINK ABOUT IT, IF YOU'D LIKE--
I DON'T REALLY HAVE TIME, BOB...
"...BECAUSE TIGER SHARK IS COMING DOWN THE HALL RIGHT NOW!"

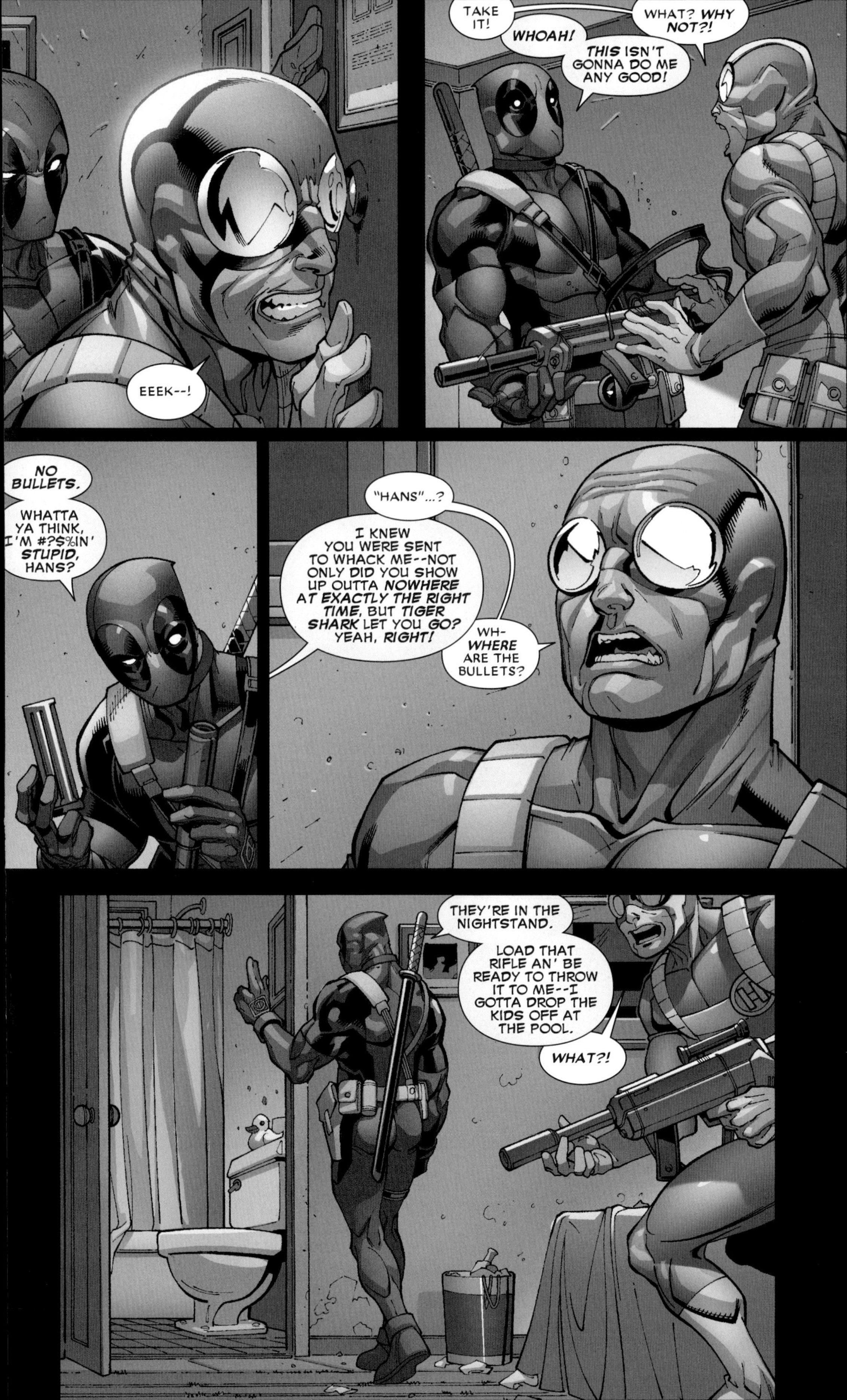
EEEK--!
TAKE IT!
WHAT? WHY NOT?!
WHOAH!
THIS ISN'T GONNA DO ME ANY GOOD!
NO BULLETS.
WHATTA YA THINK, I'M #?$%IN' STUPID, HANS?
"HANS"...?
I KNEW YOU WERE SENT TO WHACK ME--NOT ONLY DID YOU SHOW UP OUTTA NOWHERE AT EXACTLY THE RIGHT TIME, BUT TIGER SHARK LET YOU GO? YEAH, RIGHT!
WH-WHERE ARE THE BULLETS?
THEY'RE IN THE NIGHTSTAND.
LOAD THAT RIFLE AN' BE READY TO THROW IT TO ME--I GOTTA DROP THE KIDS OFF AT THE POOL.
WHAT?!

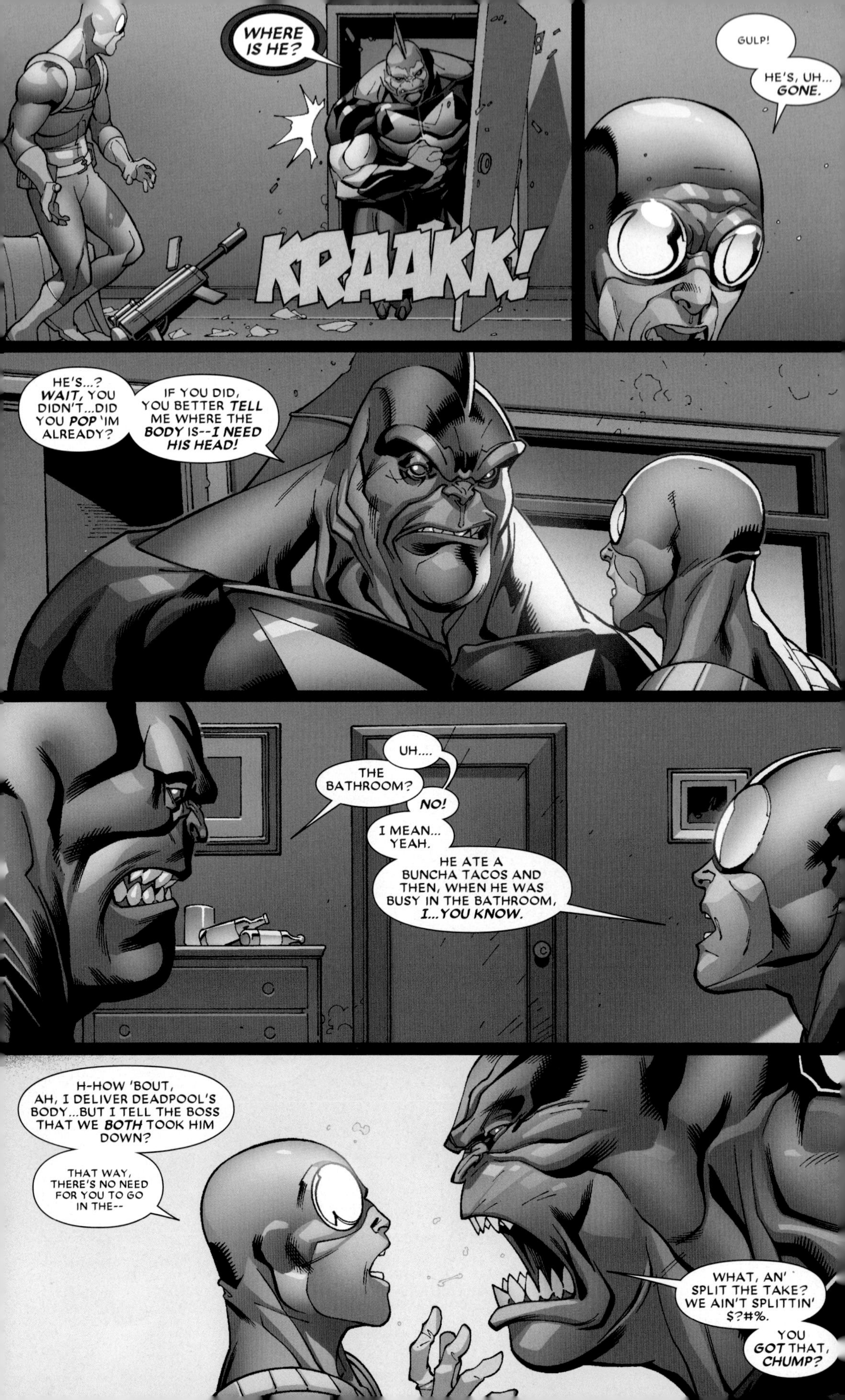
WHERE IS HE?
KRAAKK!
GULP!
HE'S, UH... GONE.
HE'S...? WAIT, YOU DIDN'T...DID YOU POP 'IM ALREADY?
IF YOU DID, YOU BETTER TELL ME WHERE THE BODY IS--I NEED HIS HEAD!
UH....
THE BATHROOM?
NO!
I MEAN... YEAH.
HE ATE A BUNCHA TACOS AND THEN, WHEN HE WAS BUSY IN THE BATHROOM, I...YOU KNOW.
H-HOW 'BOUT, AH, I DELIVER DEADPOOL'S BODY...BUT I TELL THE BOSS THAT WE BOTH TOOK HIM DOWN?
THAT WAY, THERE'S NO NEED FOR YOU TO GO IN THE--
WHAT, AN' SPLIT THE TAKE? WE AIN'T SPLITTIN' $?#%.
YOU GOT THAT, CHUMP?

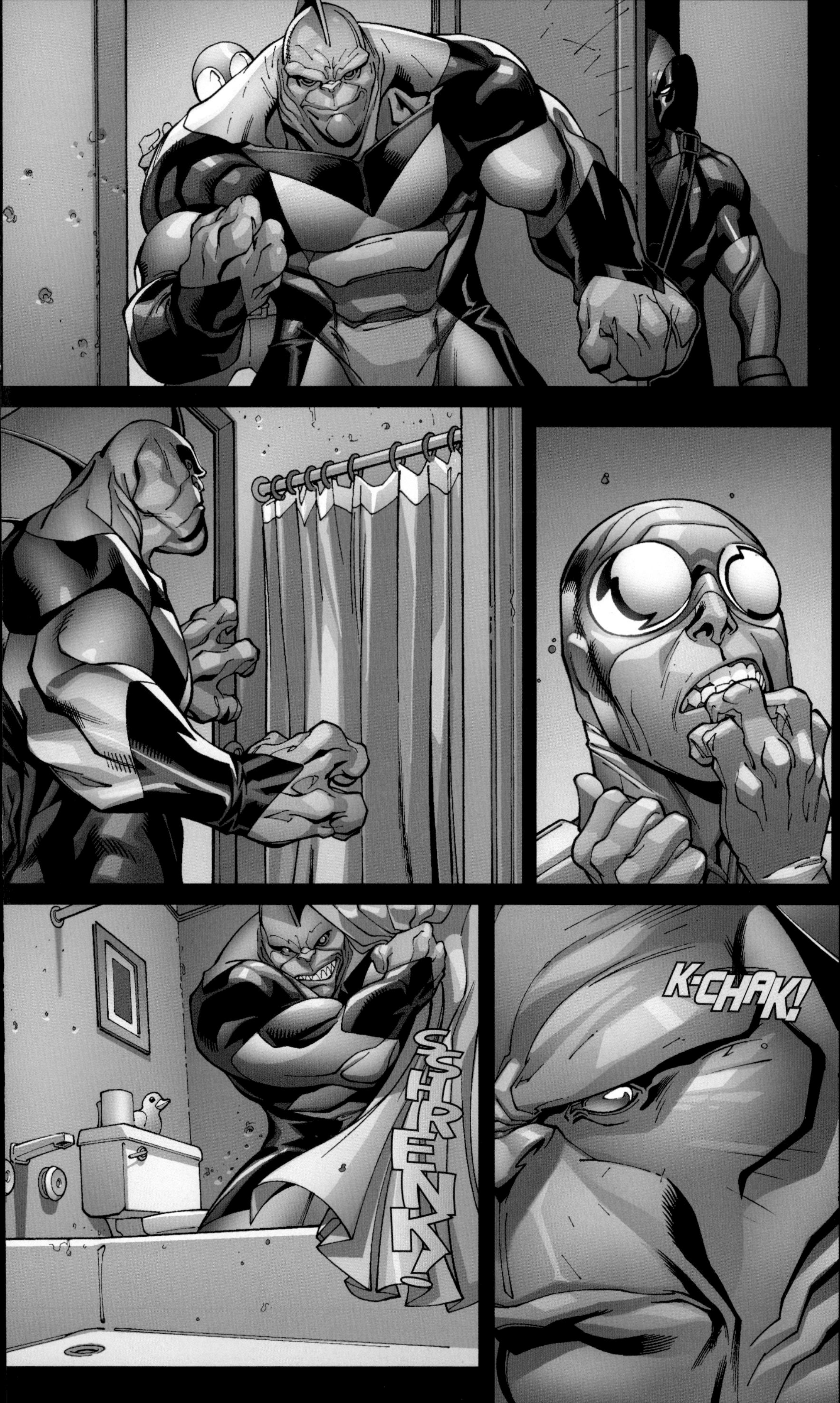
SSHRENK!
K-CHAK!

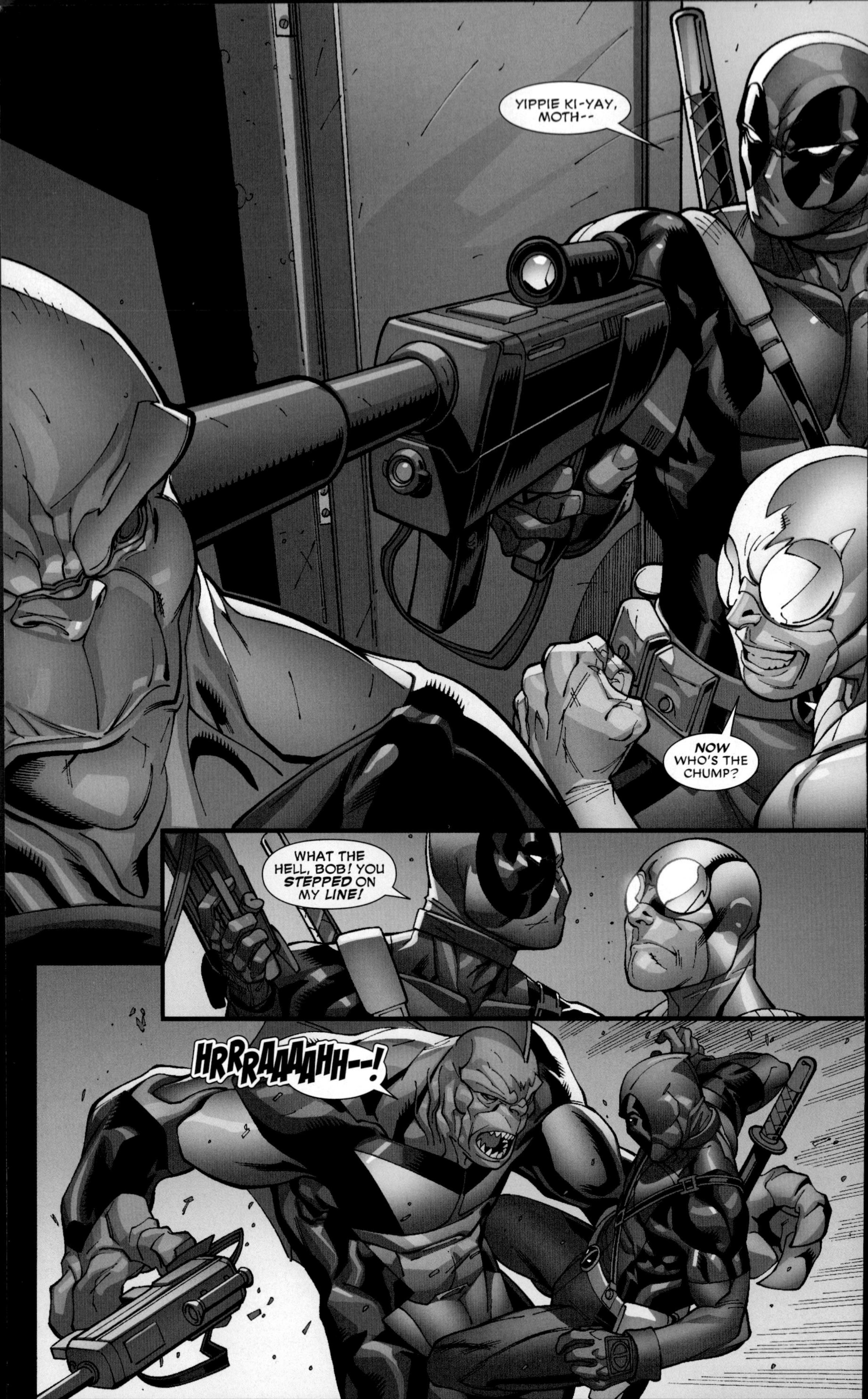
YIPPIE KI-YAY, MOTH--
NOW WHO'S THE CHUMP?
WHAT THE HELL, BOB! YOU STEPPED ON MY LINE!
HRRRAAAAHH--!

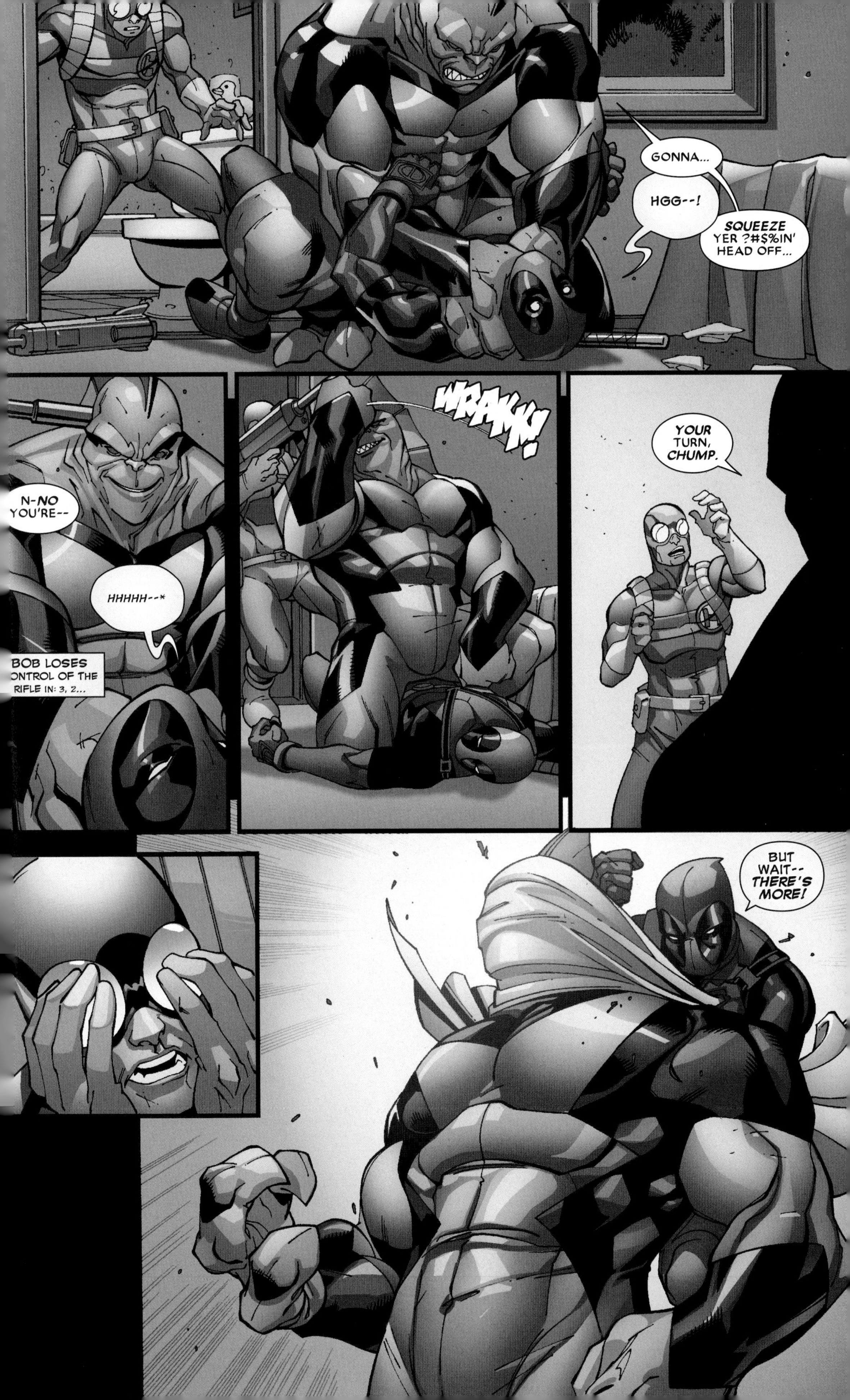
GONNA...
HGG--!
SQUEEZE YER ?#$%IN' HEAD OFF...
N-NO YOU'RE--
HHHHH--*
BOB LOSES
ONTROL OF THE
RIFLE IN: 3, 2...
WRAKK!
YOUR TURN, CHUMP.
BUT WAIT-- THERE'S MORE!

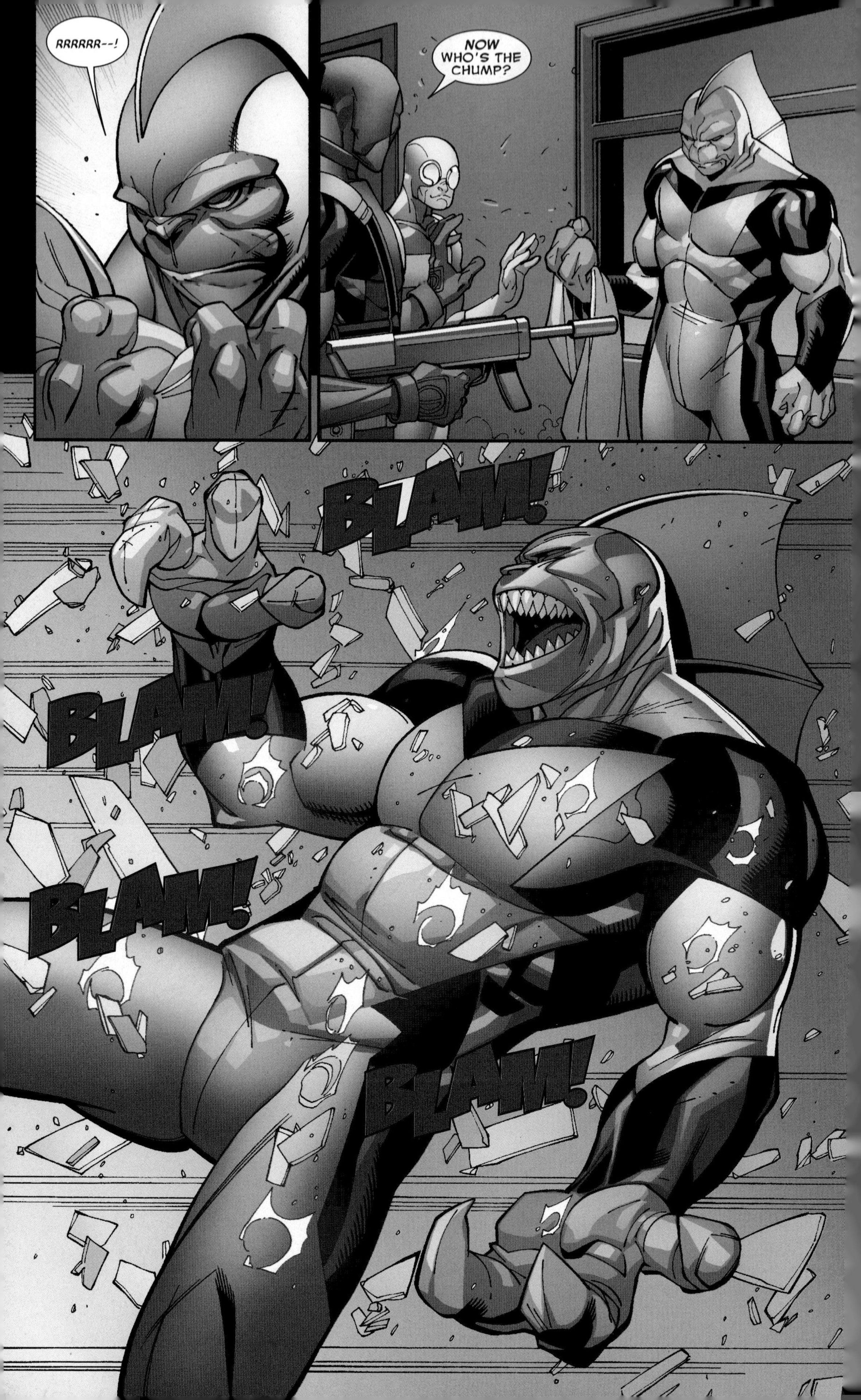
RRRRRR--!
NOW WHO'S THE CHUMP?
BLAM!
BLAM!
BLAM!
BLAM!

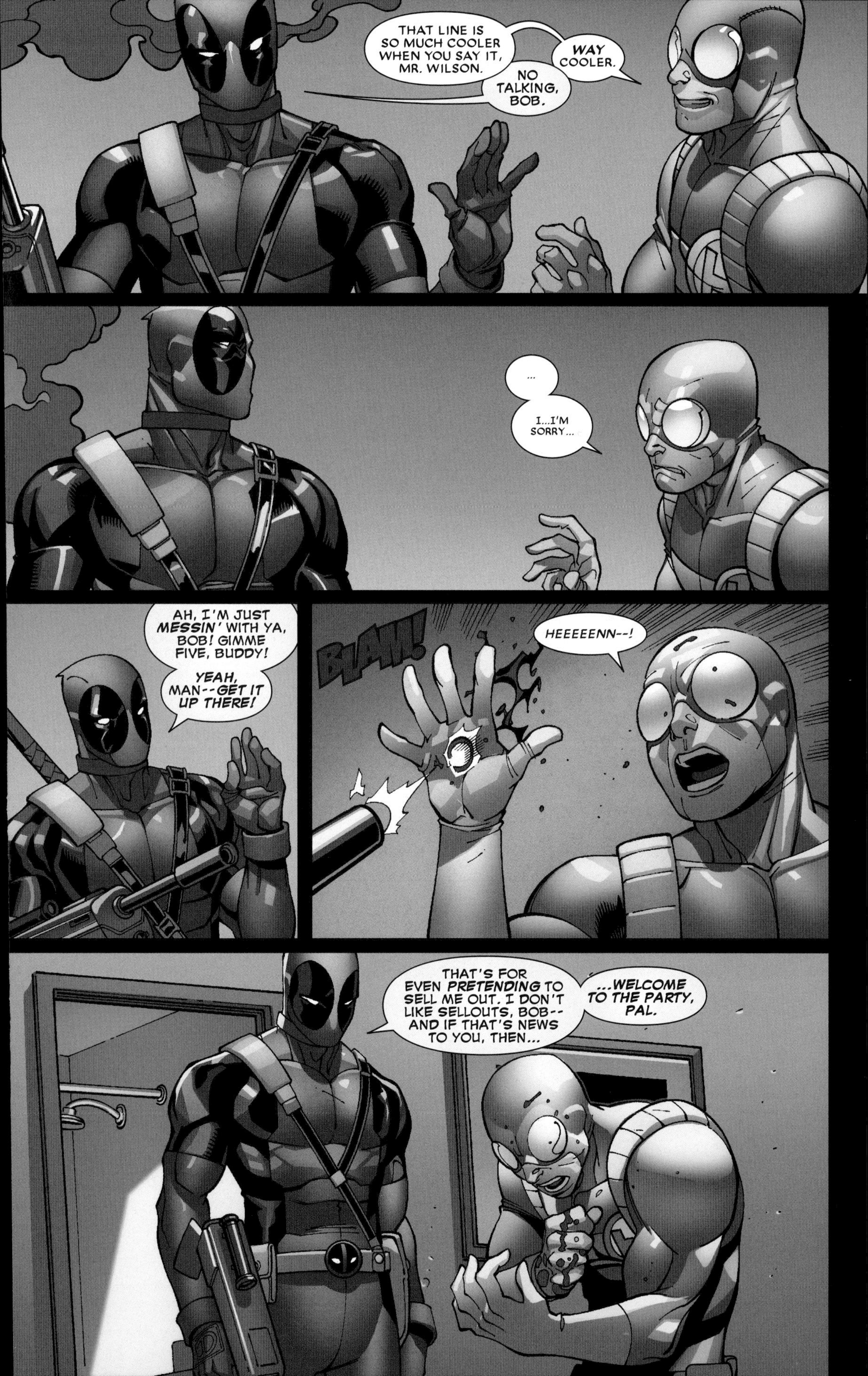
THAT LINE IS SO MUCH COOLER WHEN YOU SAY IT, MR. WILSON.
WAY COOLER.
NO TALKING, BOB.
...
I...I'M SORRY...
AH, I'M JUST MESSIN' WITH YA, BOB! GIMME FIVE, BUDDY!
YEAH, MAN--GET IT UP THERE!
BLAM!
HEEEEENN--!
THAT'S FOR EVEN PRETENDING TO SELL ME OUT. I DON'T LIKE SELLOUTS, BOB--AND IF THAT'S NEWS TO YOU, THEN...
...WELCOME TO THE PARTY, PAL.

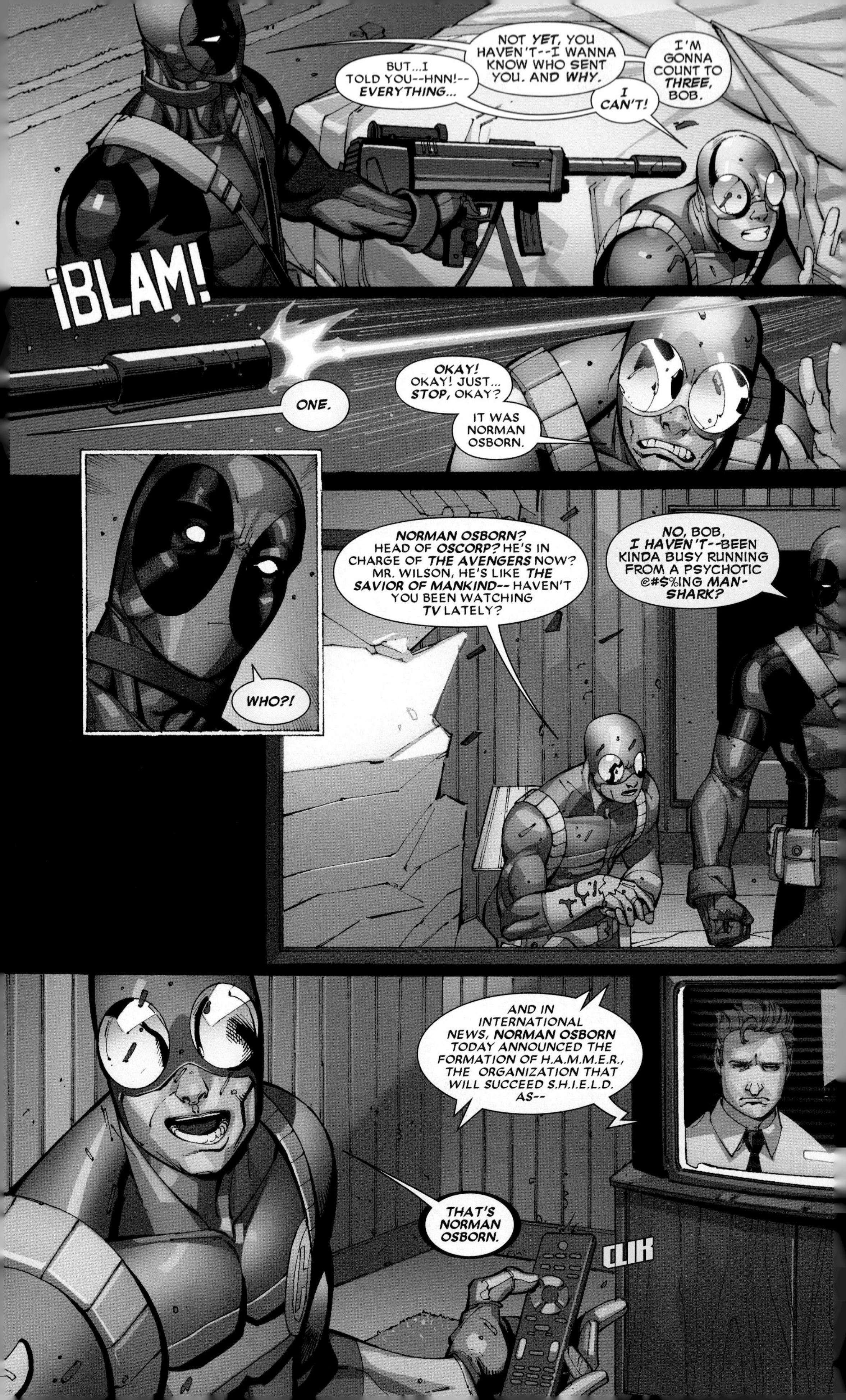

BUT...I TOLD YOU--HNN!--EVERYTHING...
NOT YET, YOU HAVEN'T--I WANNA KNOW WHO SENT YOU. AND WHY.
I CAN'T!
I'M GONNA COUNT TO THREE, BOB.
¡BLAM!
ONE.
OKAY! OKAY! JUST... STOP, OKAY?
IT WAS NORMAN OSBORN.
WHO?!
NORMAN OSBORN? HEAD OF OSCORP? HE'S IN CHARGE OF THE AVENGERS NOW? MR. WILSON, HE'S LIKE THE SAVIOR OF MANKIND-- HAVEN'T YOU BEEN WATCHING TV LATELY?
NO, BOB, I HAVEN'T--BEEN KINDA BUSY RUNNING FROM A PSYCHOTIC @#$%ING MAN-SHARK?
AND IN INTERNATIONAL NEWS, NORMAN OSBORN TODAY ANNOUNCED THE FORMATION OF H.A.M.M.E.R., THE ORGANIZATION THAT WILL SUCCEED S.H.I.E.L.D. AS--
THAT'S NORMAN OSBORN.
CLIK

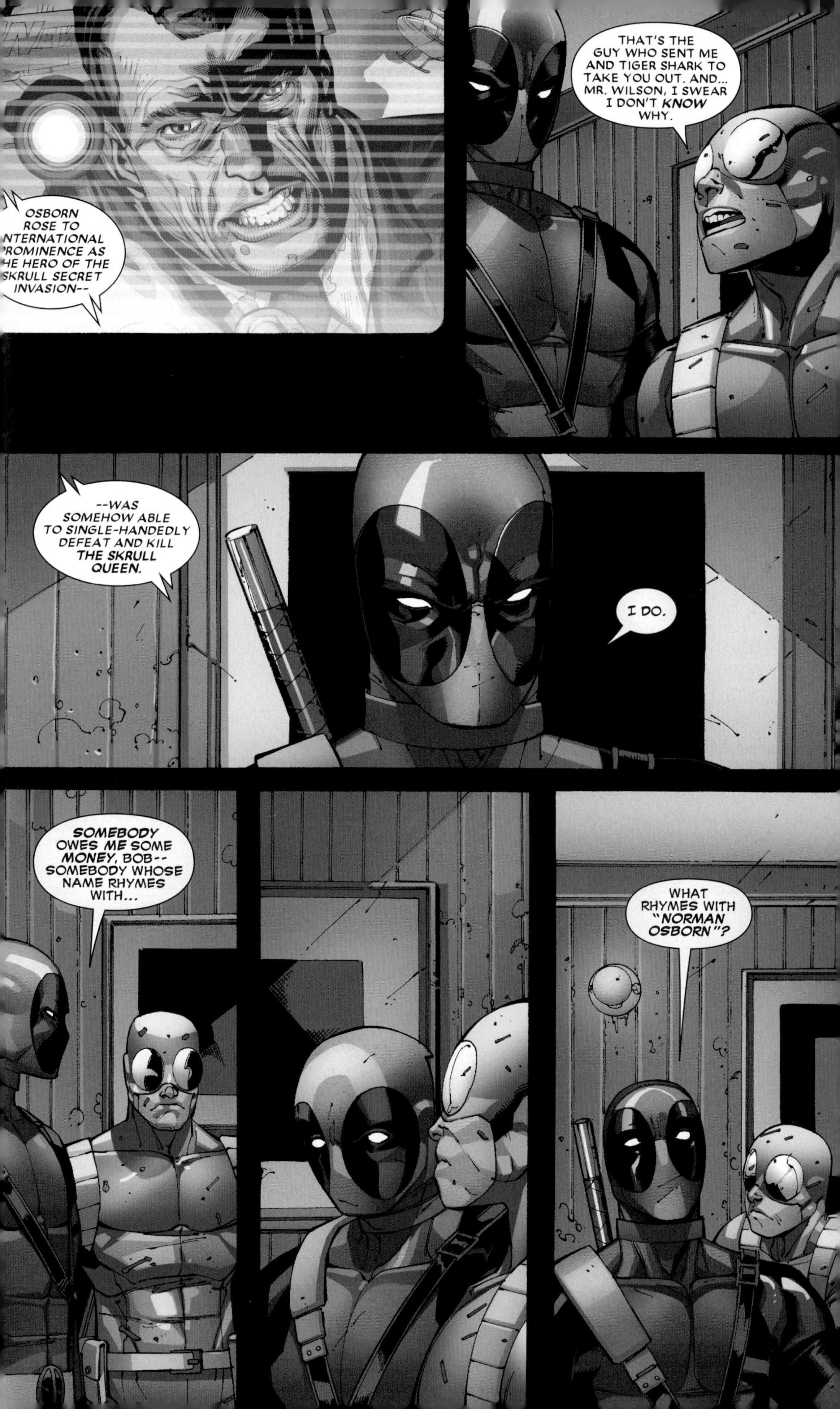
OSBORN ROSE TO INTERNATIONAL PROMINENCE AS THE HERO OF THE SKRULL SECRET INVASION--
THAT'S THE GUY WHO SENT ME AND TIGER SHARK TO TAKE YOU OUT. AND... MR. WILSON, I SWEAR I DON'T KNOW WHY.
--WAS SOMEHOW ABLE TO SINGLE-HANDEDLY DEFEAT AND KILL THE SKRULL QUEEN.
I DO.
SOMEBODY OWES ME SOME MONEY, BOB-- SOMEBODY WHOSE NAME RHYMES WITH...
WHAT RHYMES WITH "NORMAN OSBORN"?

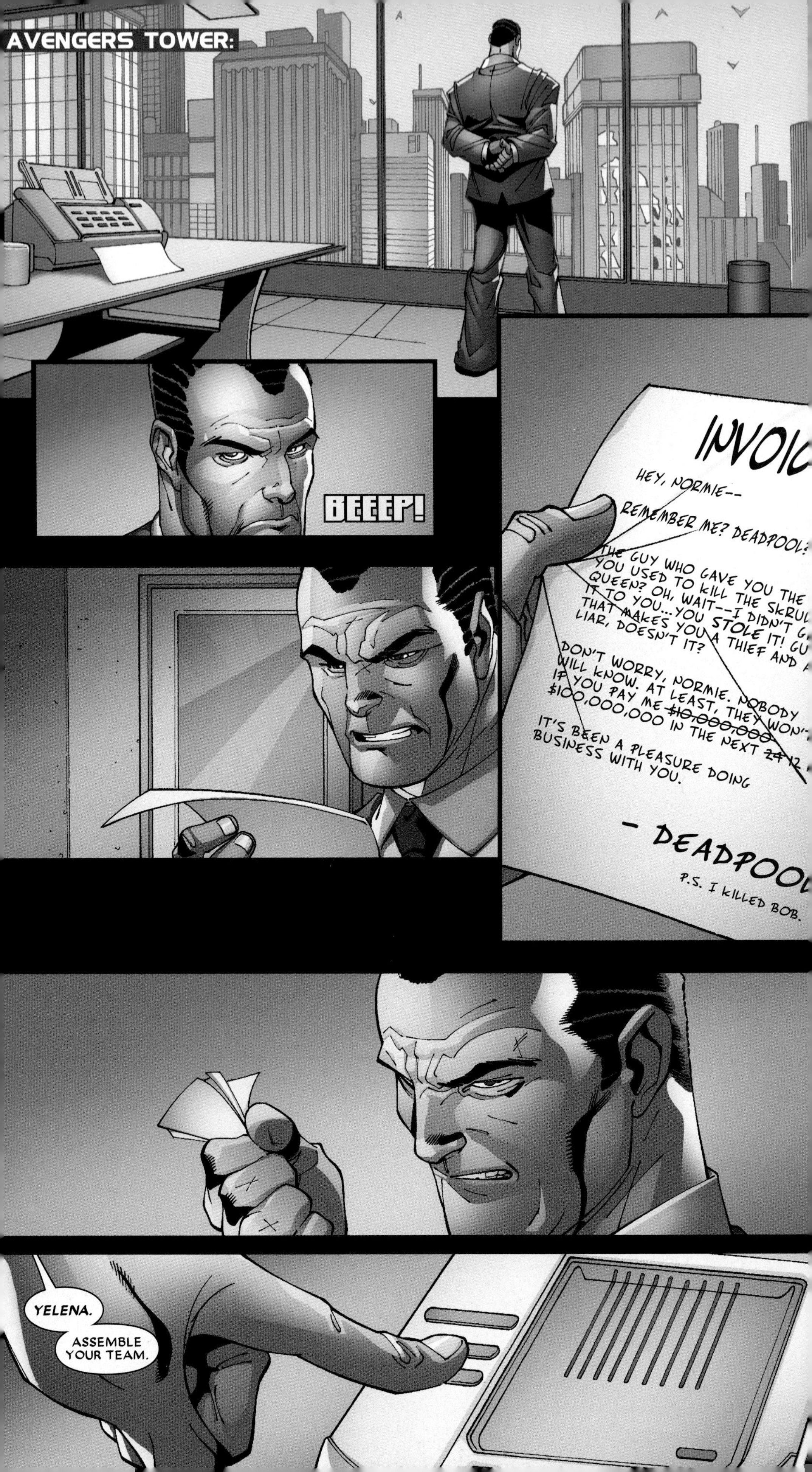

AVENGERS TOWER:
BEEEP!
INVOIC
HEY, NORMIE--
REMEMBER ME? DEADPOOL?
THE GUY WHO GAVE YOU THE
YOU USED TO KILL THE SKRUL
QUEEN? OH, WAIT--I DIDN'T G
IT TO YOU...YOU STOLE IT! GU
THAT MAKES YOU A THIEF AND
LIAR, DOESN'T IT?
DON'T WORRY, NORMIE. NOBODY
WILL KNOW. AT LEAST, THEY WON'T
IF YOU PAY ME $10,000,000
$100,000,000 IN THE NEXT 24 12
IT'S BEEN A PLEASURE DOING
BUSINESS WITH YOU.
- DEADPOOL
P.S. I KILLED BOB.
YELENA.
ASSEMBLE YOUR TEAM.

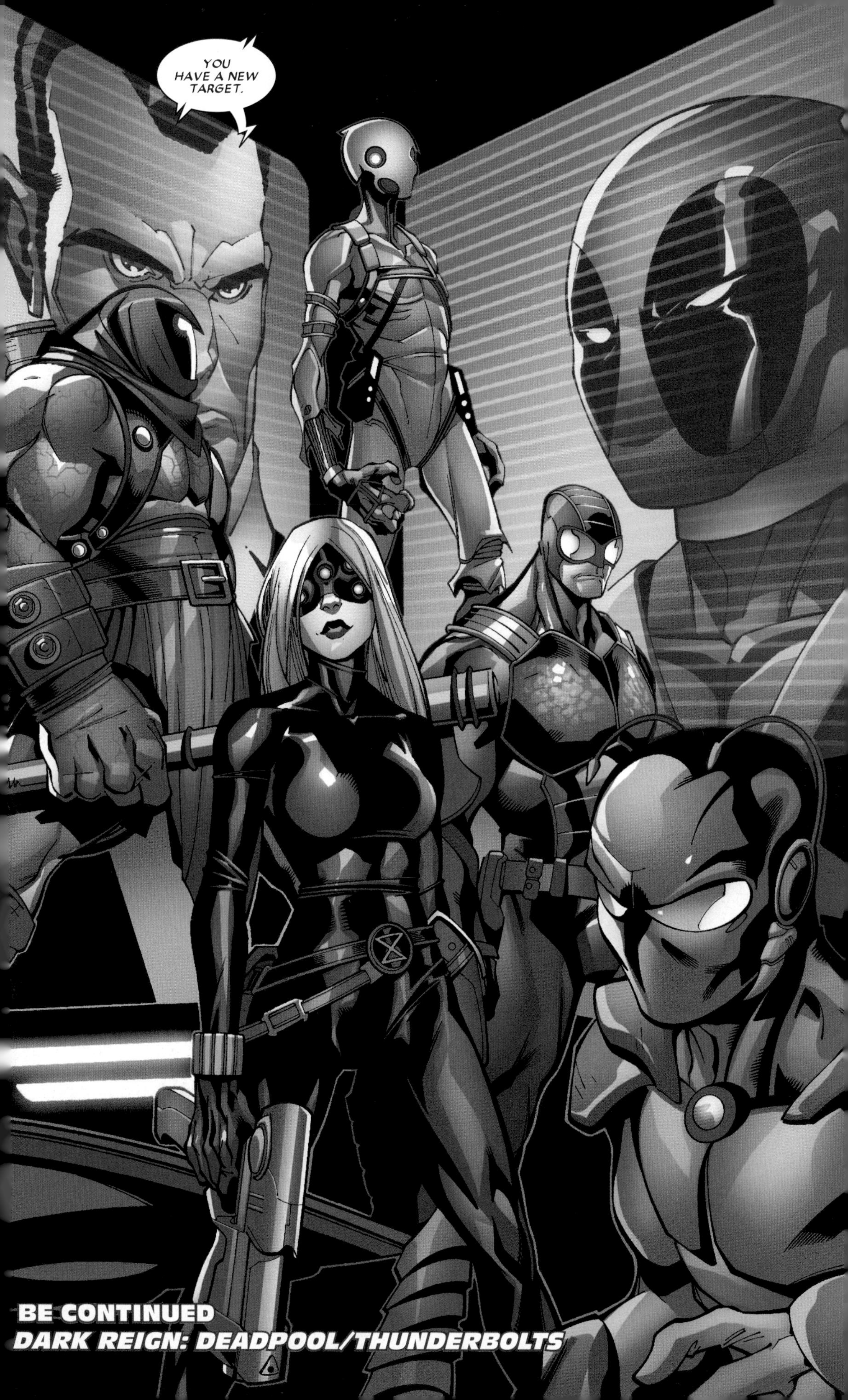

YOU HAVE A NEW TARGET.
BE CONTINUED
DARK REIGN: DEADPOOL/THUNDERBOLTS

PREVIOUSLY IN *DARK REIGN: DEADPOOL/THUNDERBOLTS*:

DEADPOOL HIRED THE REFORMED VILLAIN, TASKMASTER, TO HELP HIM TAKE ON NORMAN'S COVERT STRIKE FORCE, THE THUNDERBOLTS, AND SQUEEZE THE CASH OUT OF OSBORN. NOT ONLY DID DEADOOL AND TASKMASTER DEFEAT THE THUNDERBOLTS, BUT BY THE END OF THE BATTLE, DEADPOOL MANAGED TO STEAL OSBORN'S GOLD CARD…AND FINALLY GOT PAID! WELL…AT LEAST ENOUGH TO COVER THE MONEY HE OWED TASKMASTER. BUT WADE'S EXPECTING A PAYDAY ALL HIS OWN AND HE'S NOT FINISHED WITH NORMAN…NOT BY A LONG SHOT…

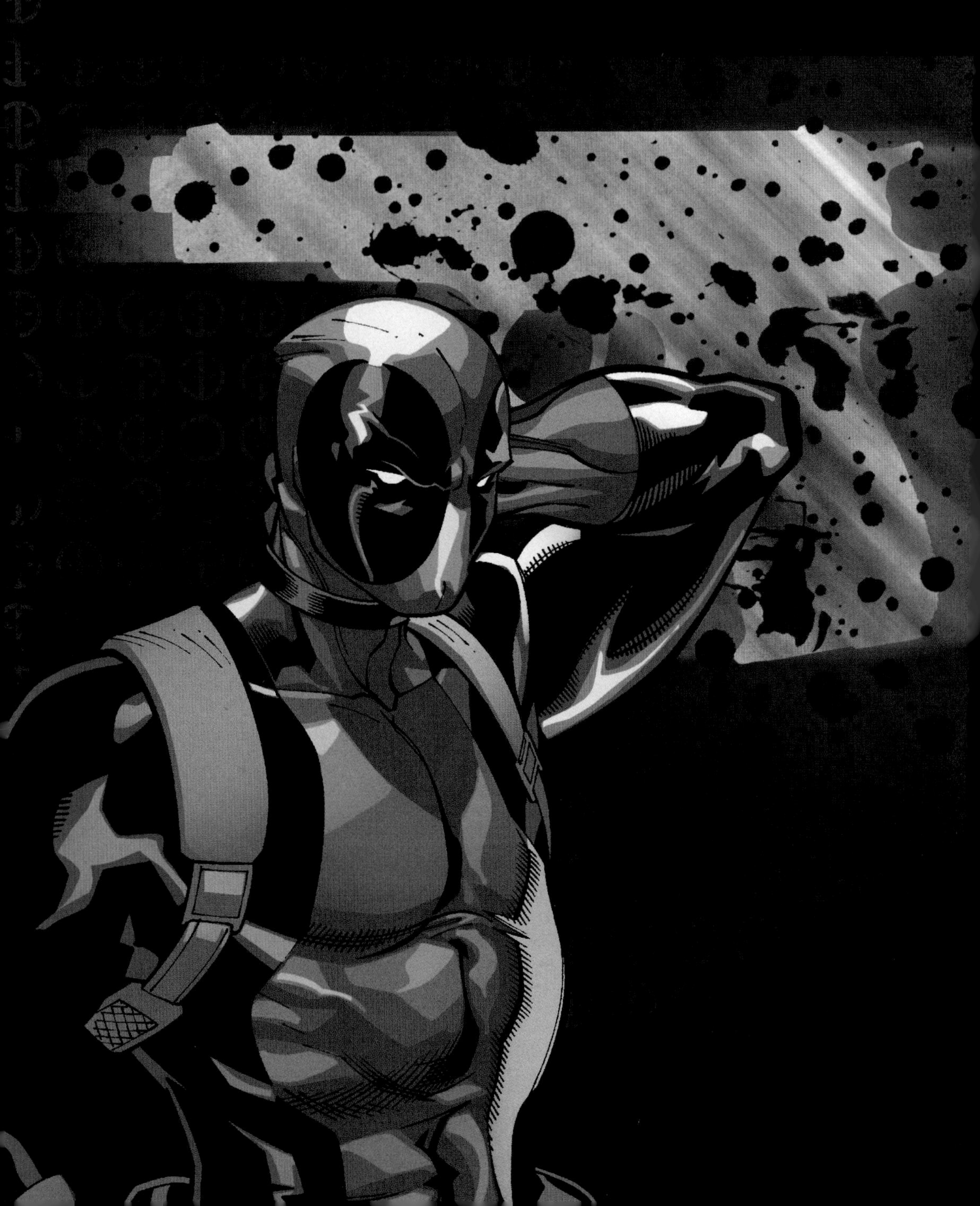

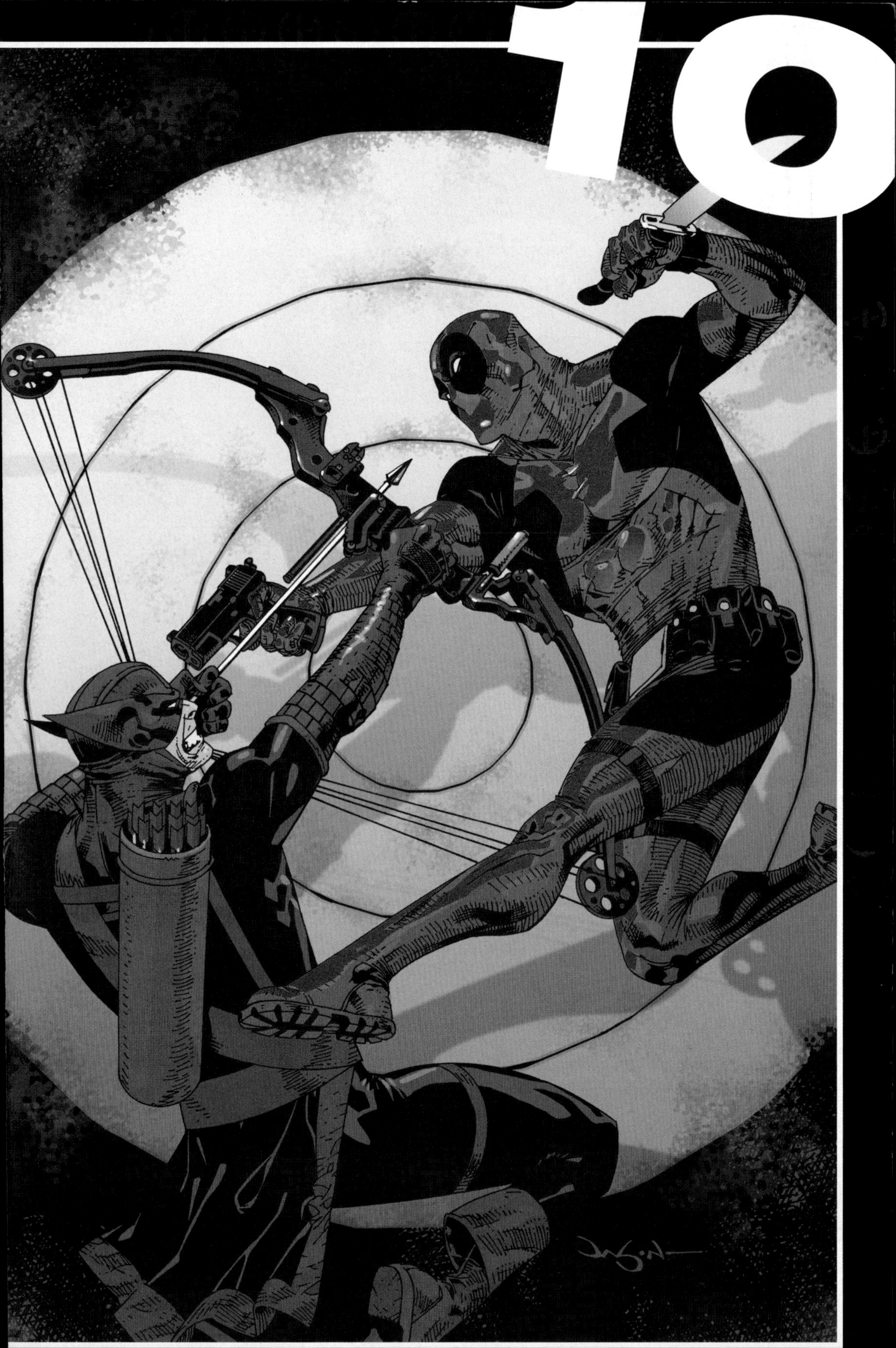
10

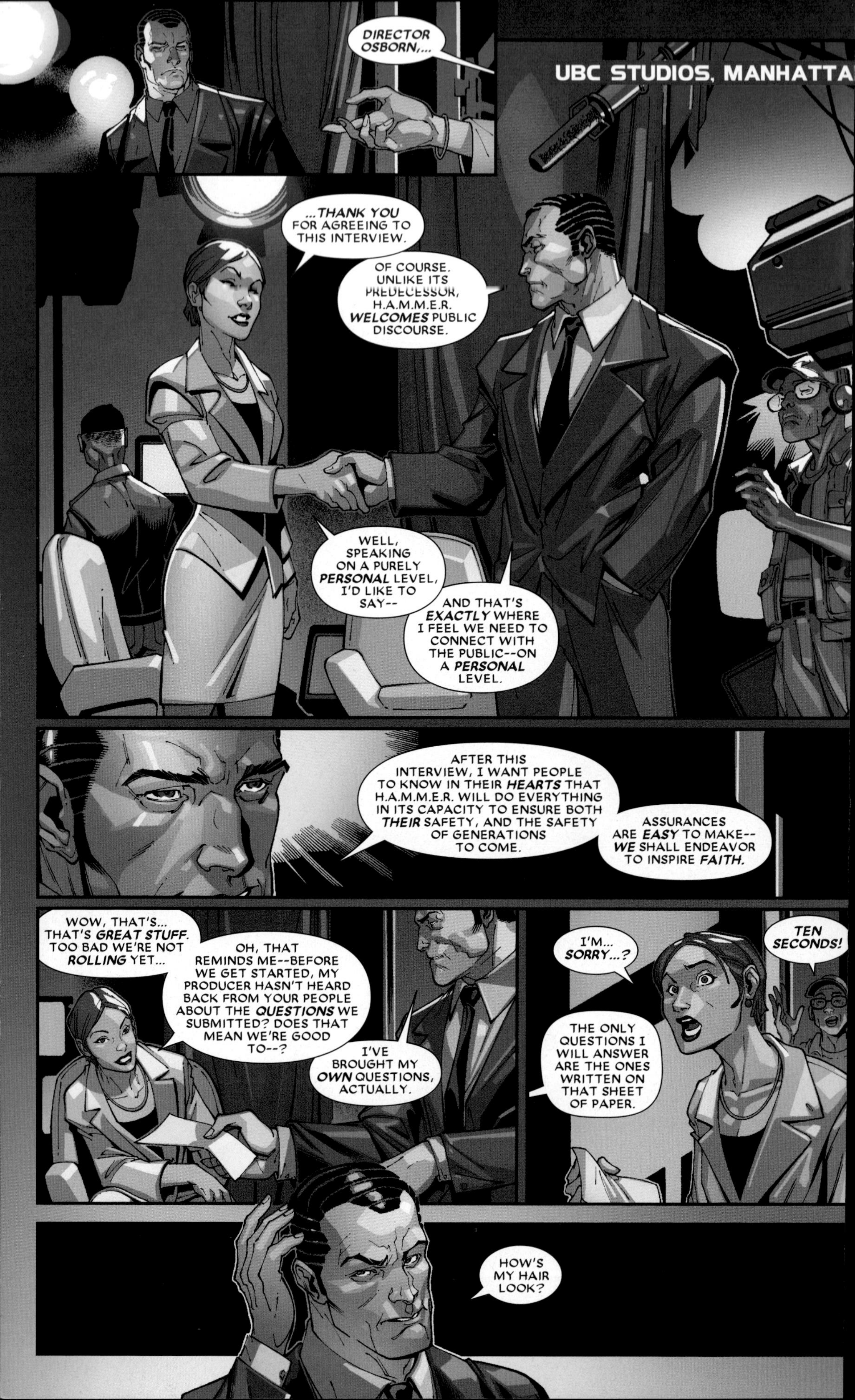

DIRECTOR OSBORN,...
UBC STUDIOS, MANHATTA
...THANK YOU FOR AGREEING TO THIS INTERVIEW.
OF COURSE. UNLIKE ITS PREDECESSOR, H.A.M.M.E.R. WELCOMES PUBLIC DISCOURSE.
WELL, SPEAKING ON A PURELY PERSONAL LEVEL, I'D LIKE TO SAY--
AND THAT'S EXACTLY WHERE I FEEL WE NEED TO CONNECT WITH THE PUBLIC--ON A PERSONAL LEVEL.
AFTER THIS INTERVIEW, I WANT PEOPLE TO KNOW IN THEIR HEARTS THAT H.A.M.M.E.R. WILL DO EVERYTHING IN ITS CAPACITY TO ENSURE BOTH THEIR SAFETY, AND THE SAFETY OF GENERATIONS TO COME.
ASSURANCES ARE EASY TO MAKE-- WE SHALL ENDEAVOR TO INSPIRE FAITH.
WOW, THAT'S... THAT'S GREAT STUFF. TOO BAD WE'RE NOT ROLLING YET...
OH, THAT REMINDS ME--BEFORE WE GET STARTED, MY PRODUCER HASN'T HEARD BACK FROM YOUR PEOPLE ABOUT THE QUESTIONS WE SUBMITTED? DOES THAT MEAN WE'RE GOOD TO--?
I'VE BROUGHT MY OWN QUESTIONS, ACTUALLY.
I'M... SORRY...?
TEN SECONDS!
THE ONLY QUESTIONS I WILL ANSWER ARE THE ONES WRITTEN ON THAT SHEET OF PAPER.
HOW'S MY HAIR LOOK?

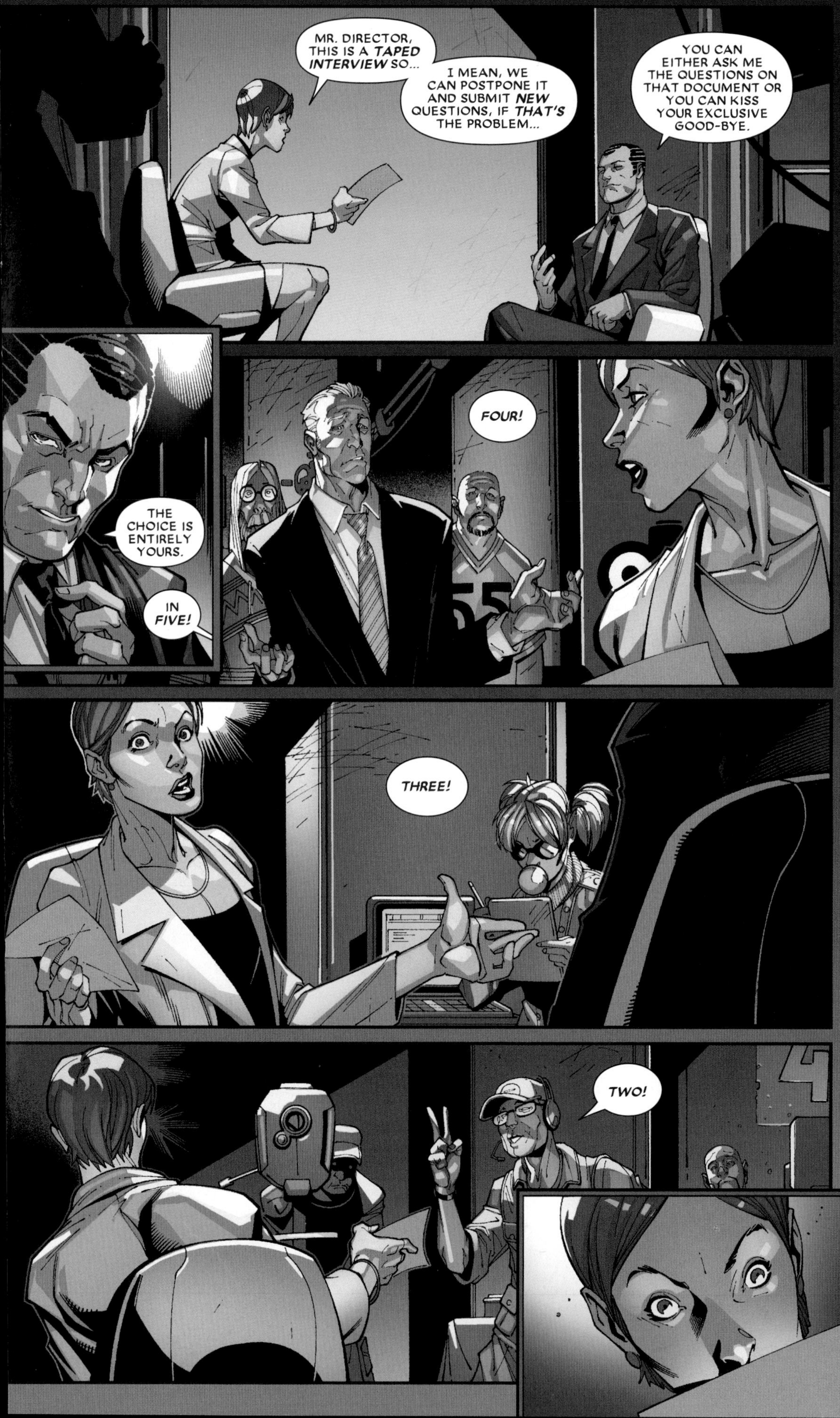
MR. DIRECTOR, THIS IS A *TAPED INTERVIEW* SO...
I MEAN, WE CAN POSTPONE IT AND SUBMIT *NEW* QUESTIONS, IF *THAT'S* THE PROBLEM...
YOU CAN EITHER ASK ME THE QUESTIONS ON THAT DOCUMENT OR YOU CAN KISS YOUR EXCLUSIVE GOOD-BYE.
THE CHOICE IS ENTIRELY YOURS.
IN *FIVE!*
FOUR!
THREE!
TWO!

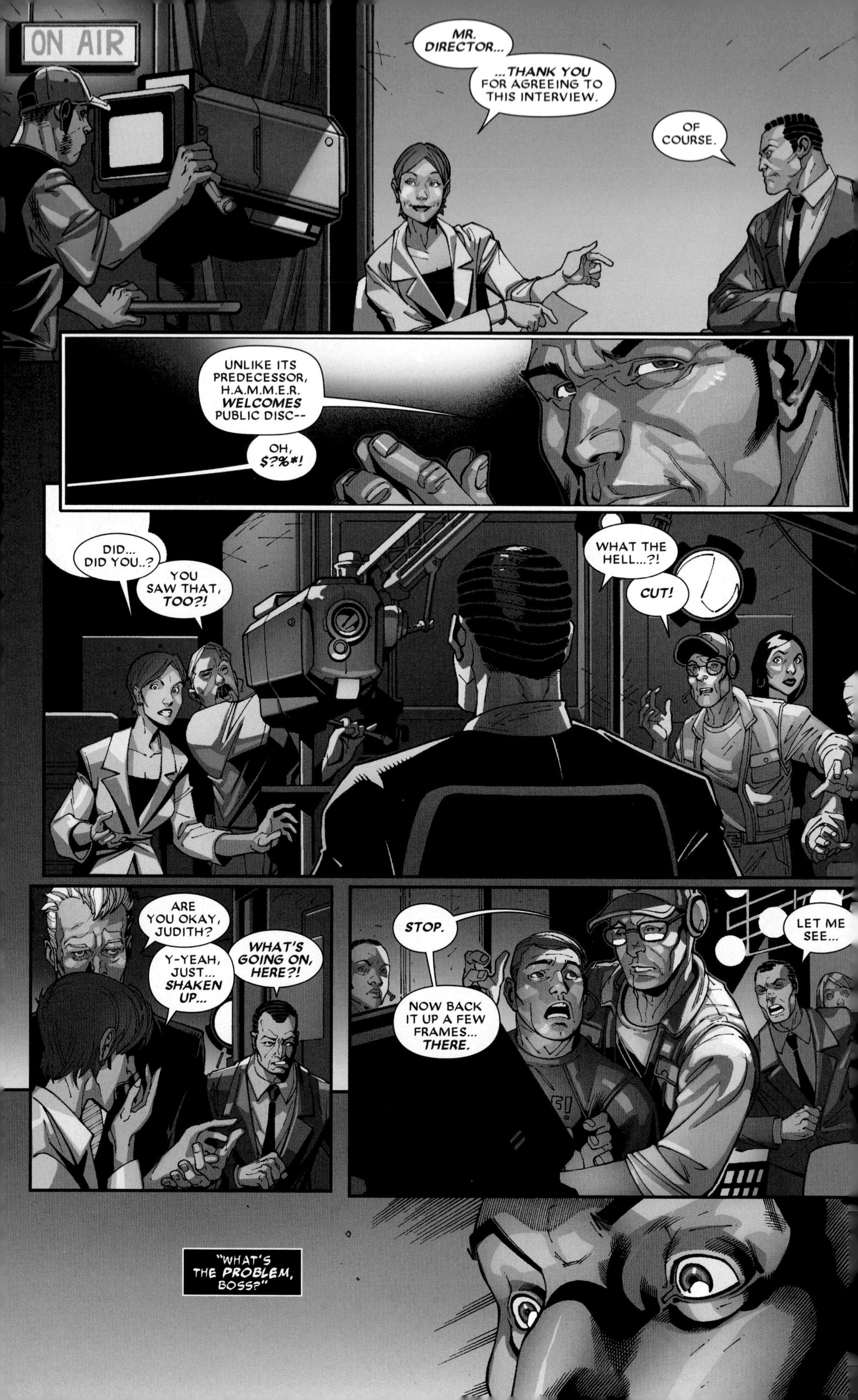
ON AIR
MR. DIRECTOR...
...THANK YOU FOR AGREEING TO THIS INTERVIEW.
OF COURSE.
UNLIKE ITS PREDECESSOR, H.A.M.M.E.R. WELCOMES PUBLIC DISC--
OH, $?%*!
DID... DID YOU..?
YOU SAW THAT, TOO?!
WHAT THE HELL...?!
CUT!
ARE YOU OKAY, JUDITH?
Y-YEAH, JUST... SHAKEN UP...
WHAT'S GOING ON, HERE?!
STOP.
NOW BACK IT UP A FEW FRAMES... THERE.
LET ME SEE...
"WHAT'S THE PROBLEM, BOSS?"

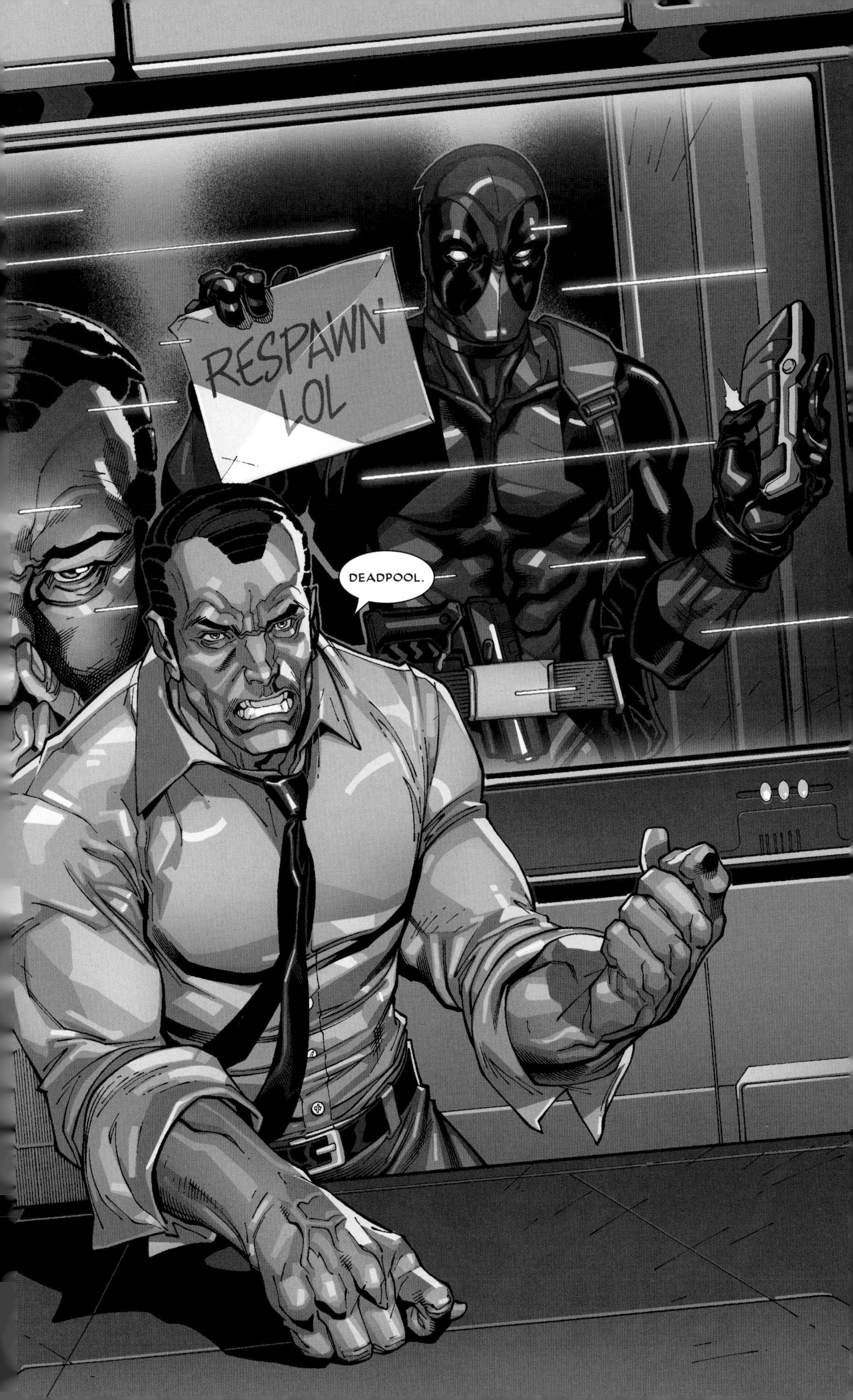
RESPAWN LOL
DEADPOOL.

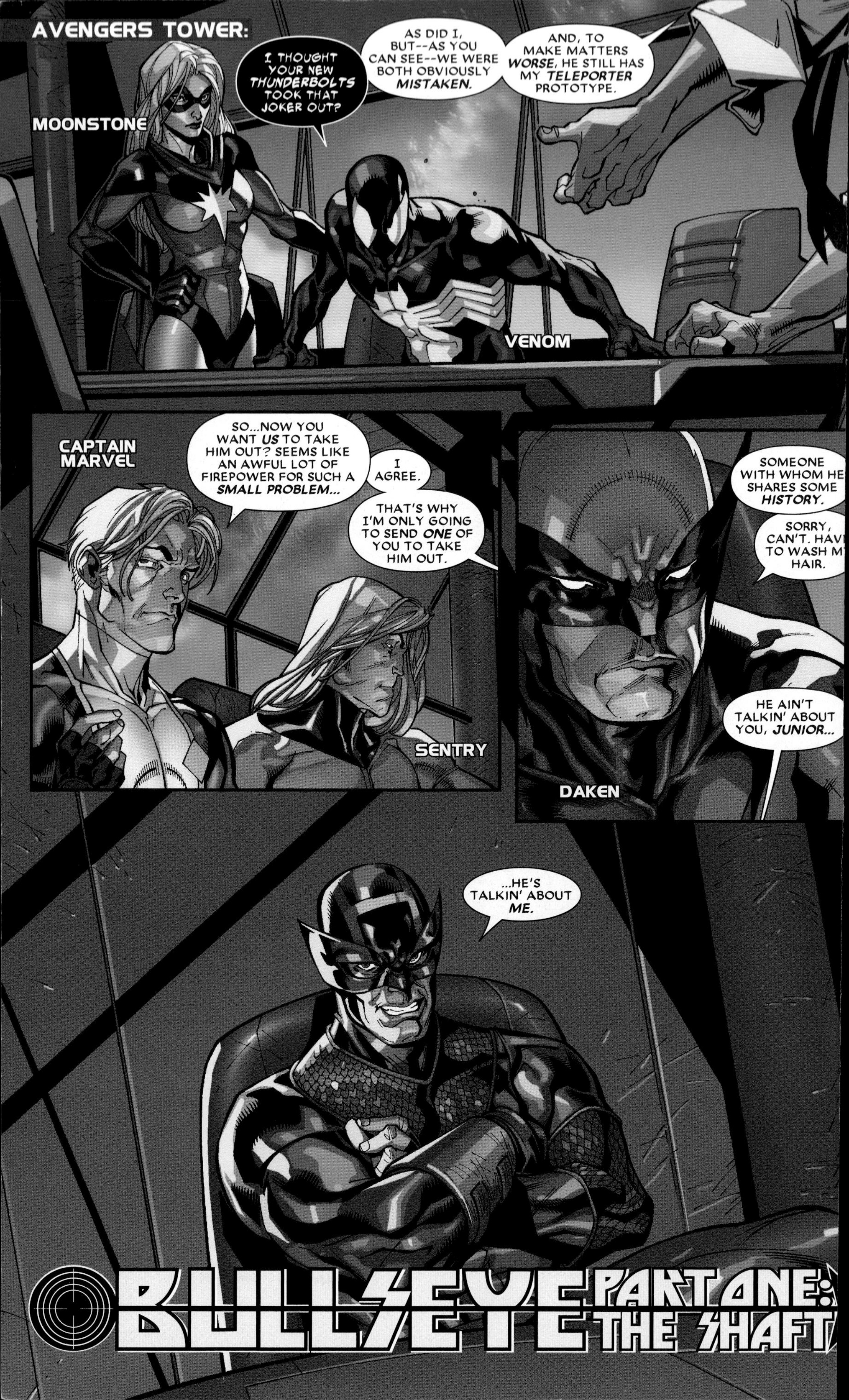
AVENGERS TOWER:
I THOUGHT YOUR NEW THUNDERBOLTS TOOK THAT JOKER OUT?
AS DID I, BUT--AS YOU CAN SEE--WE WERE BOTH OBVIOUSLY MISTAKEN.
AND, TO MAKE MATTERS WORSE, HE STILL HAS MY TELEPORTER PROTOTYPE.
MOONSTONE
VENOM
CAPTAIN MARVEL
SO...NOW YOU WANT US TO TAKE HIM OUT? SEEMS LIKE AN AWFUL LOT OF FIREPOWER FOR SUCH A SMALL PROBLEM...
I AGREE.
THAT'S WHY I'M ONLY GOING TO SEND ONE OF YOU TO TAKE HIM OUT.
SENTRY
SOMEONE WITH WHOM HE SHARES SOME HISTORY.
SORRY, CAN'T. HAVE TO WASH MY HAIR.
HE AIN'T TALKIN' ABOUT YOU, JUNIOR...
DAKEN
...HE'S TALKIN' ABOUT ME.
BULLSEYE
PART ONE: THE SHAFT

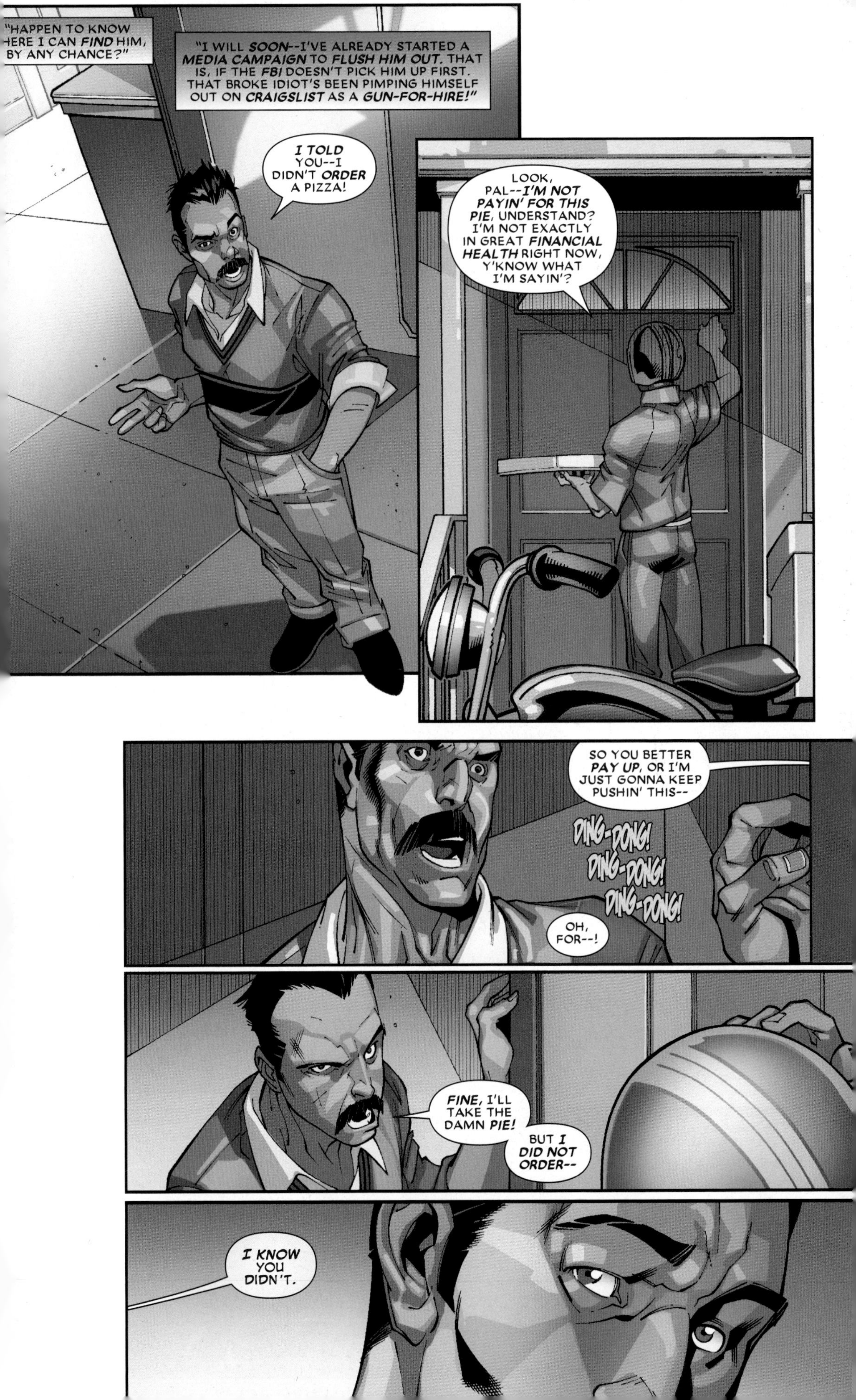
"HAPPEN TO KNOW
HERE I CAN FIND HIM,
BY ANY CHANCE?"
"I WILL SOON--I'VE ALREADY STARTED A MEDIA CAMPAIGN TO FLUSH HIM OUT. THAT IS, IF THE FBI DOESN'T PICK HIM UP FIRST. THAT BROKE IDIOT'S BEEN PIMPING HIMSELF OUT ON CRAIGSLIST AS A GUN-FOR-HIRE!"
I TOLD YOU--I DIDN'T ORDER A PIZZA!
LOOK, PAL--I'M NOT PAYIN' FOR THIS PIE, UNDERSTAND? I'M NOT EXACTLY IN GREAT FINANCIAL HEALTH RIGHT NOW, Y'KNOW WHAT I'M SAYIN'?
SO YOU BETTER PAY UP, OR I'M JUST GONNA KEEP PUSHIN' THIS--
DING-DONG! DING-DONG! DING-DONG!
OH, FOR--!
FINE, I'LL TAKE THE DAMN PIE!
BUT I DID NOT ORDER--
I KNOW YOU DIDN'T.

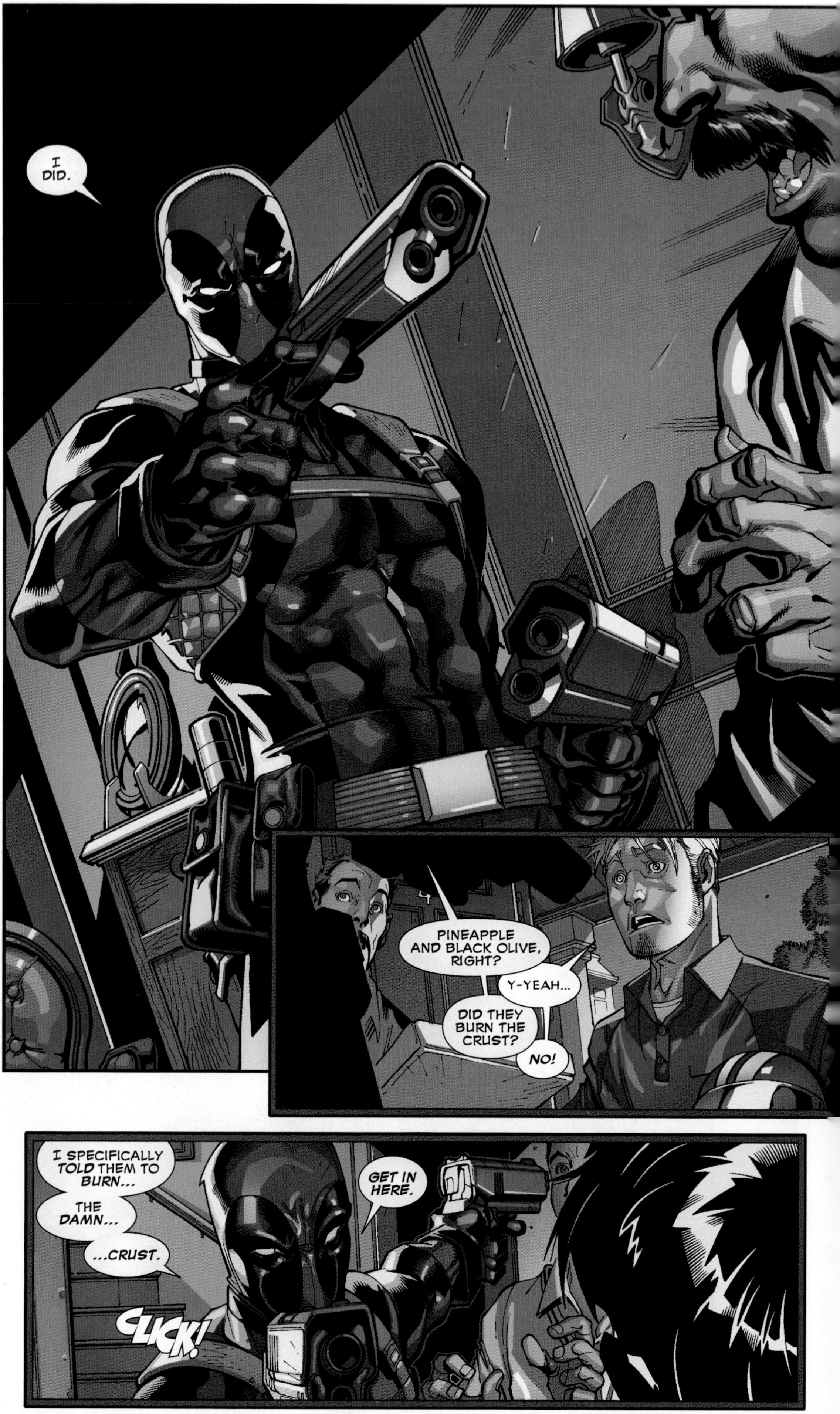
I DID.
PINEAPPLE AND BLACK OLIVE, RIGHT?
Y-YEAH...
DID THEY BURN THE CRUST?
NO!
I SPECIFICALLY *TOLD* THEM TO *BURN*...
THE *DAMN*...
...CRUST.
GET IN HERE.
CLICK!

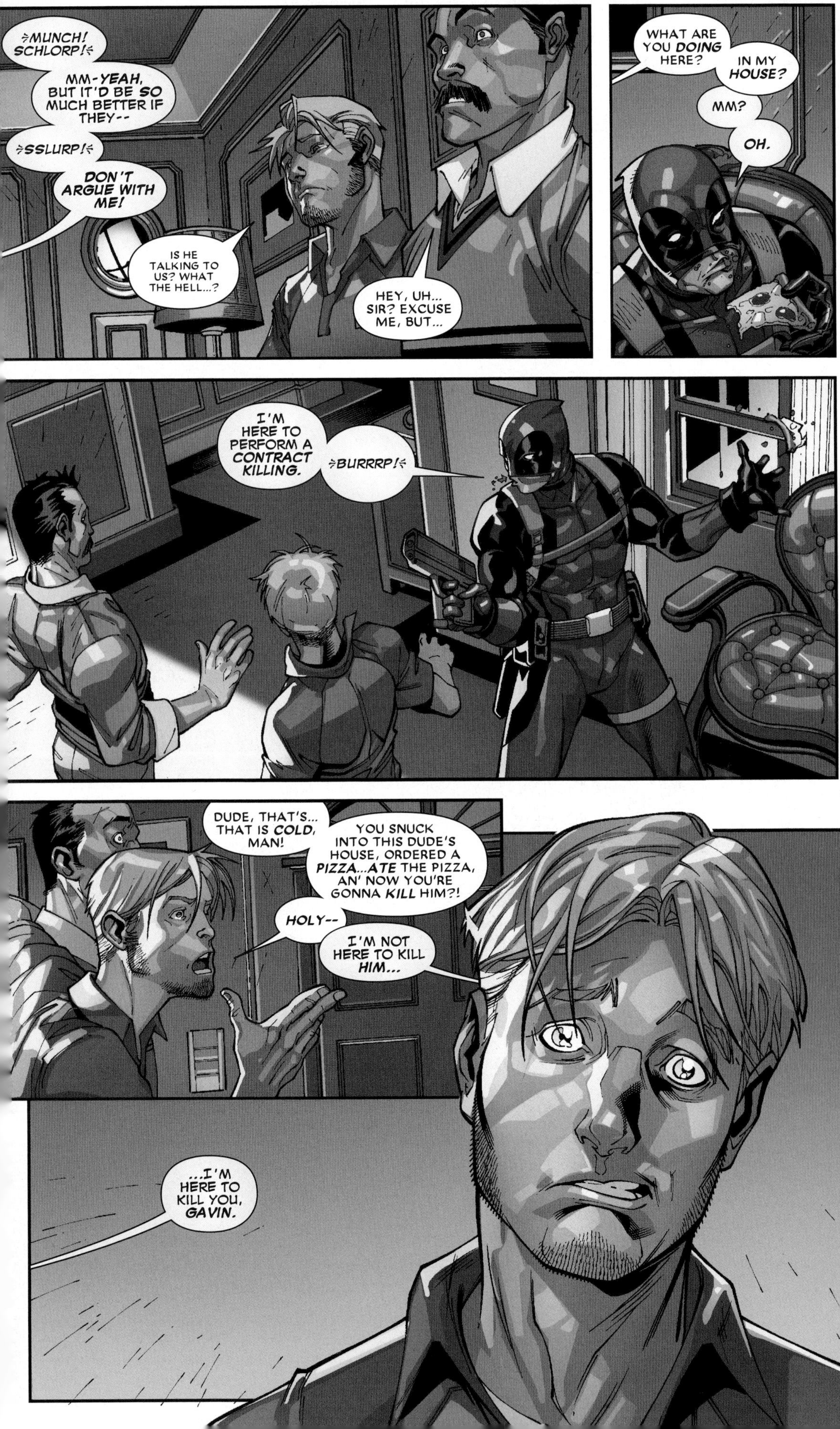

⇒MUNCH! SCHLORP!⇐
MM-YEAH, BUT IT'D BE SO MUCH BETTER IF THEY--
⇒SSLURP!⇐
DON'T ARGUE WITH ME!
IS HE TALKING TO US? WHAT THE HELL...?
HEY, UH... SIR? EXCUSE ME, BUT...
WHAT ARE YOU DOING HERE?
IN MY HOUSE?
MM?
OH.
I'M HERE TO PERFORM A CONTRACT KILLING.
⇒BURRRP!⇐
DUDE, THAT'S... THAT IS COLD, MAN!
YOU SNUCK INTO THIS DUDE'S HOUSE, ORDERED A PIZZA...ATE THE PIZZA, AN' NOW YOU'RE GONNA KILL HIM?!
HOLY--
I'M NOT HERE TO KILL HIM...
...I'M HERE TO KILL YOU, GAVIN.

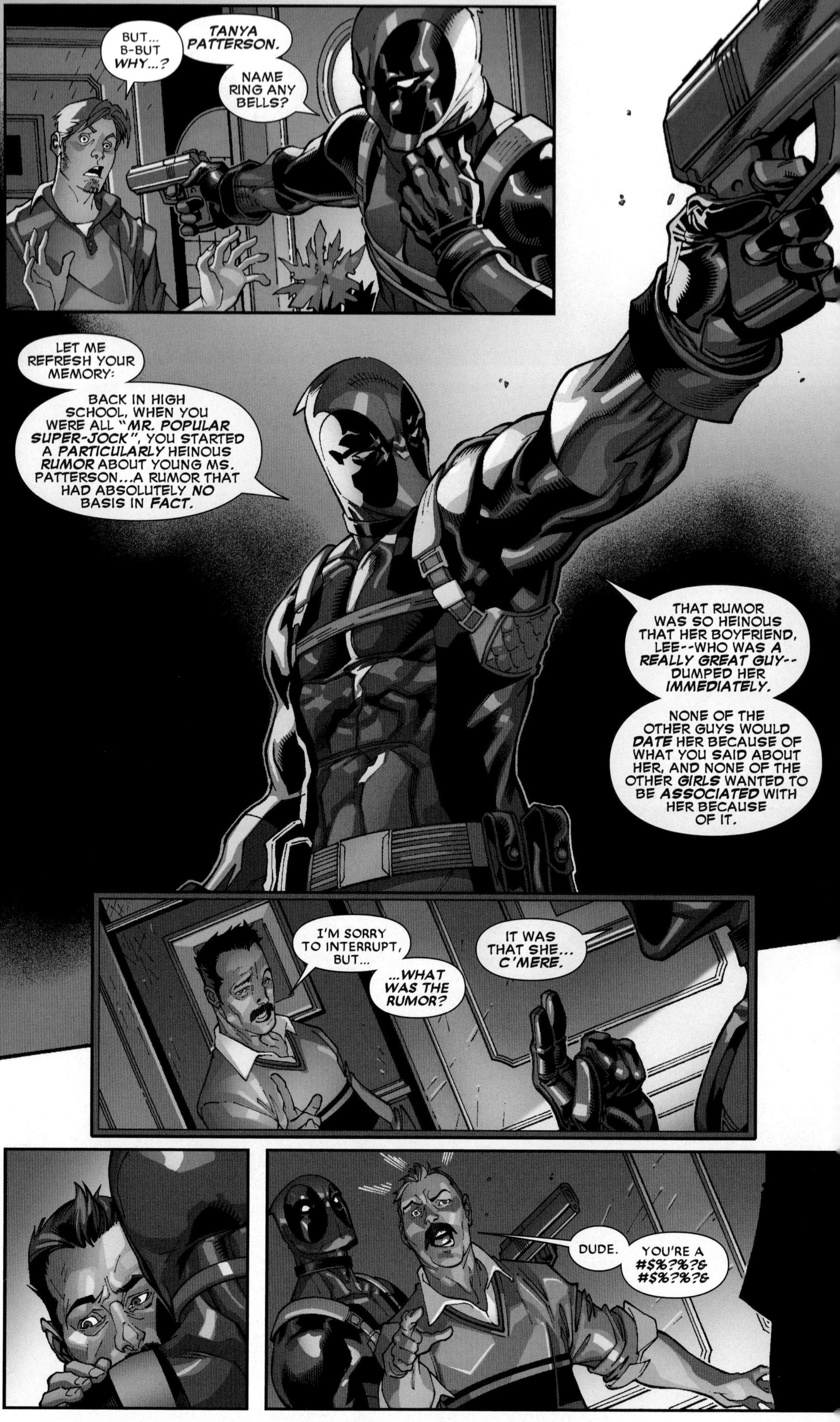

TANYA PATTERSON.
BUT... B-BUT WHY...?
NAME RING ANY BELLS?
LET ME REFRESH YOUR MEMORY:
BACK IN HIGH SCHOOL, WHEN YOU WERE ALL "MR. POPULAR SUPER-JOCK", YOU STARTED A PARTICULARLY HEINOUS RUMOR ABOUT YOUNG MS. PATTERSON...A RUMOR THAT HAD ABSOLUTELY NO BASIS IN FACT.
THAT RUMOR WAS SO HEINOUS THAT HER BOYFRIEND, LEE--WHO WAS A REALLY GREAT GUY--DUMPED HER IMMEDIATELY.
NONE OF THE OTHER GUYS WOULD DATE HER BECAUSE OF WHAT YOU SAID ABOUT HER, AND NONE OF THE OTHER GIRLS WANTED TO BE ASSOCIATED WITH HER BECAUSE OF IT.
I'M SORRY TO INTERRUPT, BUT...
...WHAT WAS THE RUMOR?
IT WAS THAT SHE... C'MERE.
DUDE.
YOU'RE A #$%?%?& #$%?%?&

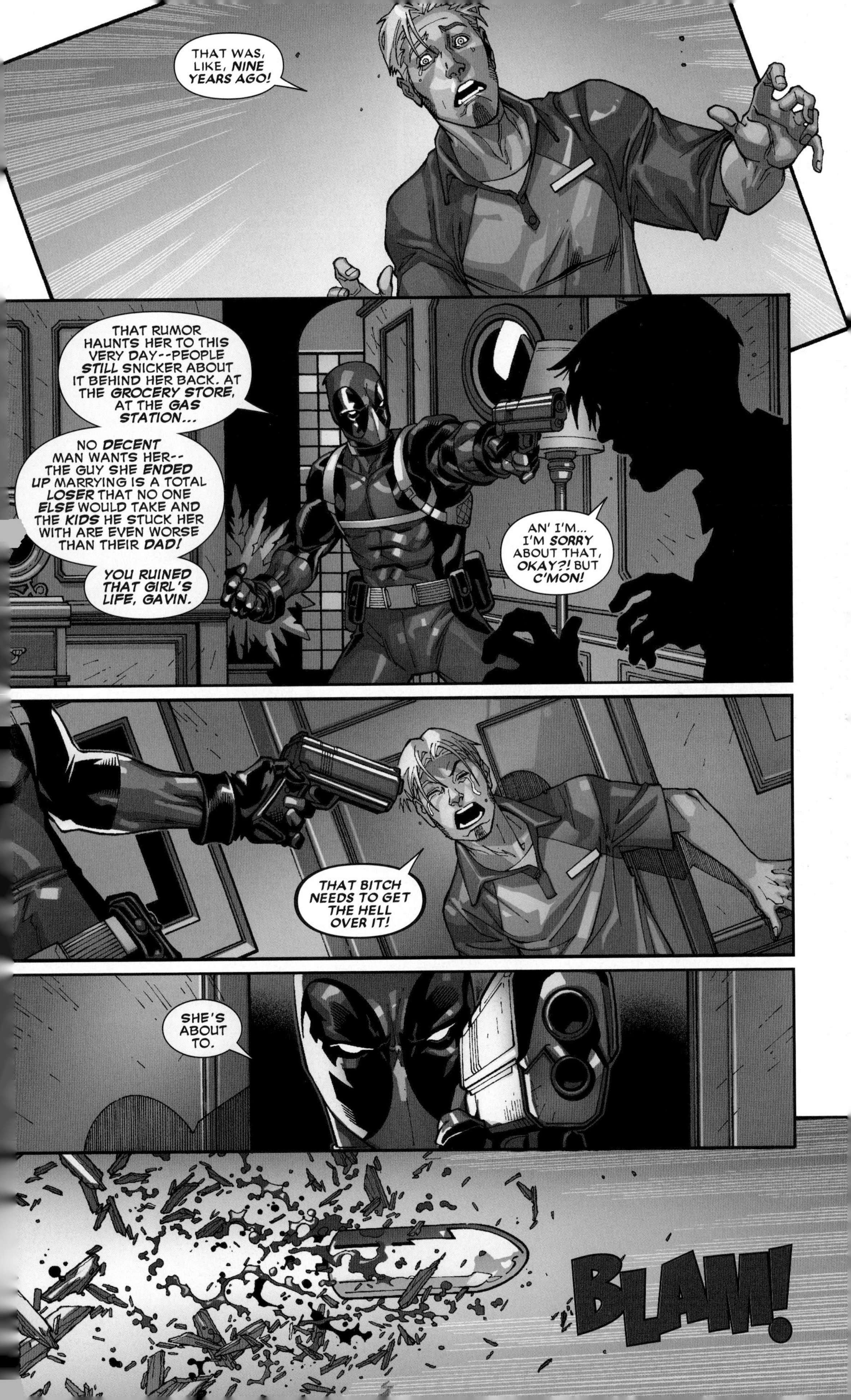
THAT WAS, LIKE, NINE YEARS AGO!
THAT RUMOR HAUNTS HER TO THIS VERY DAY--PEOPLE STILL SNICKER ABOUT IT BEHIND HER BACK. AT THE GROCERY STORE, AT THE GAS STATION...
NO DECENT MAN WANTS HER--THE GUY SHE ENDED UP MARRYING IS A TOTAL LOSER THAT NO ONE ELSE WOULD TAKE AND THE KIDS HE STUCK HER WITH ARE EVEN WORSE THAN THEIR DAD!
YOU RUINED THAT GIRL'S LIFE, GAVIN.
AN' I'M... I'M SORRY ABOUT THAT, OKAY?! BUT C'MON!
THAT BITCH NEEDS TO GET THE HELL OVER IT!
SHE'S ABOUT TO.
BLAM!

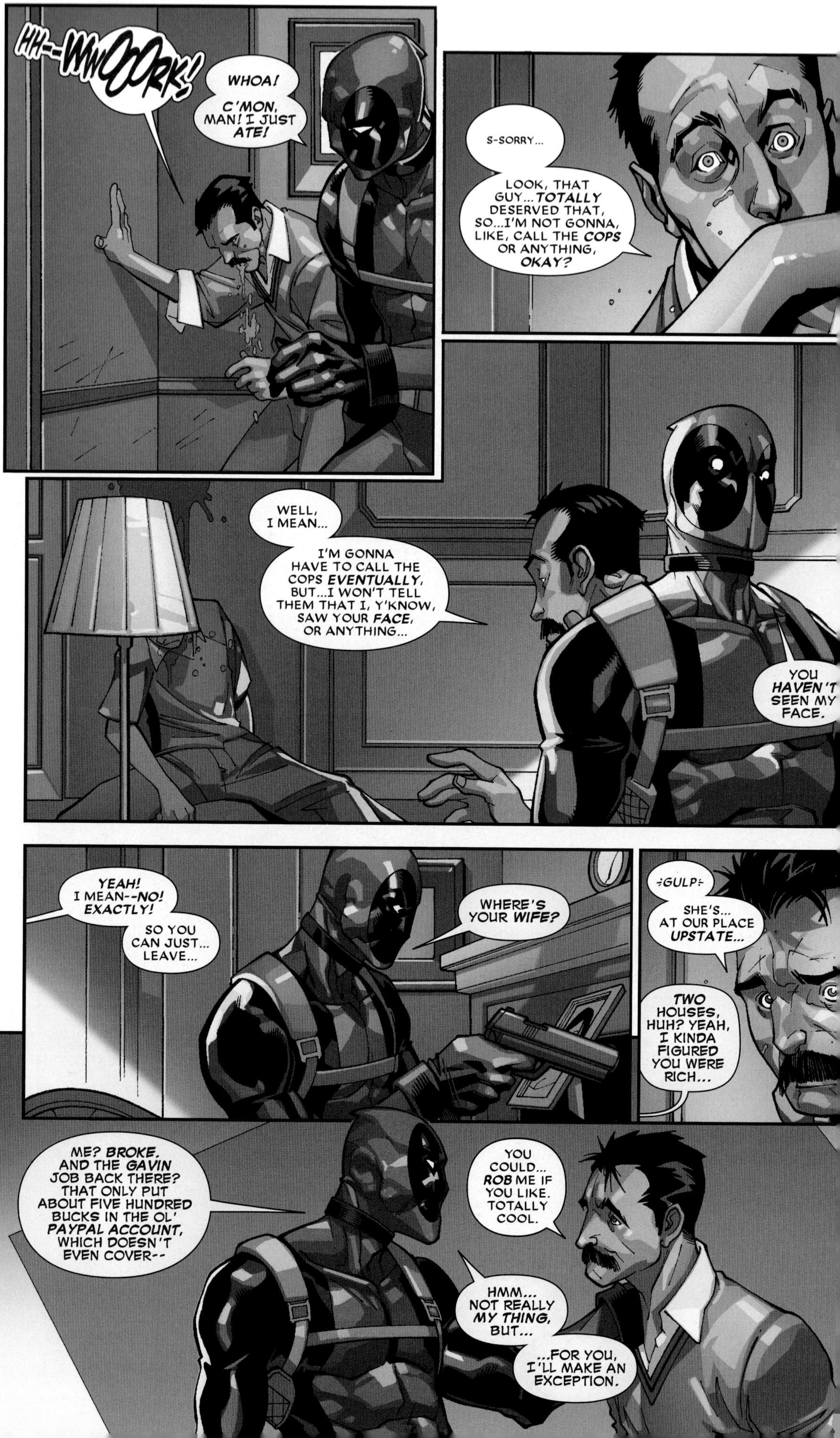

HH--WWOOORK!
WHOA!
C'MON, MAN! I JUST ATE!
S-SORRY...
LOOK, THAT GUY... TOTALLY DESERVED THAT, SO...I'M NOT GONNA, LIKE, CALL THE COPS OR ANYTHING, OKAY?
WELL, I MEAN...
I'M GONNA HAVE TO CALL THE COPS EVENTUALLY, BUT...I WON'T TELL THEM THAT I, Y'KNOW, SAW YOUR FACE, OR ANYTHING...
YOU HAVEN'T SEEN MY FACE.
YEAH! I MEAN--NO! EXACTLY!
SO YOU CAN JUST... LEAVE...
WHERE'S YOUR WIFE?
GULP
SHE'S... AT OUR PLACE UPSTATE...
TWO HOUSES, HUH? YEAH, I KINDA FIGURED YOU WERE RICH...
ME? BROKE. AND THE GAVIN JOB BACK THERE? THAT ONLY PUT ABOUT FIVE HUNDRED BUCKS IN THE OL' PAYPAL ACCOUNT, WHICH DOESN'T EVEN COVER--
YOU COULD... ROB ME IF YOU LIKE. TOTALLY COOL.
HMM... NOT REALLY MY THING, BUT...
...FOR YOU, I'LL MAKE AN EXCEPTION.

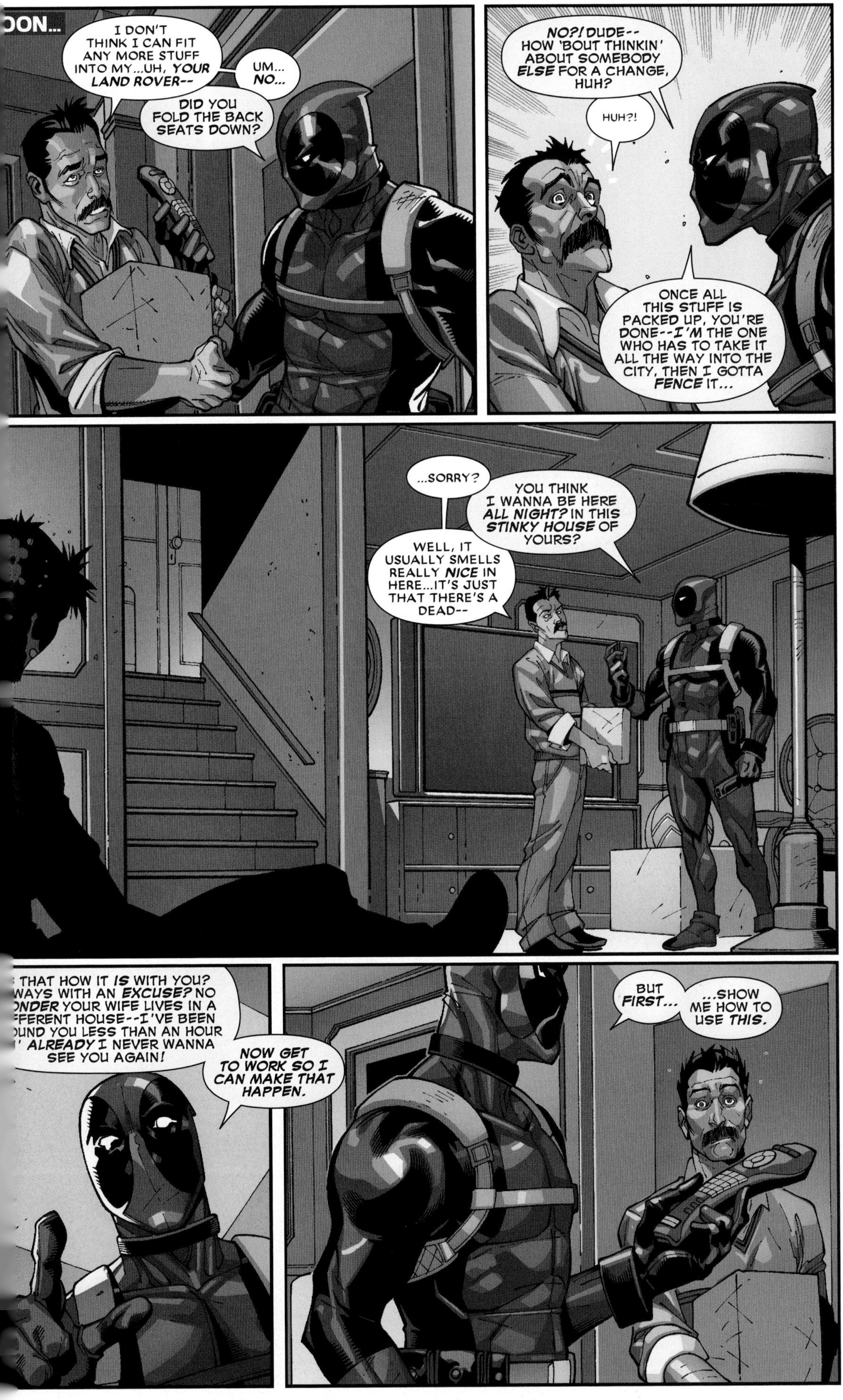
OON...
I DON'T THINK I CAN FIT ANY MORE STUFF INTO MY...UH, YOUR LAND ROVER--
UM... NO...
DID YOU FOLD THE BACK SEATS DOWN?
NO?! DUDE-- HOW 'BOUT THINKIN' ABOUT SOMEBODY ELSE FOR A CHANGE, HUH?
HUH?!
ONCE ALL THIS STUFF IS PACKED UP, YOU'RE DONE--I'M THE ONE WHO HAS TO TAKE IT ALL THE WAY INTO THE CITY, THEN I GOTTA FENCE IT...
...SORRY?
YOU THINK I WANNA BE HERE ALL NIGHT? IN THIS STINKY HOUSE OF YOURS?
WELL, IT USUALLY SMELLS REALLY NICE IN HERE...IT'S JUST THAT THERE'S A DEAD--
THAT HOW IT IS WITH YOU? WAYS WITH AN EXCUSE? NO ONDER YOUR WIFE LIVES IN A FFERENT HOUSE--I'VE BEEN OUND YOU LESS THAN AN HOUR ' ALREADY I NEVER WANNA SEE YOU AGAIN!
NOW GET TO WORK SO I CAN MAKE THAT HAPPEN.
BUT FIRST...
...SHOW ME HOW TO USE THIS.

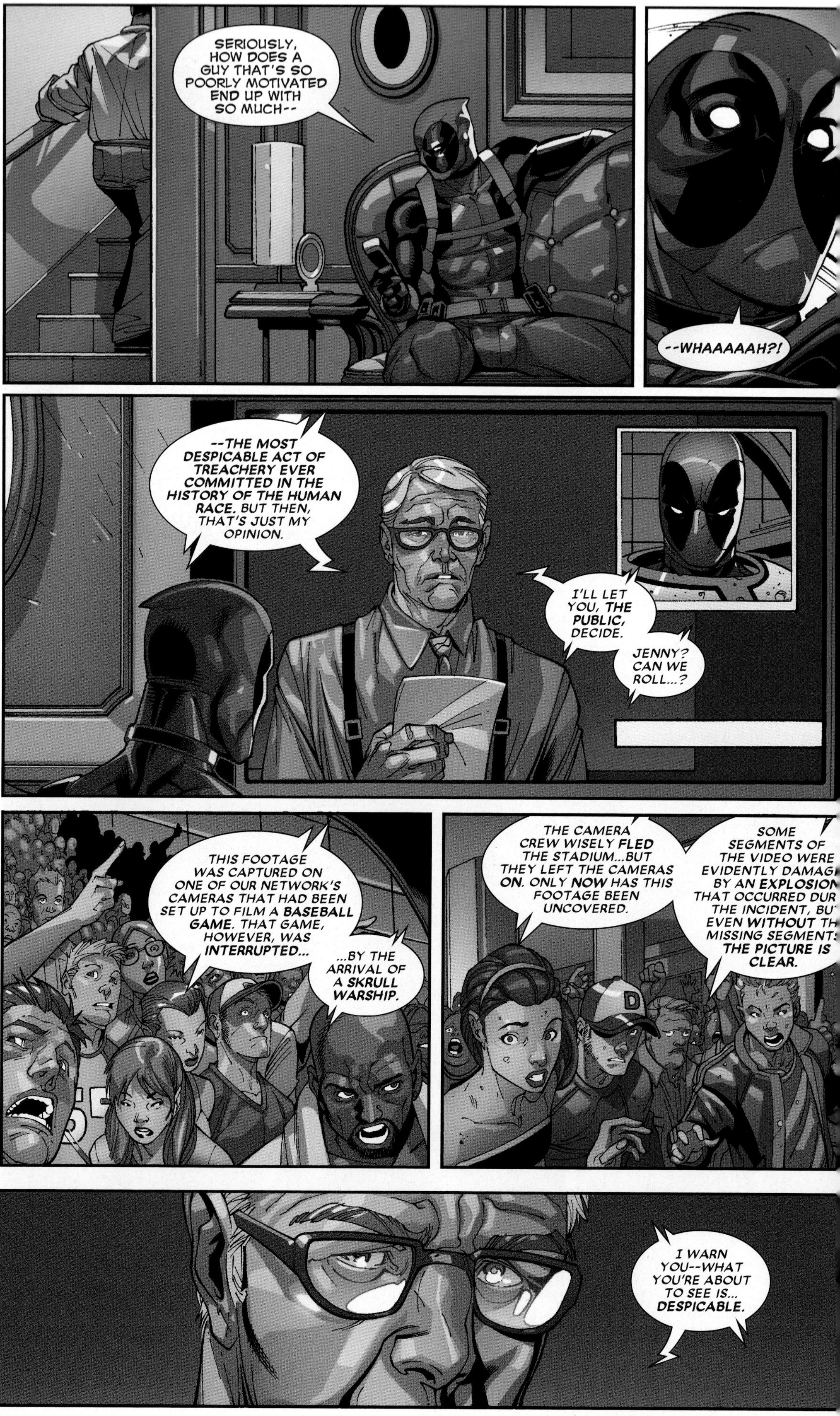
SERIOUSLY, HOW DOES A GUY THAT'S SO POORLY MOTIVATED END UP WITH SO MUCH--
--WHAAAAAH?!
--THE MOST DESPICABLE ACT OF TREACHERY EVER COMMITTED IN THE HISTORY OF THE HUMAN RACE. BUT THEN, THAT'S JUST MY OPINION.
I'LL LET YOU, THE PUBLIC, DECIDE.
JENNY? CAN WE ROLL...?
THIS FOOTAGE WAS CAPTURED ON ONE OF OUR NETWORK'S CAMERAS THAT HAD BEEN SET UP TO FILM A BASEBALL GAME. THAT GAME, HOWEVER, WAS INTERRUPTED...
...BY THE ARRIVAL OF A SKRULL WARSHIP.
THE CAMERA CREW WISELY FLED THE STADIUM...BUT THEY LEFT THE CAMERAS ON. ONLY NOW HAS THIS FOOTAGE BEEN UNCOVERED.
SOME SEGMENTS OF THE VIDEO WERE EVIDENTLY DAMAG BY AN EXPLOSION THAT OCCURRED DUR THE INCIDENT, BUT EVEN WITHOUT TH MISSING SEGMENT THE PICTURE IS CLEAR.
I WARN YOU--WHAT YOU'RE ABOUT TO SEE IS... DESPICABLE.

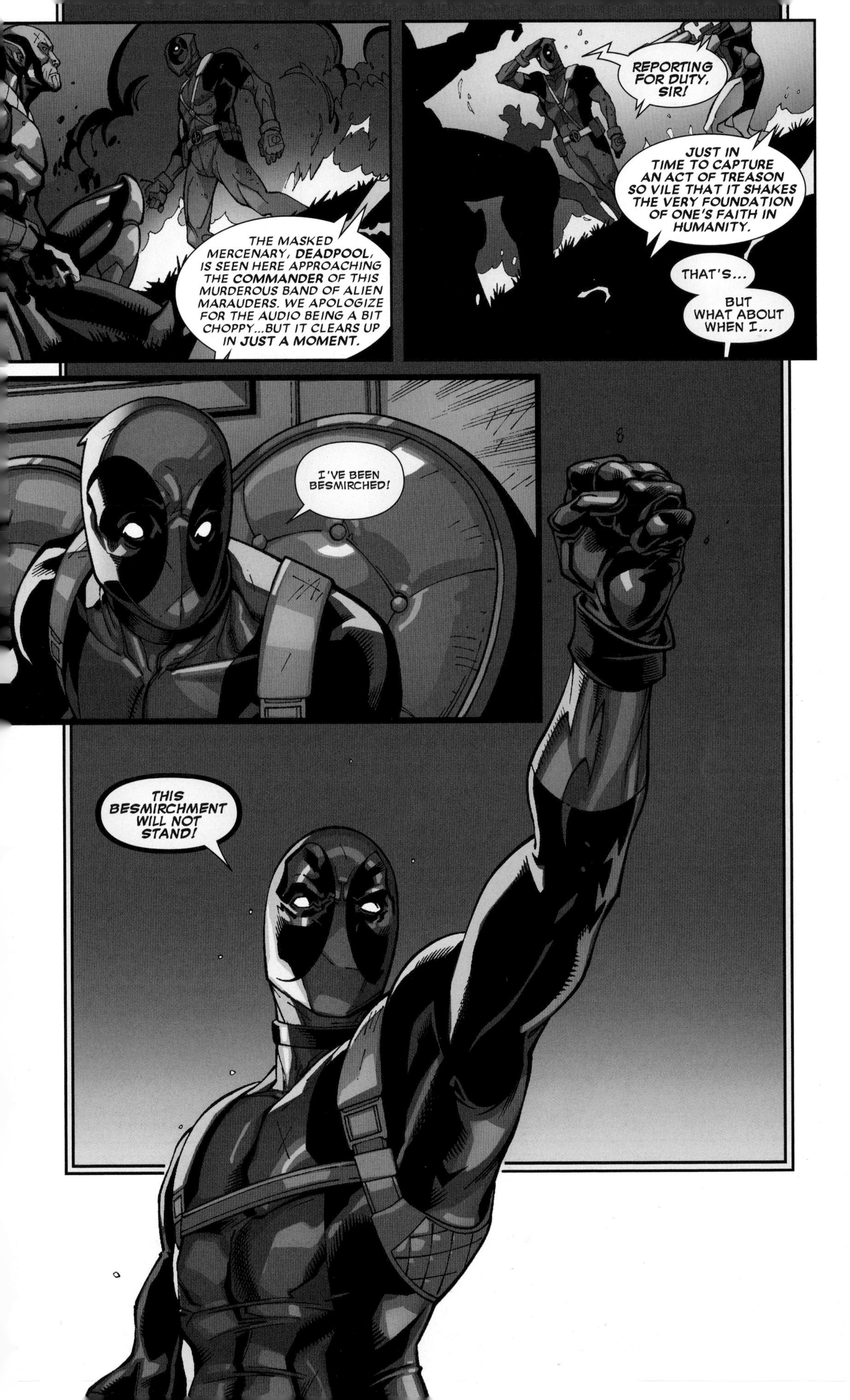
THE MASKED MERCENARY, DEADPOOL, IS SEEN HERE APPROACHING THE COMMANDER OF THIS MURDEROUS BAND OF ALIEN MARAUDERS. WE APOLOGIZE FOR THE AUDIO BEING A BIT CHOPPY...BUT IT CLEARS UP IN JUST A MOMENT.
REPORTING FOR DUTY, SIR!
JUST IN TIME TO CAPTURE AN ACT OF TREASON SO VILE THAT IT SHAKES THE VERY FOUNDATION OF ONE'S FAITH IN HUMANITY.
THAT'S...
BUT WHAT ABOUT WHEN I...
I'VE BEEN BESMIRCHED!
THIS BESMIRCHMENT WILL NOT STAND!

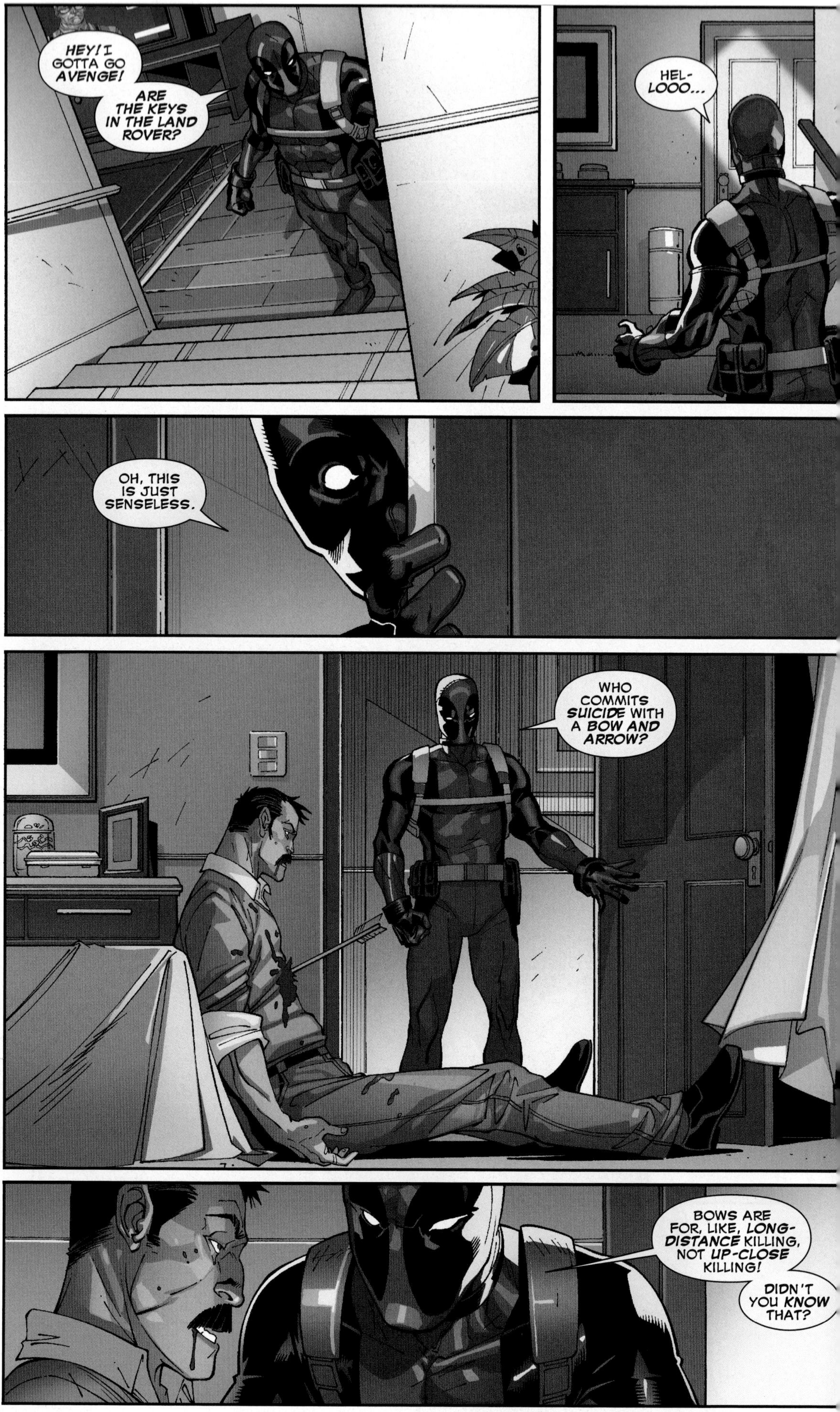
HEY! I GOTTA GO AVENGE!
ARE THE KEYS IN THE LAND ROVER?
HEL-LOOO...
OH, THIS IS JUST SENSELESS.
WHO COMMITS SUICIDE WITH A BOW AND ARROW?
BOWS ARE FOR, LIKE, LONG-DISTANCE KILLING, NOT UP-CLOSE KILLING!
DIDN'T YOU KNOW THAT?

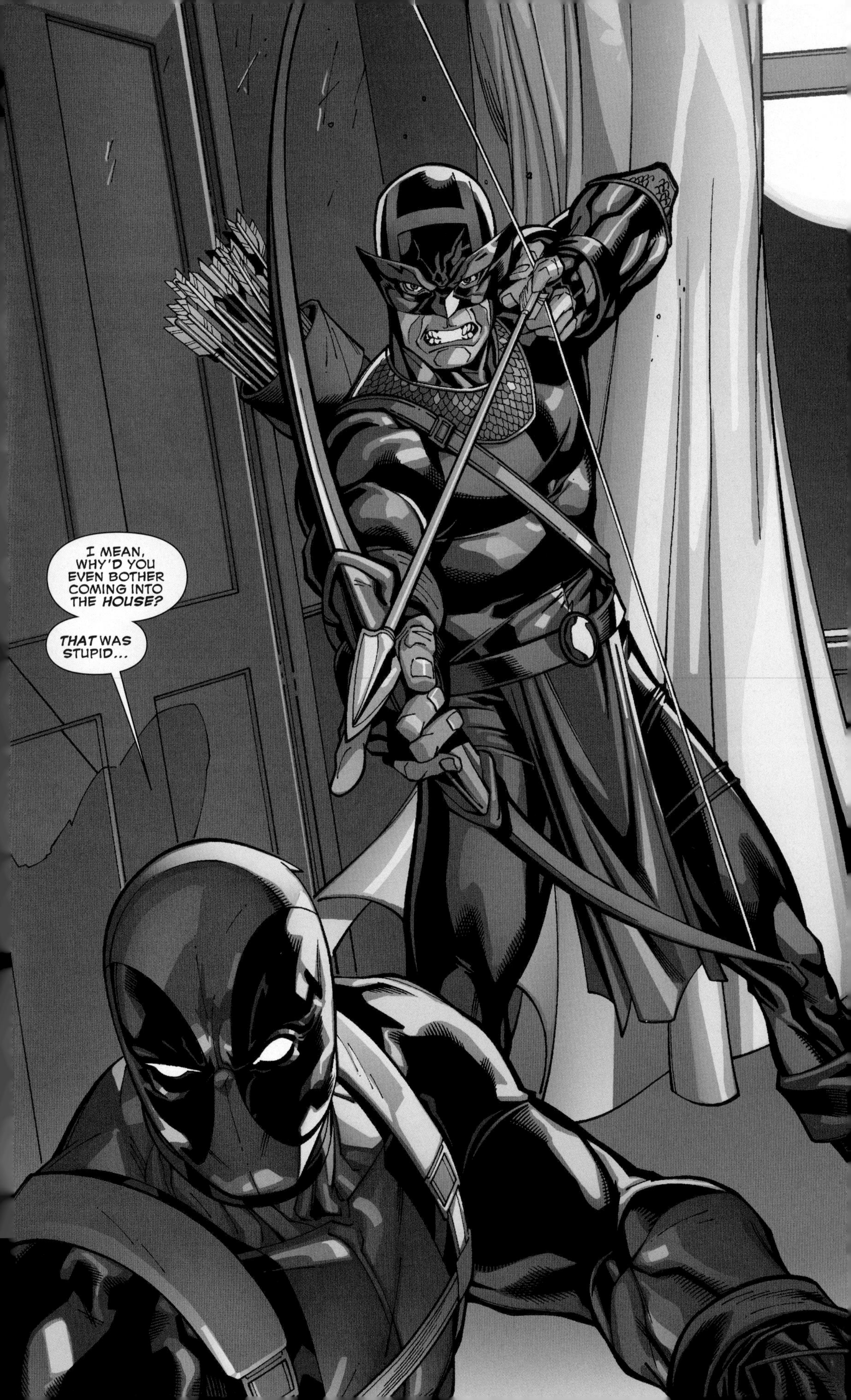
I MEAN, WHY'D YOU EVEN BOTHER COMING INTO THE *HOUSE?*
THAT WAS STUPID...

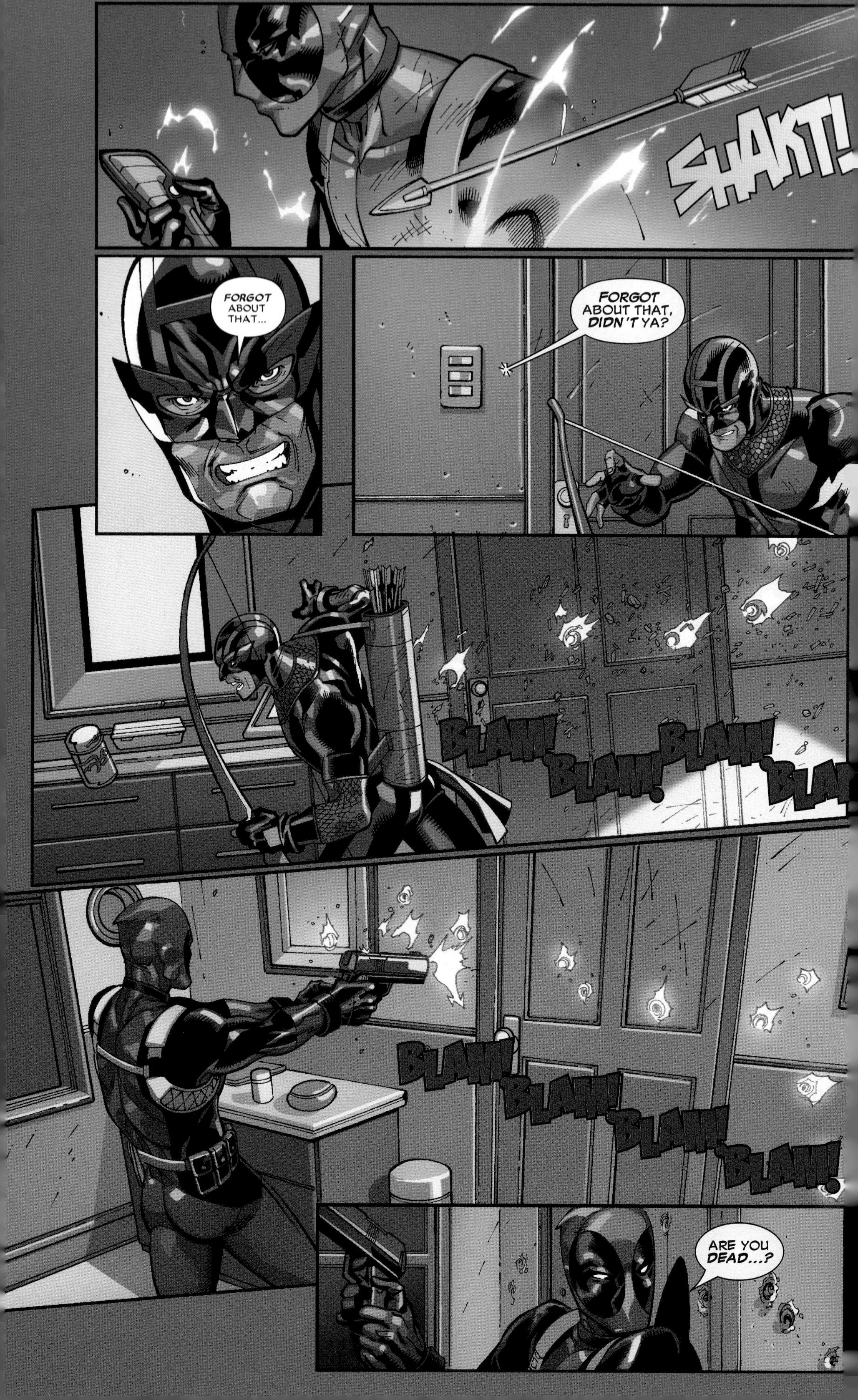
SHAKT!
FORGOT ABOUT THAT...
FORGOT ABOUT THAT, *DIDN'T* YA?
BLAM! BLAM! BLAM! BLAM!
BLAM! BLAM! BLAM! BLAM!
ARE YOU *DEAD...?*

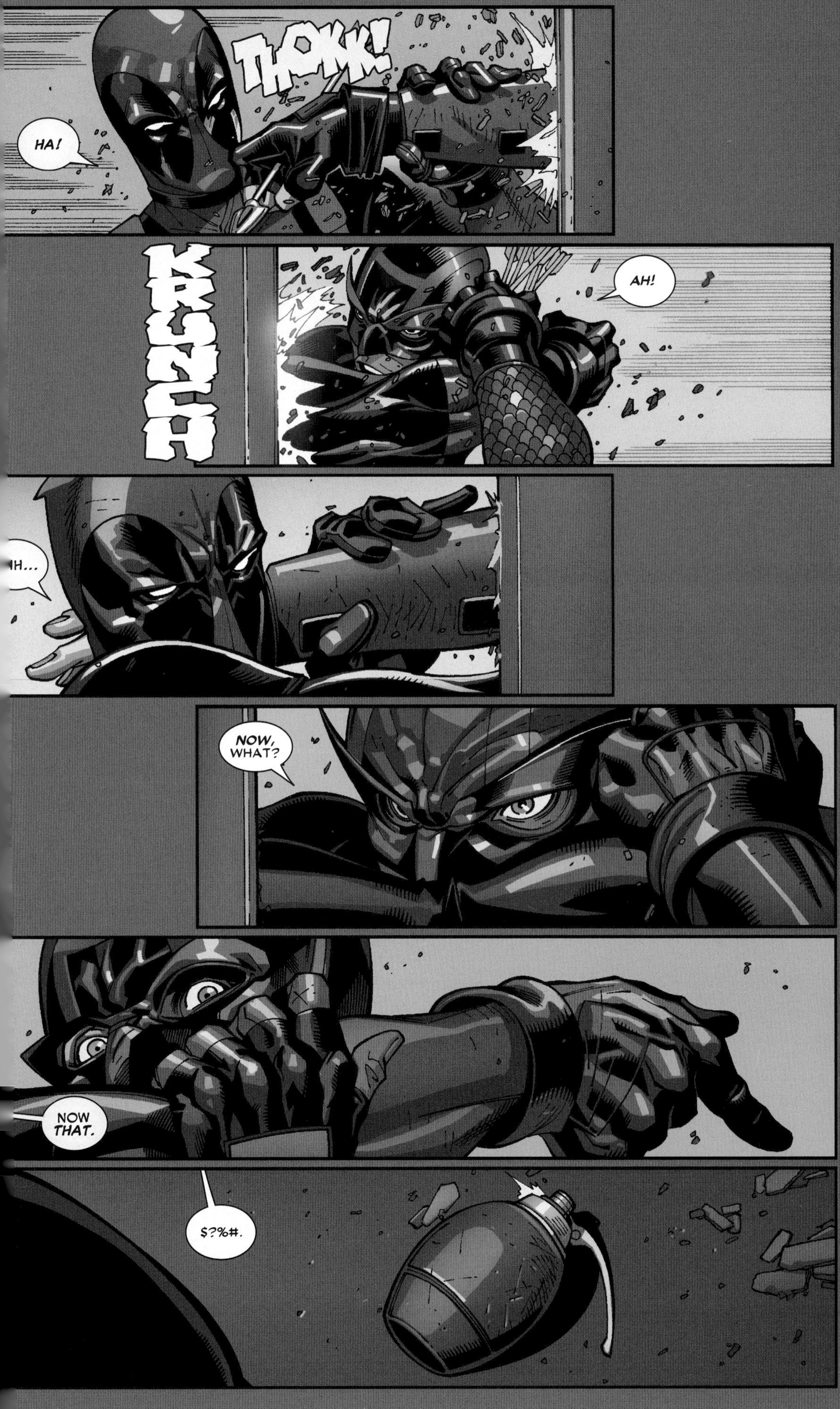
THOKK!
HA!
KRUNCH
AH!
NOW, WHAT?
NOW THAT.
$?%#.

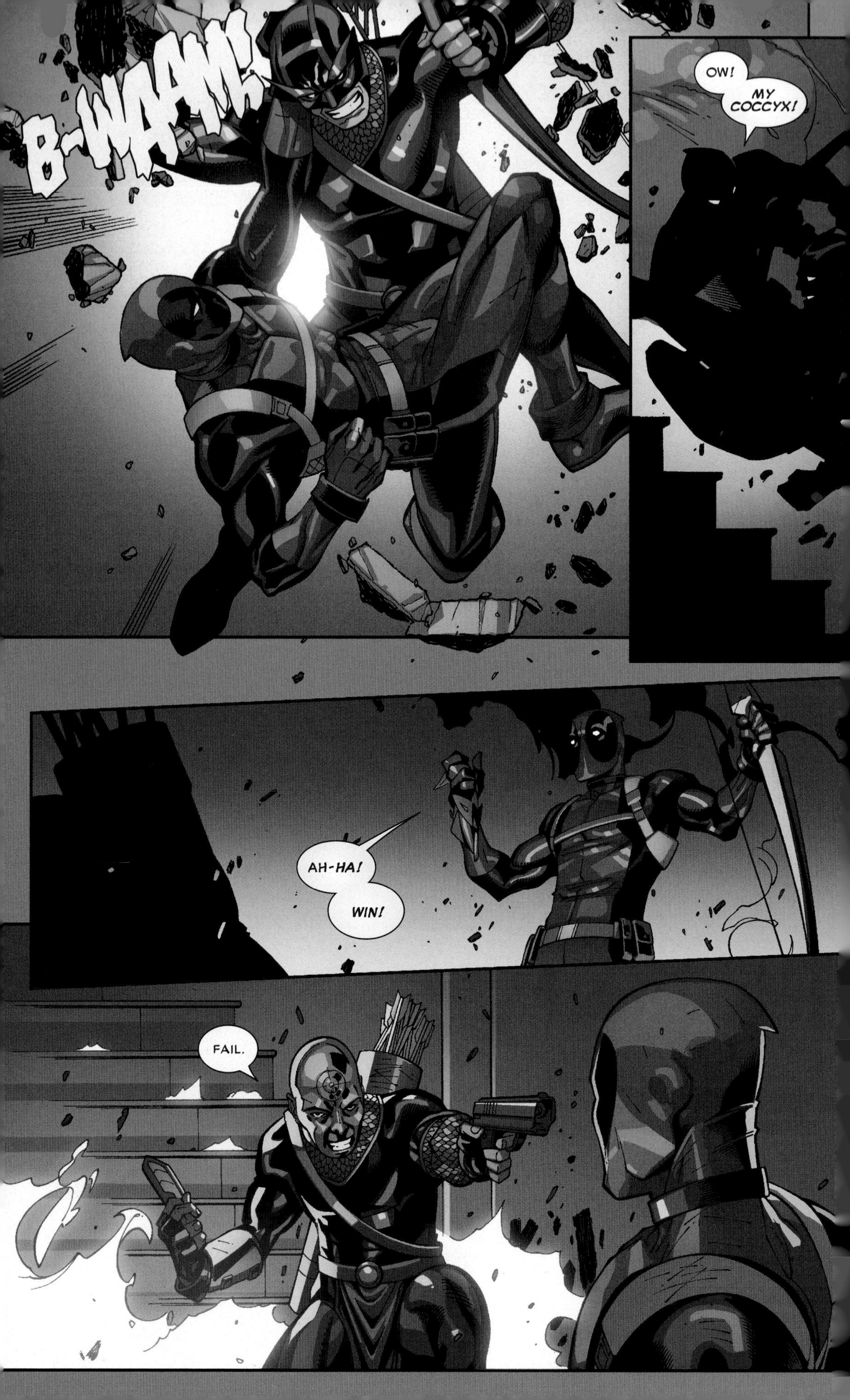
B-WAAM!
OW!
MY COCCYX!
AH-HA!
WIN!
FAIL.

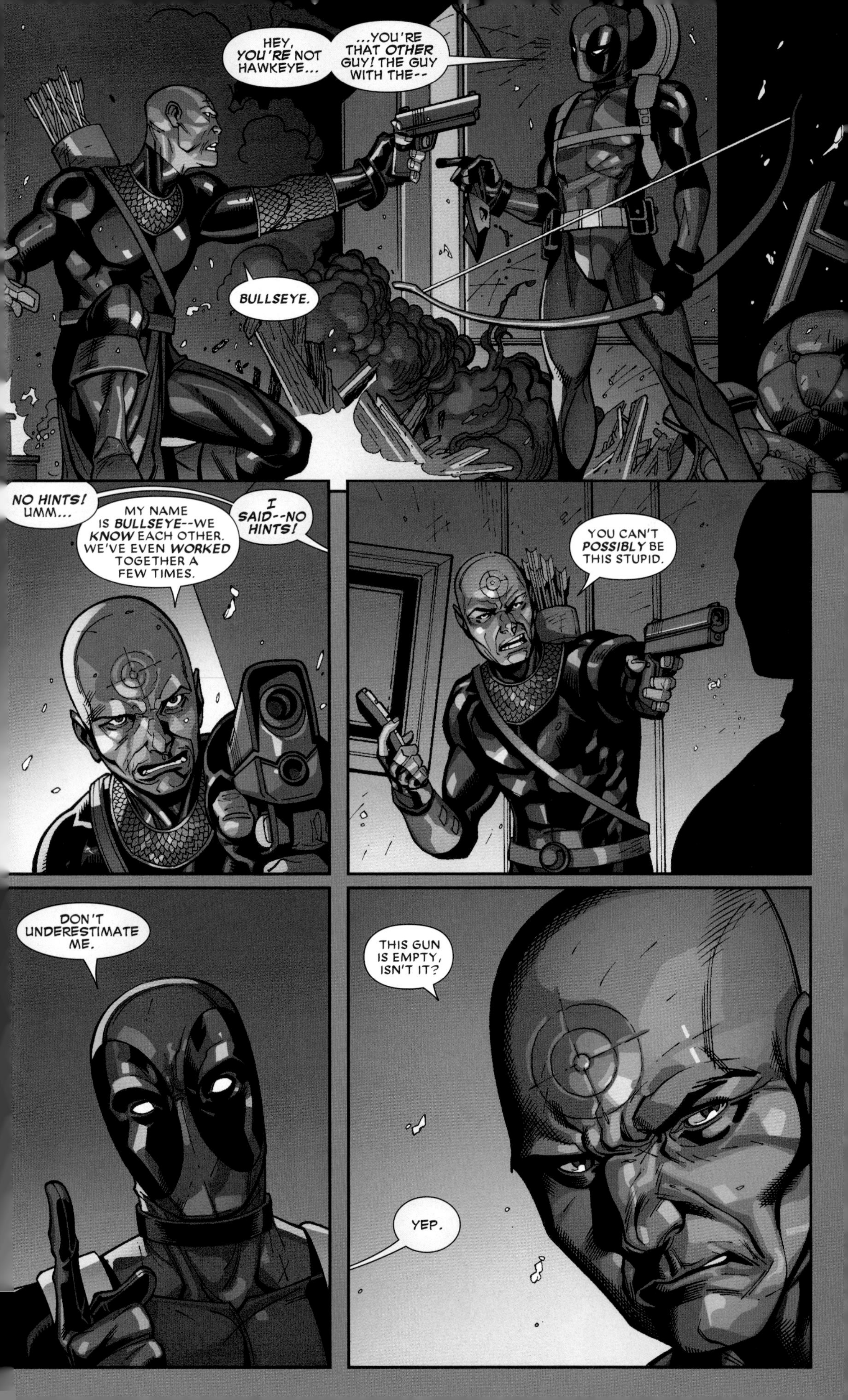
HEY, *YOU'RE* NOT HAWKEYE...
...YOU'RE THAT *OTHER* GUY! THE GUY WITH THE--
BULLSEYE.
NO HINTS! UMM...
MY NAME IS *BULLSEYE*--WE *KNOW* EACH OTHER. WE'VE EVEN *WORKED* TOGETHER A FEW TIMES.
I SAID--NO HINTS!
YOU CAN'T *POSSIBLY* BE THIS STUPID.
DON'T UNDERESTIMATE ME.
THIS GUN IS EMPTY, ISN'T IT?
YEP.

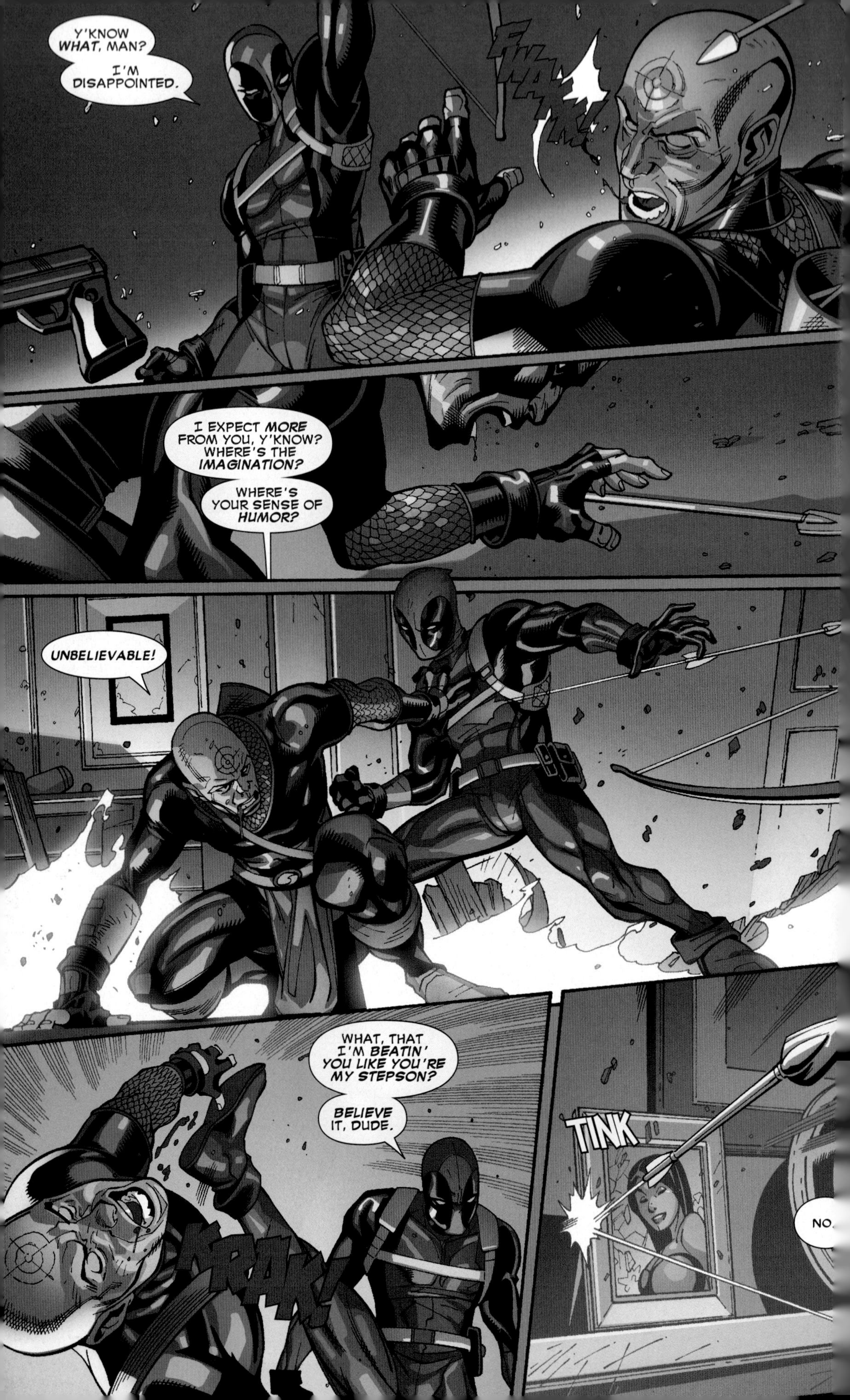
Y'KNOW WHAT, MAN?
I'M DISAPPOINTED.
FWAK!
I EXPECT MORE FROM YOU, Y'KNOW? WHERE'S THE IMAGINATION?
WHERE'S YOUR SENSE OF HUMOR?
UNBELIEVABLE!
WHAT, THAT I'M BEATIN' YOU LIKE YOU'RE MY STEPSON?
BELIEVE IT, DUDE.
TINK
NO.

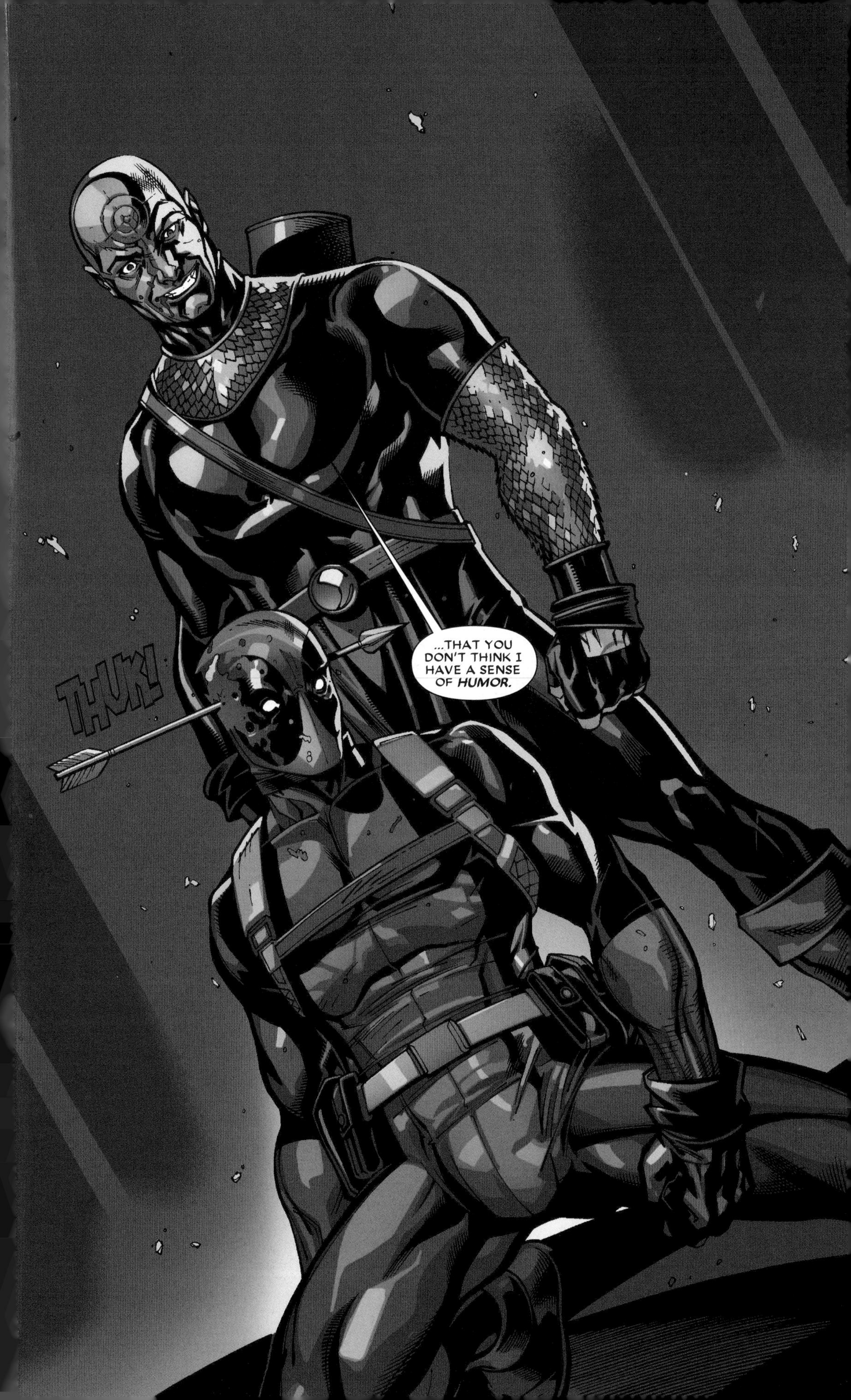
THUK!
...THAT YOU DON'T THINK I HAVE A SENSE OF *HUMOR.*

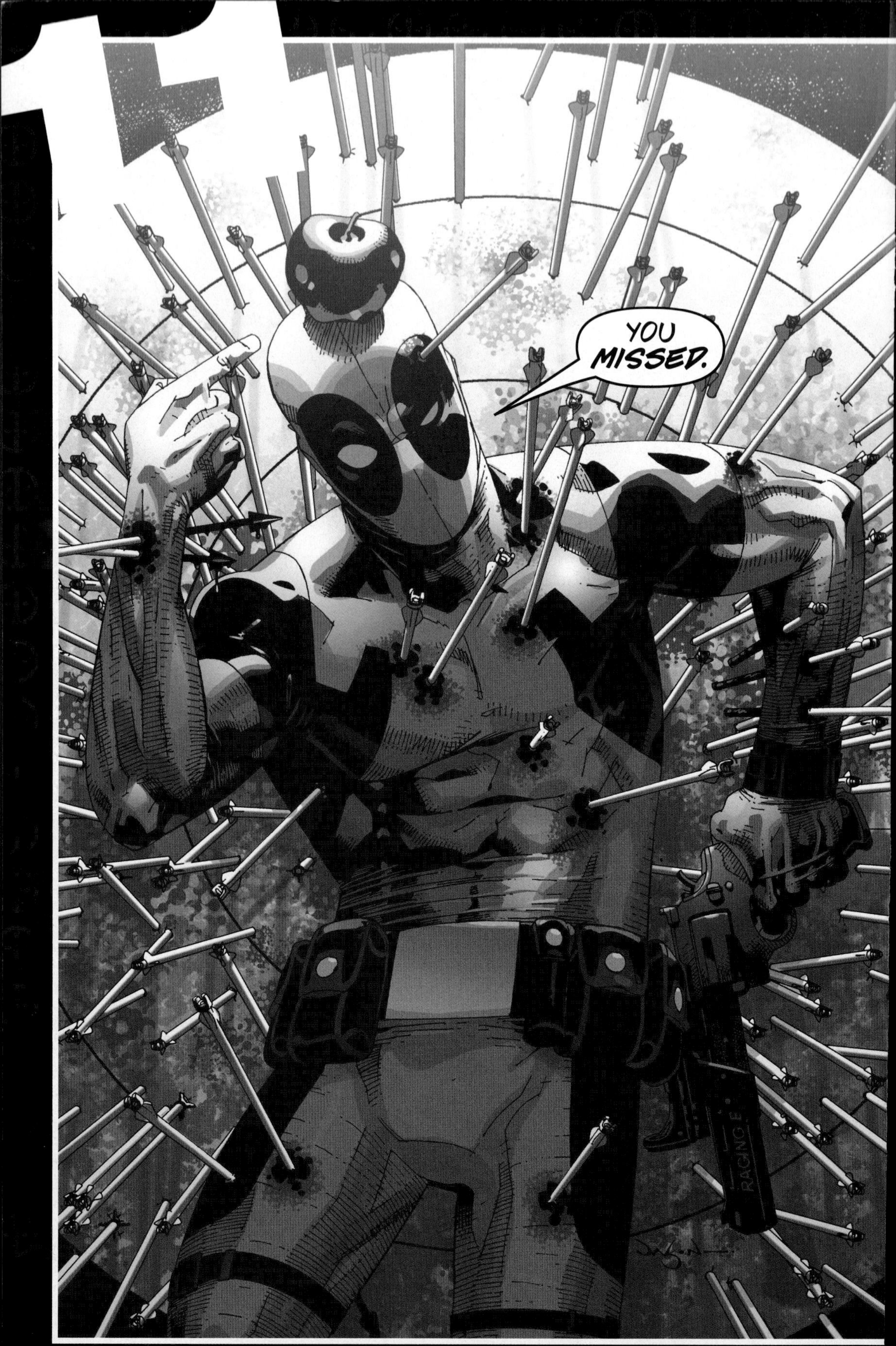
YOU MISSED.

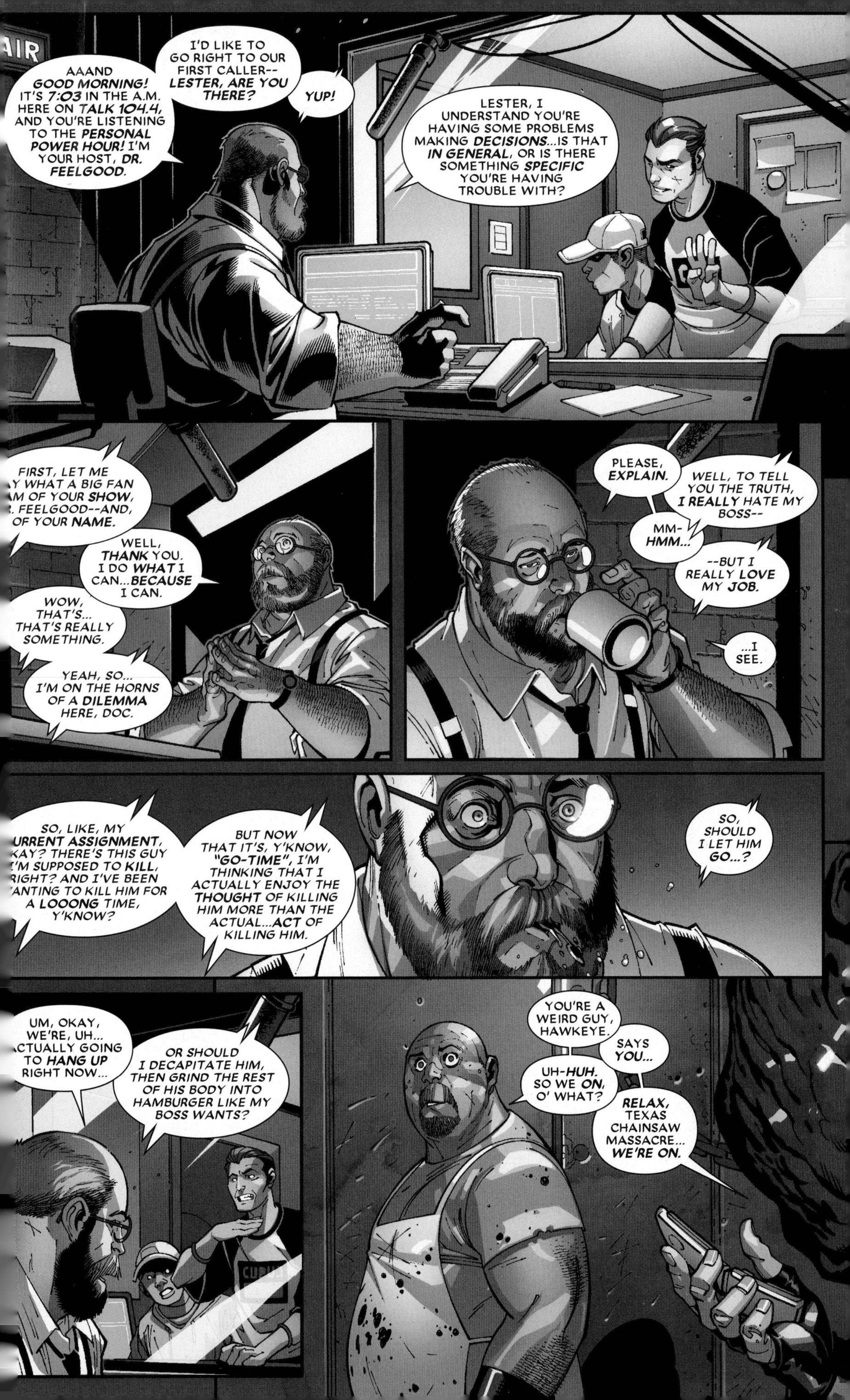
AIR
AAAND GOOD MORNING! IT'S 7:03 IN THE A.M. HERE ON TALK 104.4, AND YOU'RE LISTENING TO THE PERSONAL POWER HOUR! I'M YOUR HOST, DR. FEELGOOD.
I'D LIKE TO GO RIGHT TO OUR FIRST CALLER-- LESTER, ARE YOU THERE?
YUP!
LESTER, I UNDERSTAND YOU'RE HAVING SOME PROBLEMS MAKING DECISIONS...IS THAT IN GENERAL, OR IS THERE SOMETHING SPECIFIC YOU'RE HAVING TROUBLE WITH?
FIRST, LET ME Y WHAT A BIG FAN M OF YOUR SHOW, . FEELGOOD--AND, OF YOUR NAME.
WELL, THANK YOU. I DO WHAT I CAN...BECAUSE I CAN.
WOW, THAT'S... THAT'S REALLY SOMETHING.
YEAH, SO... I'M ON THE HORNS OF A DILEMMA HERE, DOC.
PLEASE, EXPLAIN.
WELL, TO TELL YOU THE TRUTH, I REALLY HATE MY BOSS--
MM-HMM...
--BUT I REALLY LOVE MY JOB.
...I SEE.
SO, LIKE, MY URRENT ASSIGNMENT, KAY? THERE'S THIS GUY I'M SUPPOSED TO KILL, RIGHT? AND I'VE BEEN ANTING TO KILL HIM FOR A LOOONG TIME, Y'KNOW?
BUT NOW THAT IT'S, Y'KNOW, "GO-TIME", I'M THINKING THAT I ACTUALLY ENJOY THE THOUGHT OF KILLING HIM MORE THAN THE ACTUAL...ACT OF KILLING HIM.
SO, SHOULD I LET HIM GO...?
UM, OKAY, WE'RE, UH... CTUALLY GOING TO HANG UP RIGHT NOW...
OR SHOULD I DECAPITATE HIM, THEN GRIND THE REST OF HIS BODY INTO HAMBURGER LIKE MY BOSS WANTS?
YOU'RE A WEIRD GUY, HAWKEYE.
SAYS YOU...
UH-HUH. SO WE ON, O' WHAT?
RELAX, TEXAS CHAINSAW MASSACRE... WE'RE ON.

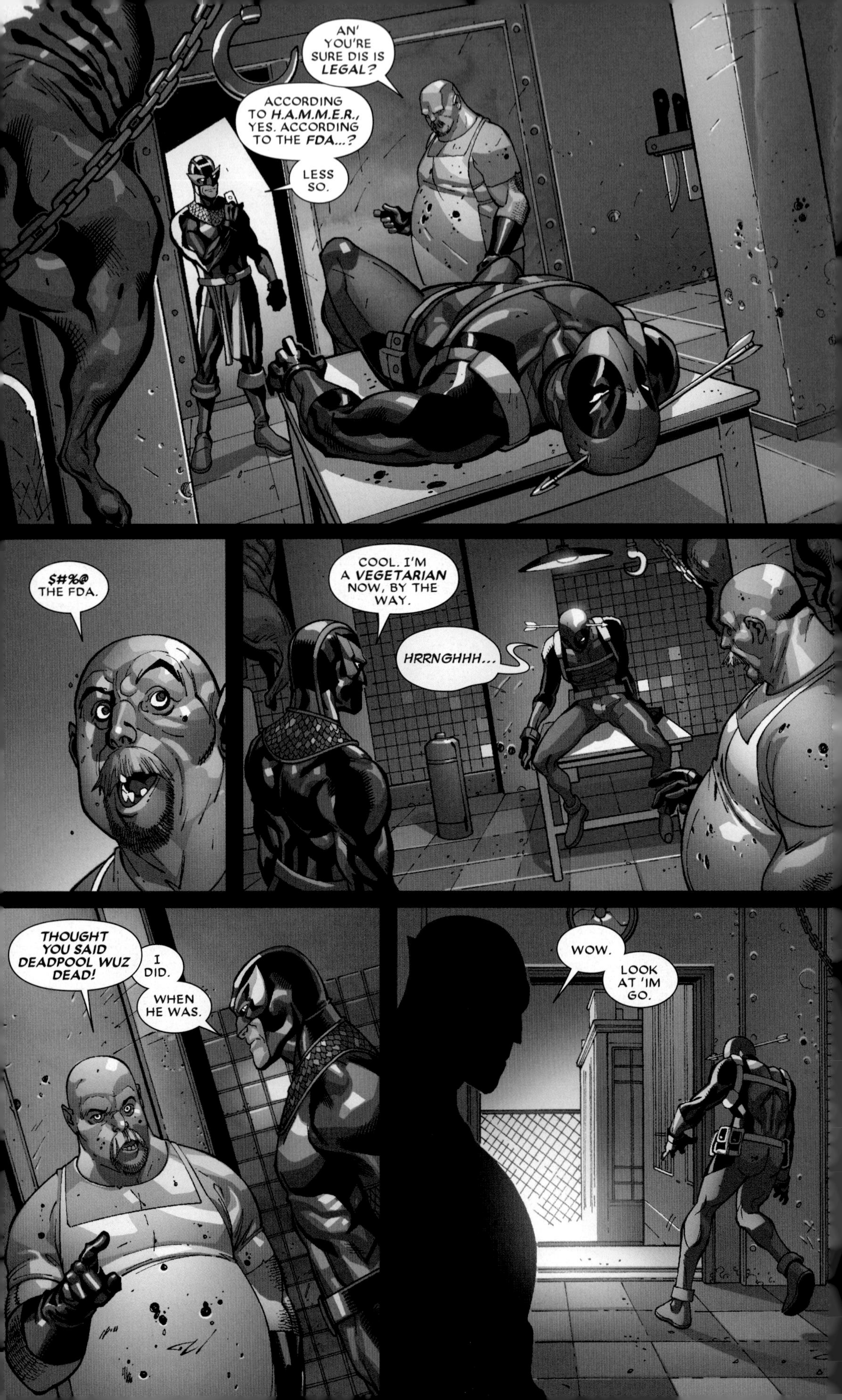
AN' YOU'RE SURE DIS IS LEGAL?
ACCORDING TO H.A.M.M.E.R., YES. ACCORDING TO THE FDA...?
LESS SO.
$#%@ THE FDA.
COOL. I'M A VEGETARIAN NOW, BY THE WAY.
HRRNGHHH...
THOUGHT YOU SAID DEADPOOL WUZ DEAD!
I DID.
WHEN HE WAS.
WOW.
LOOK AT 'IM GO.

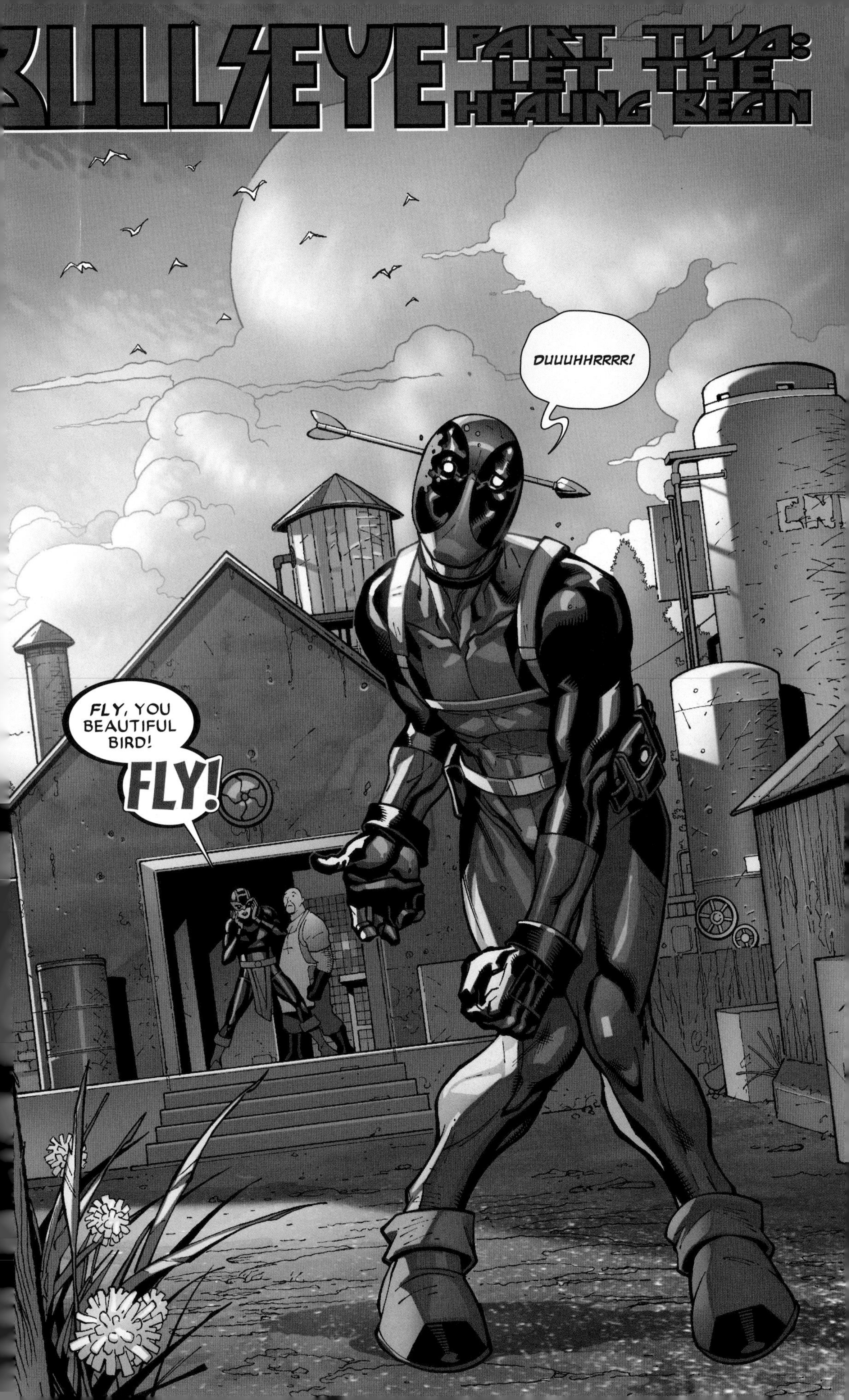
BULLSEYE
PART TWO: LET THE HEALING BEGIN
DUUUHHRRRR!
FLY, YOU BEAUTIFUL BIRD!
FLY!

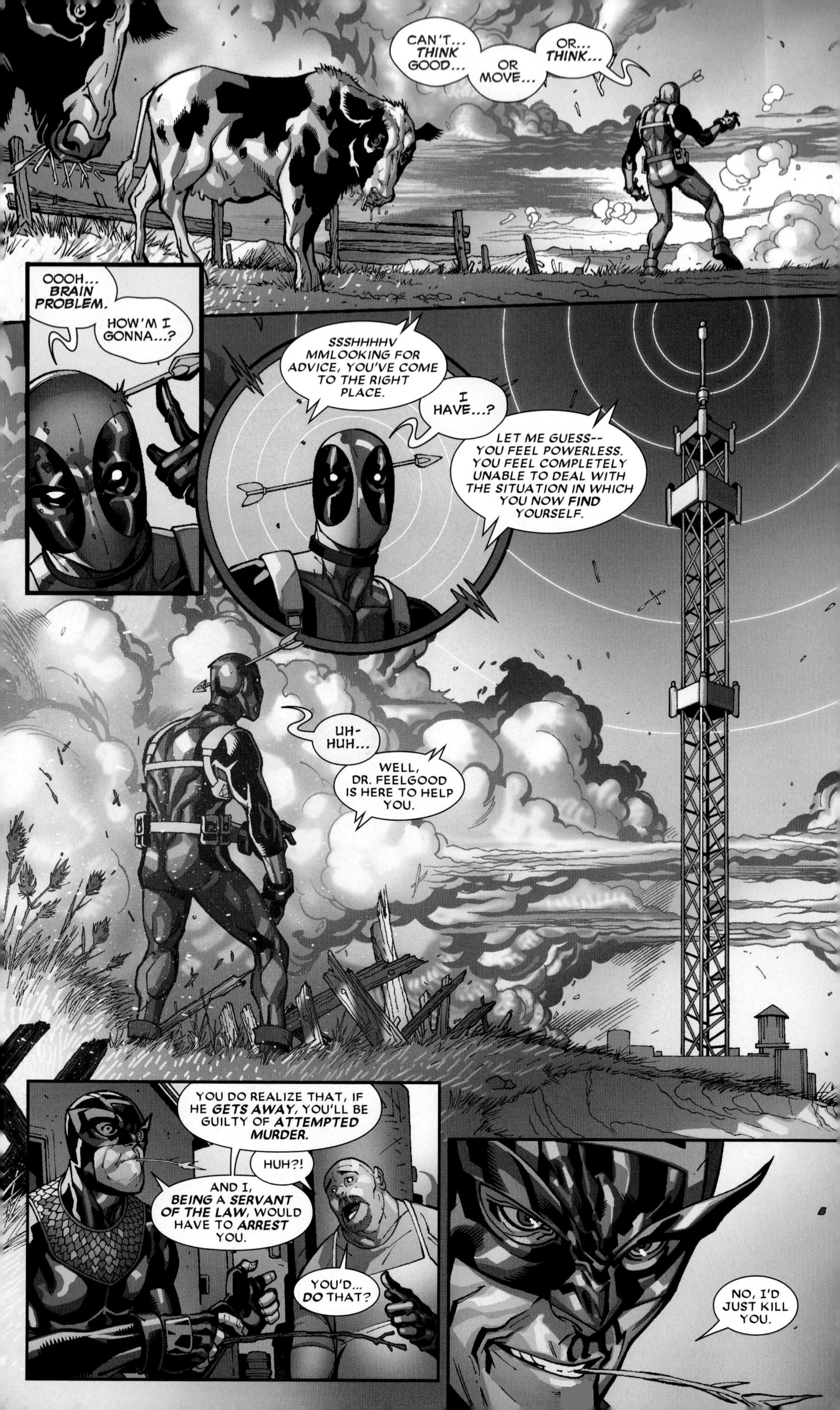
CAN'T... THINK GOOD...
OR MOVE...
OR... THINK...
OOOH... BRAIN PROBLEM.
HOW'M I GONNA...?
SSSHHHHV MMLOOKING FOR ADVICE, YOU'VE COME TO THE RIGHT PLACE.
I HAVE...?
LET ME GUESS-- YOU FEEL POWERLESS. YOU FEEL COMPLETELY UNABLE TO DEAL WITH THE SITUATION IN WHICH YOU NOW FIND YOURSELF.
UH-HUH...
WELL, DR. FEELGOOD IS HERE TO HELP YOU.
YOU DO REALIZE THAT, IF HE GETS AWAY, YOU'LL BE GUILTY OF ATTEMPTED MURDER.
HUH?!
AND I, BEING A SERVANT OF THE LAW, WOULD HAVE TO ARREST YOU.
YOU'D... DO THAT?
NO, I'D JUST KILL YOU.

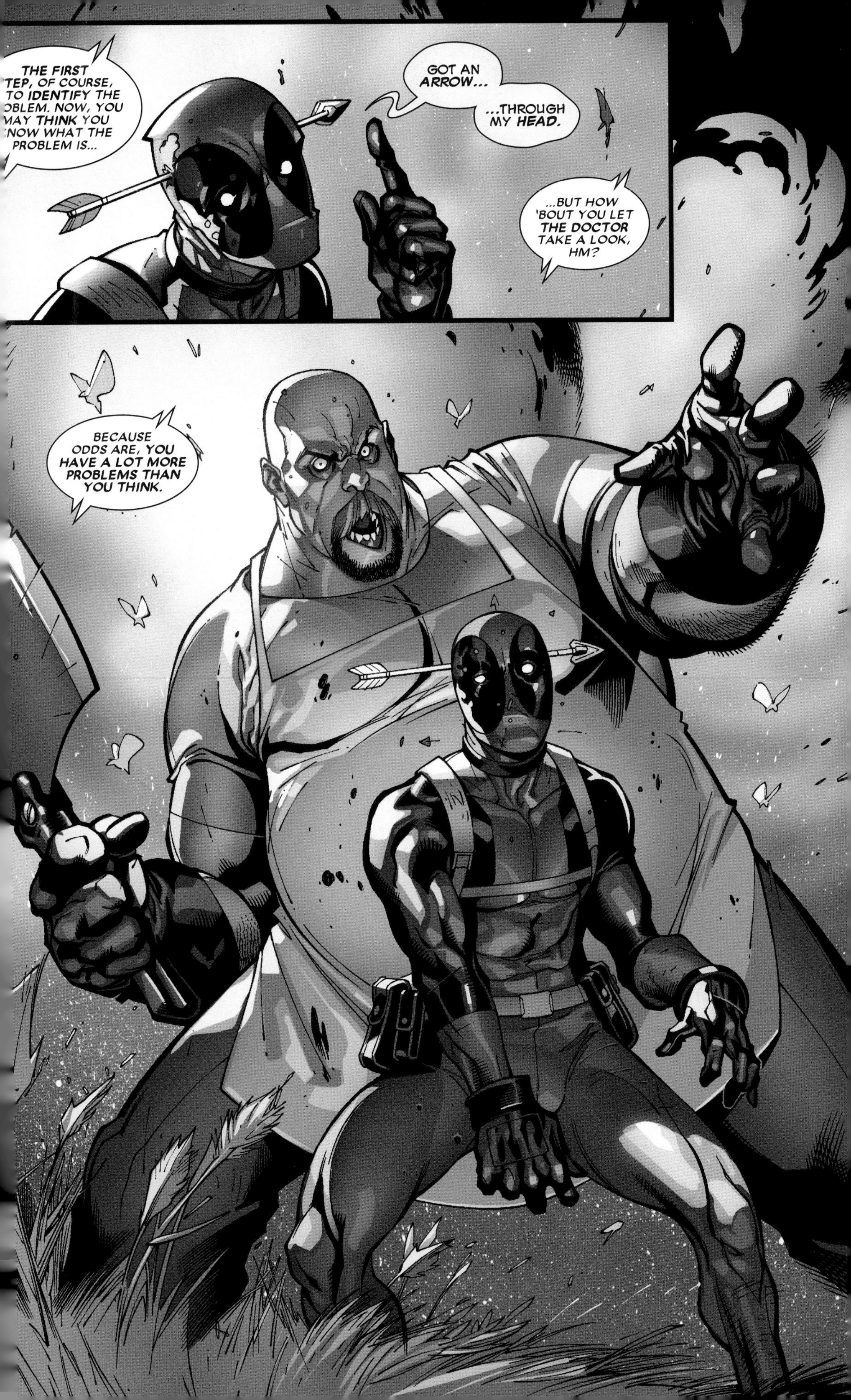
THE FIRST TEP, OF COURSE, TO IDENTIFY THE OBLEM. NOW, YOU MAY THINK YOU NOW WHAT THE PROBLEM IS...
GOT AN ARROW...
...THROUGH MY HEAD.
...BUT HOW 'BOUT YOU LET THE DOCTOR TAKE A LOOK, HM?
BECAUSE ODDS ARE, YOU HAVE A LOT MORE PROBLEMS THAN YOU THINK.

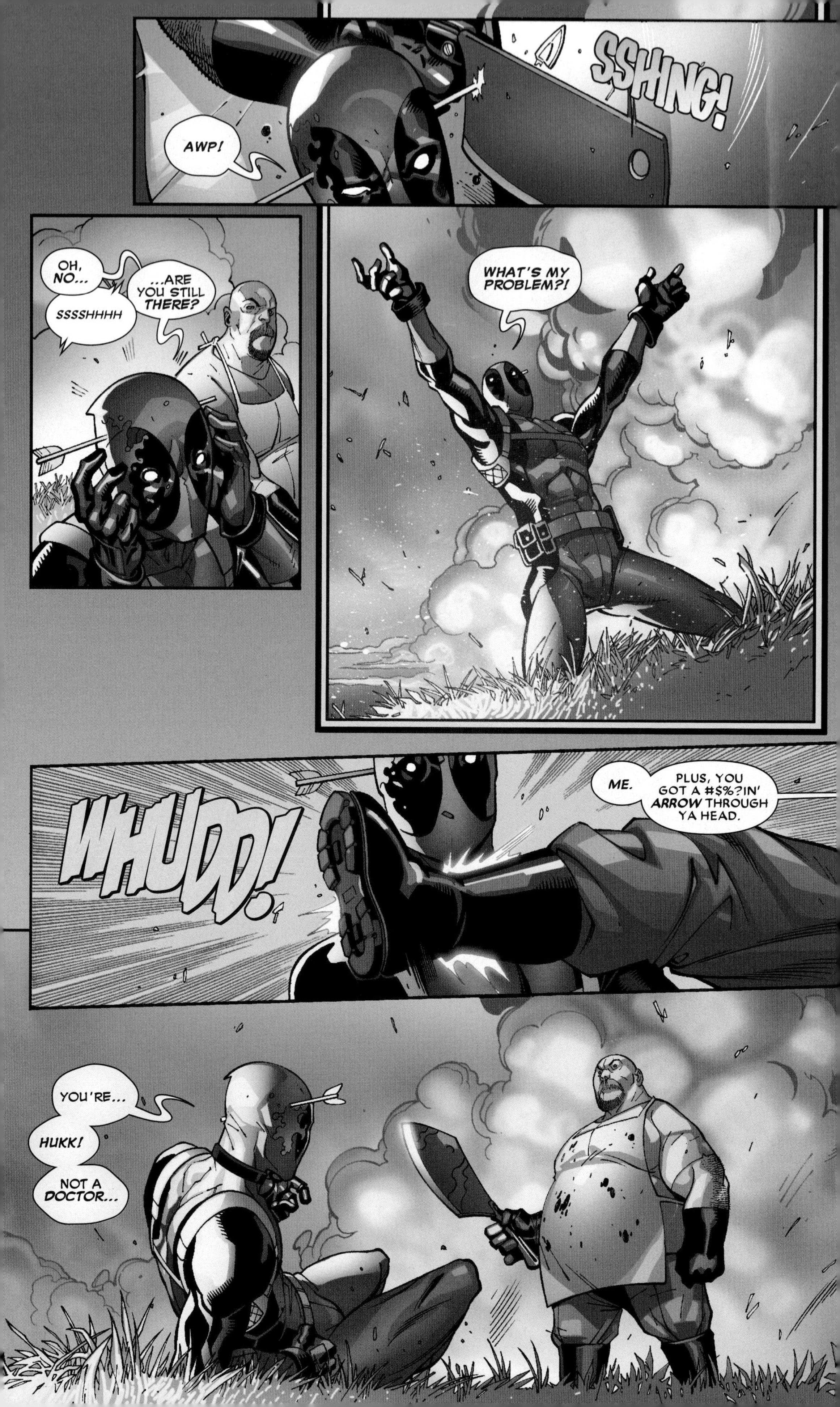
SSHING!
AWP!
OH, NO...
SSSSHHHH
...ARE YOU STILL THERE?
WHAT'S MY PROBLEM?!
WHUDD!
ME.
PLUS, YOU GOT A #$%?IN' ARROW THROUGH YA HEAD.
YOU'RE...
HUKK!
NOT A DOCTOR...

YES, WADE... ...I AM A DOCTOR.

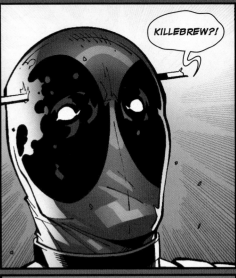

KILLEBREW?!

HAH?

AAAAIIIIEEEEE!

KRAK!

OH, #@#$.

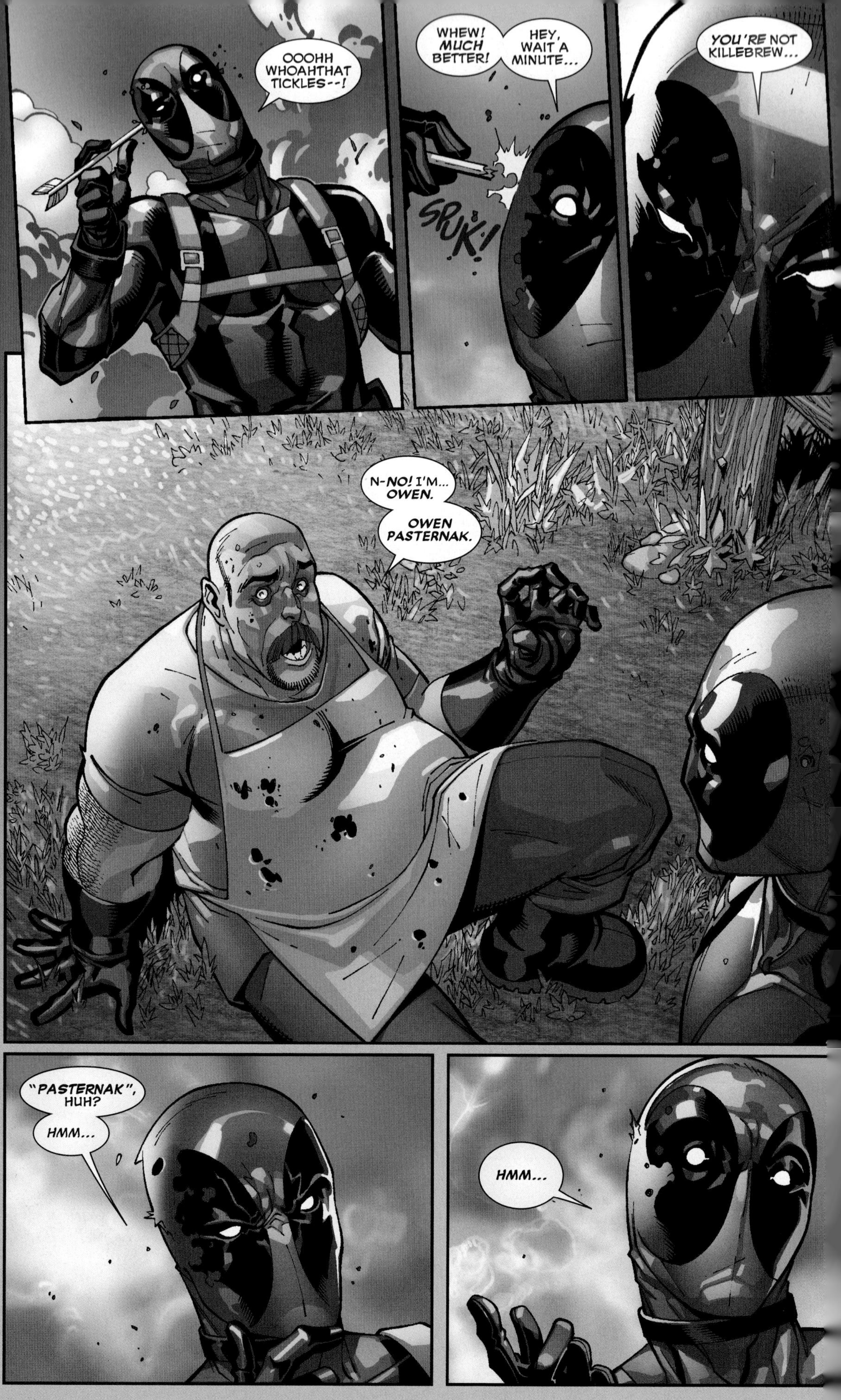
OOOHH WHOAHTHAT TICKLES--!
WHEW! MUCH BETTER!
HEY, WAIT A MINUTE...
SPUK!
YOU'RE NOT KILLEBREW...
N-NO! I'M... OWEN.
OWEN PASTERNAK.
"PASTERNAK", HUH?
HMM...
HMM...

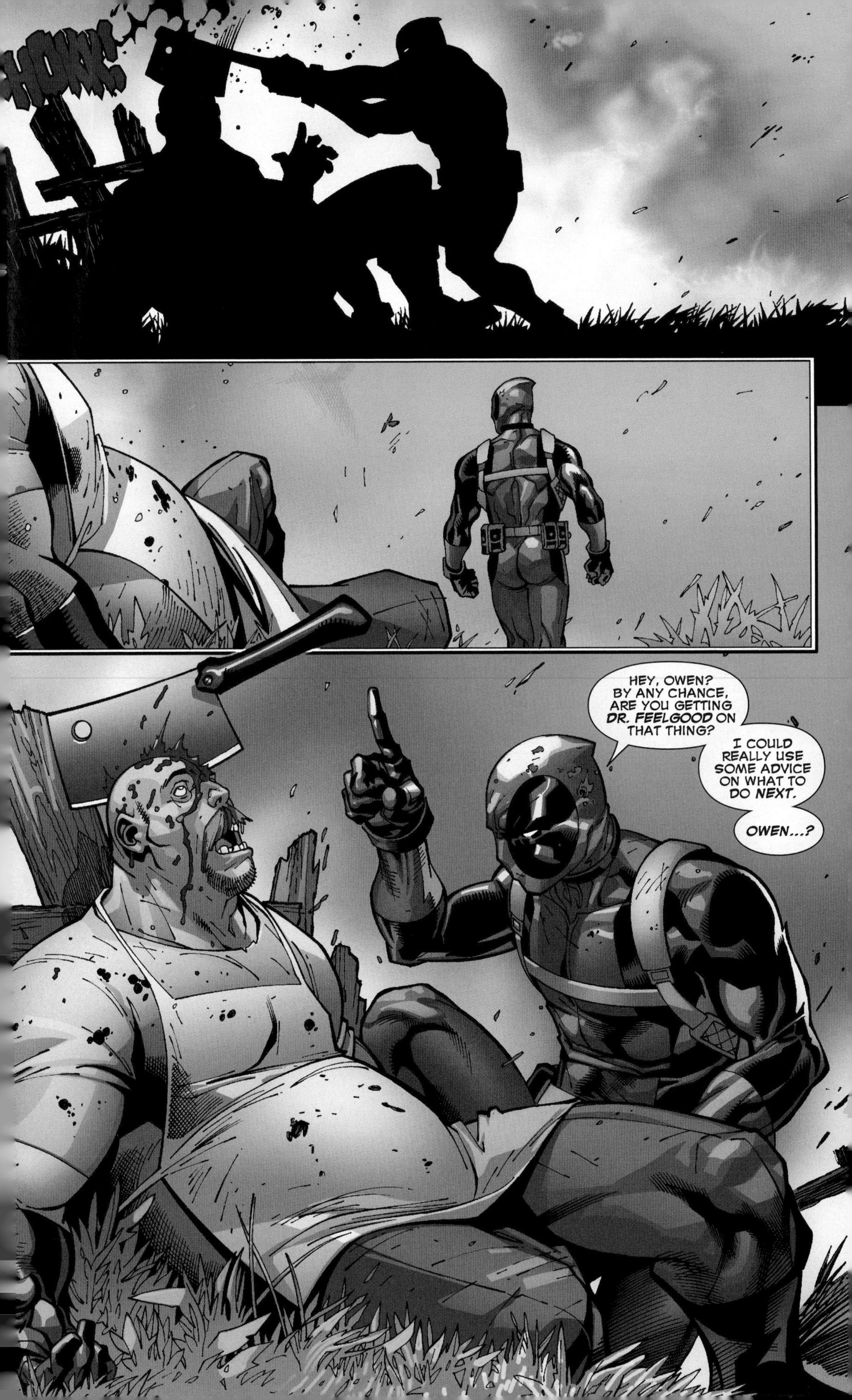
HOKK!
HEY, OWEN? BY ANY CHANCE, ARE YOU GETTING DR. FEELGOOD ON THAT THING?
I COULD REALLY USE SOME ADVICE ON WHAT TO DO NEXT.
OWEN...?

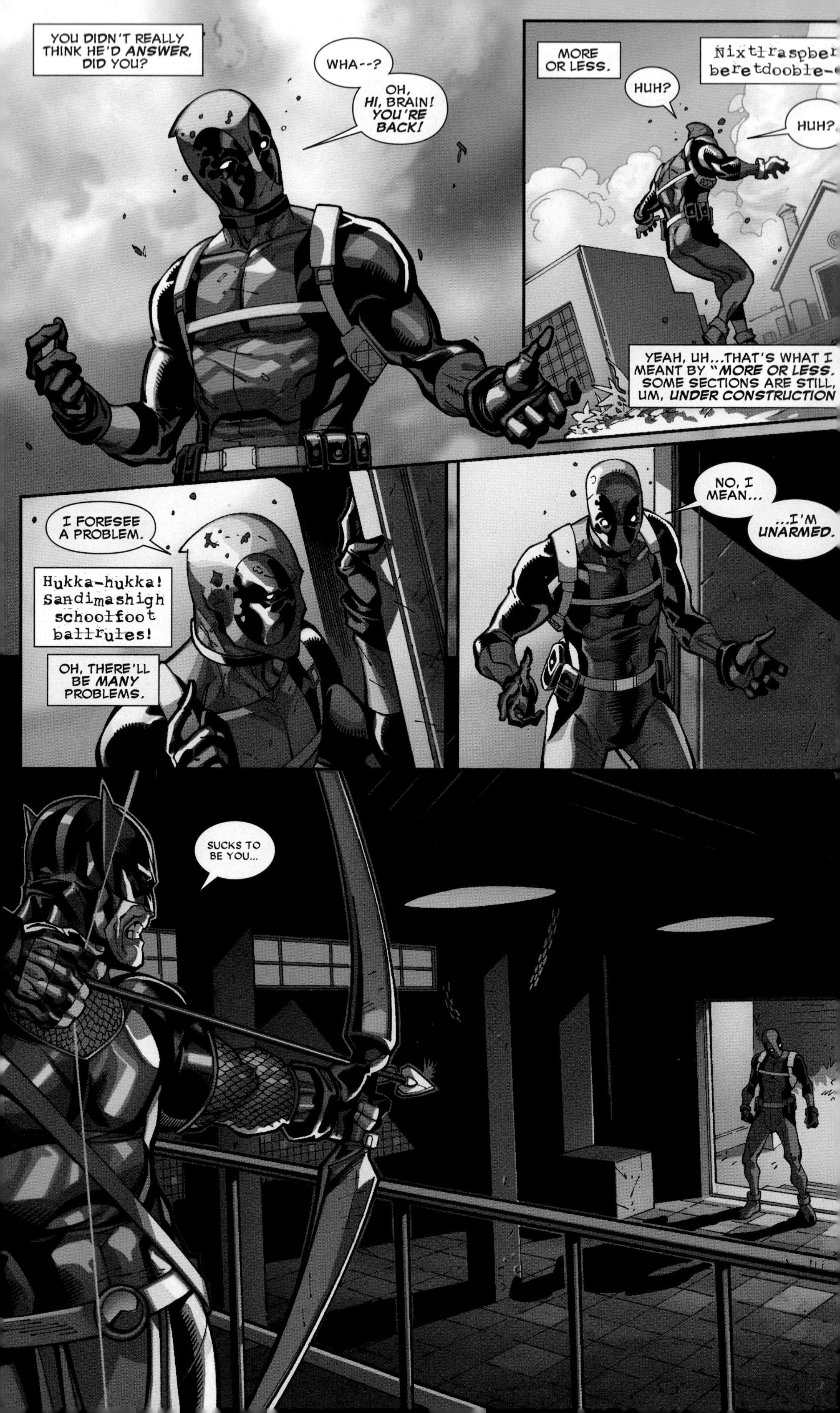
YOU DIDN'T REALLY THINK HE'D ANSWER, DID YOU?
WHA--?
OH, HI, BRAIN! YOU'RE BACK!
MORE OR LESS.
Nixtlraspber beretdooble-
HUH?
HUH?
YEAH, UH...THAT'S WHAT I MEANT BY "MORE OR LESS." SOME SECTIONS ARE STILL, UM, UNDER CONSTRUCTION
I FORESEE A PROBLEM.
Hukka-hukka! Sandimashigh schoolfoot ballrules!
OH, THERE'LL BE MANY PROBLEMS.
NO, I MEAN...
...I'M UNARMED.
SUCKS TO BE YOU...

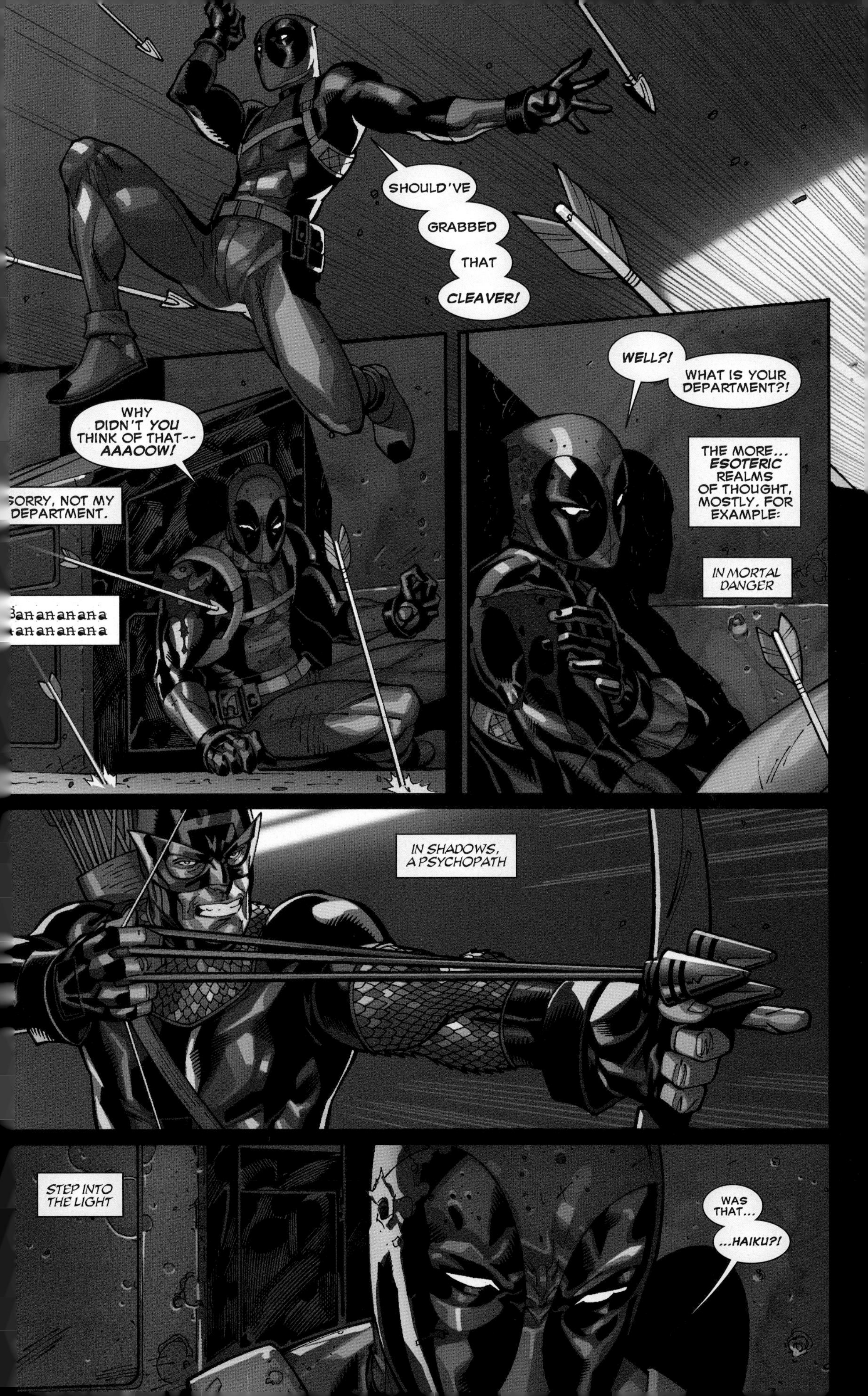
SHOULD'VE
GRABBED
THAT
CLEAVER!
WHY DIDN'T YOU THINK OF THAT--AAAOOW!
SORRY, NOT MY DEPARTMENT.
Banananana
Banananana
WELL?!
WHAT IS YOUR DEPARTMENT?!
THE MORE... ESOTERIC REALMS OF THOUGHT, MOSTLY. FOR EXAMPLE:
IN MORTAL DANGER
IN SHADOWS, A PSYCHOPATH
STEP INTO THE LIGHT
WAS THAT...
...HAIKU?!

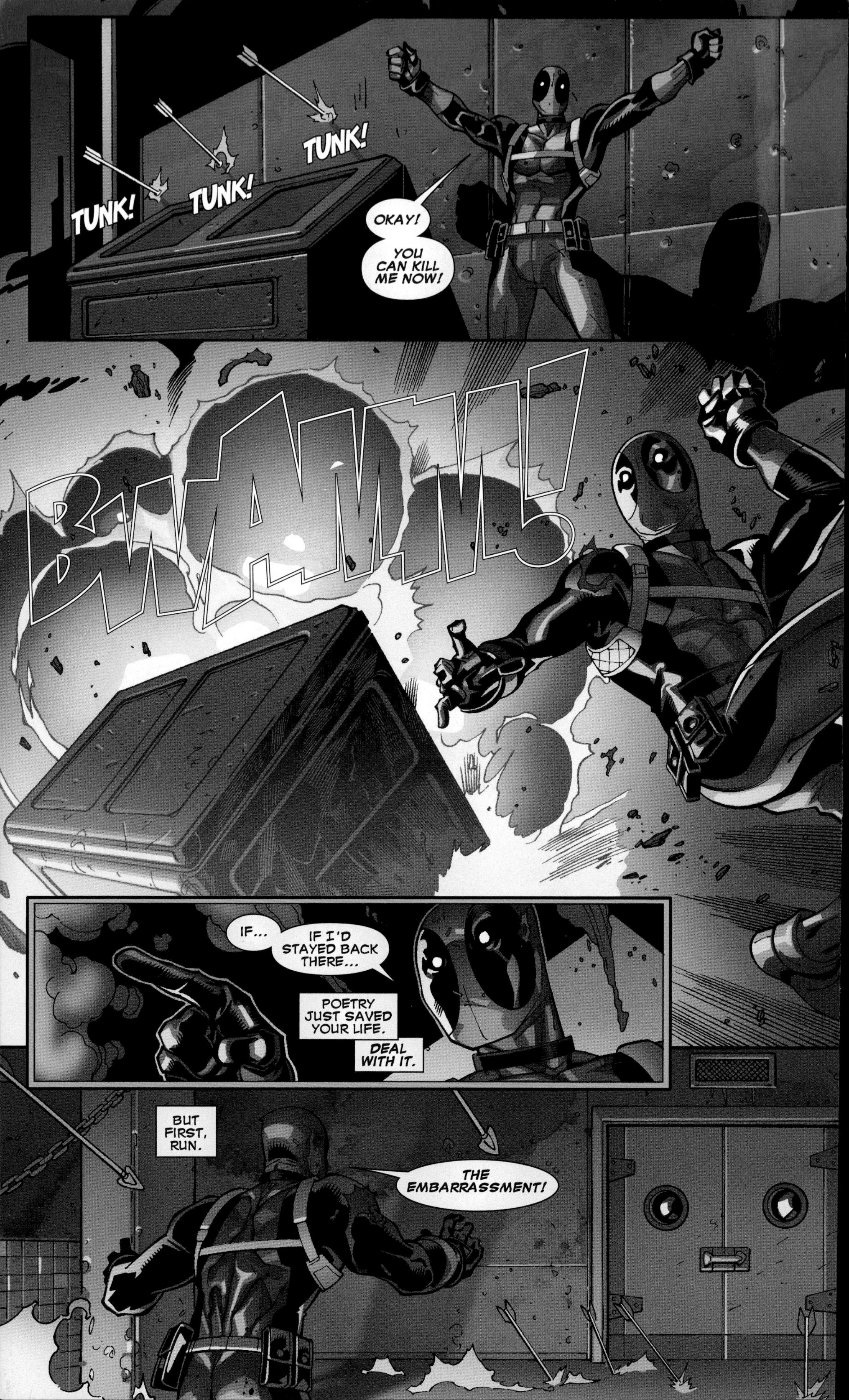
TUNK!
TUNK!
TUNK!
OKAY!
YOU CAN KILL ME NOW!
BWAMM!
IF...
IF I'D STAYED BACK THERE...
POETRY JUST SAVED YOUR LIFE.
DEAL WITH IT.
BUT FIRST, RUN.
THE EMBARRASSMENT!

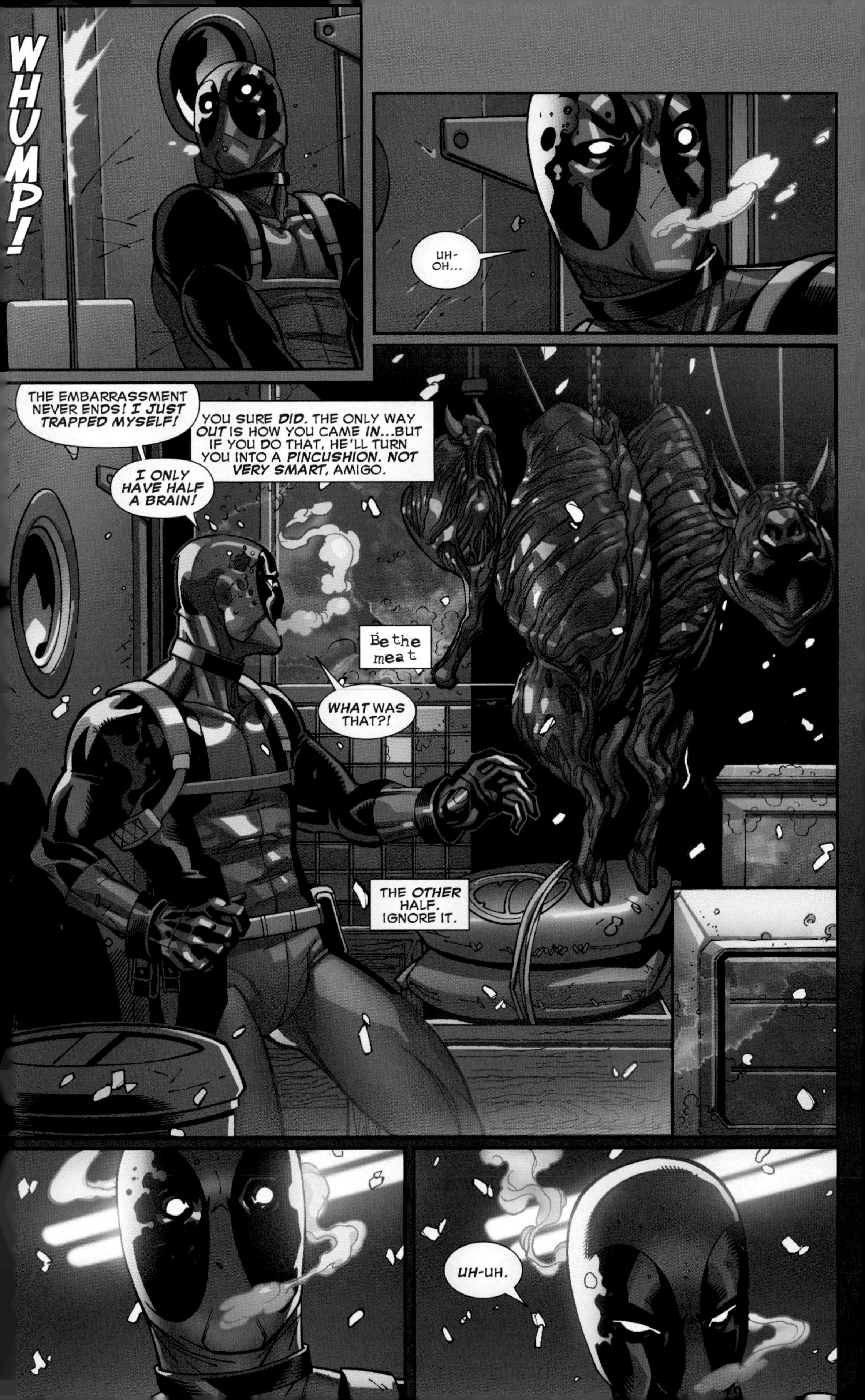
WHUMP!
UH-OH...
THE EMBARRASSMENT NEVER ENDS! I JUST TRAPPED MYSELF!
YOU SURE DID. THE ONLY WAY OUT IS HOW YOU CAME IN...BUT IF YOU DO THAT, HE'LL TURN YOU INTO A PINCUSHION. NOT VERY SMART, AMIGO.
I ONLY HAVE HALF A BRAIN!
Be the meat
WHAT WAS THAT?!
THE OTHER HALF. IGNORE IT.
UH-UH.

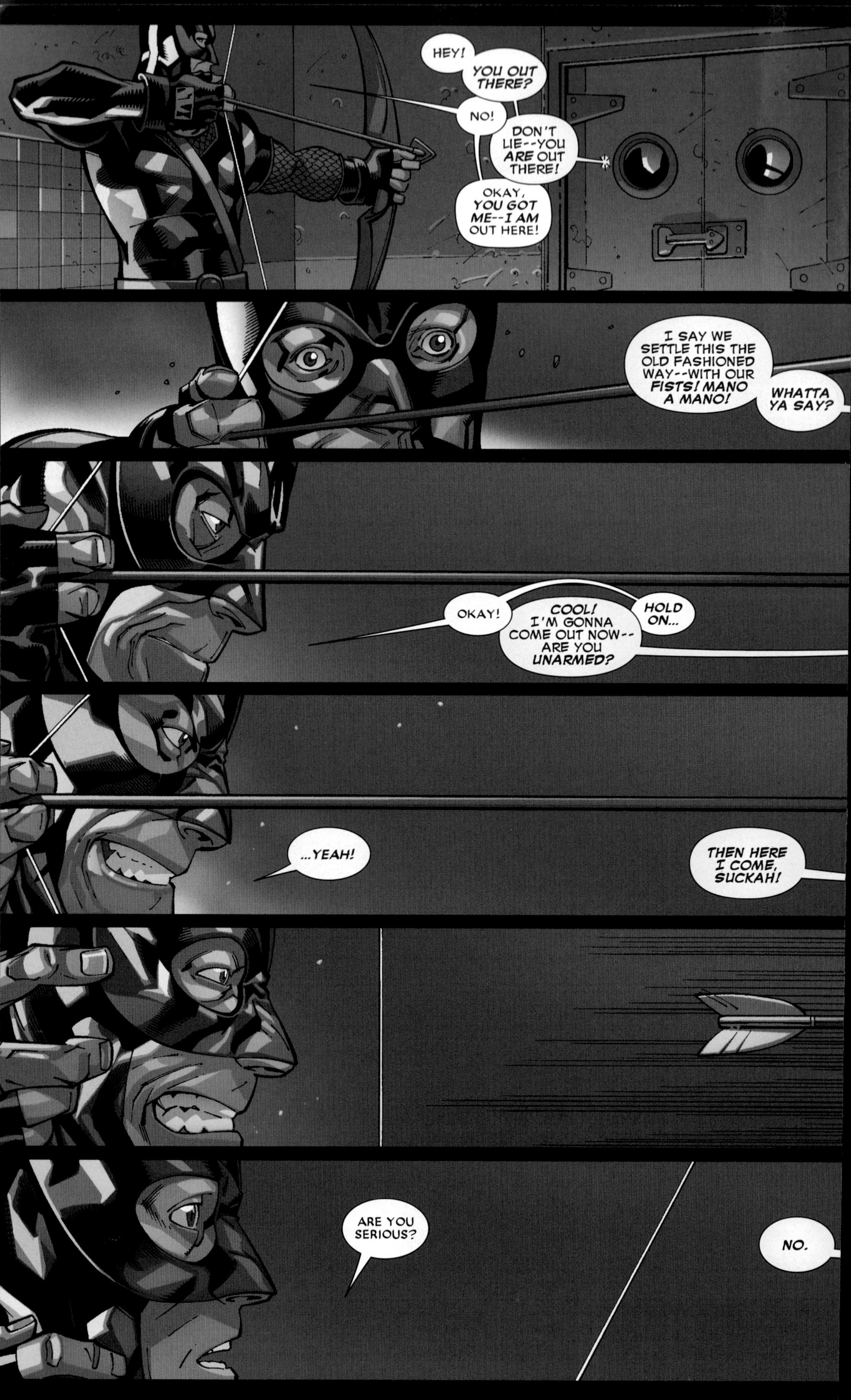
HEY!
YOU OUT THERE?
NO!
DON'T LIE--YOU ARE OUT THERE!
OKAY, YOU GOT ME--I AM OUT HERE!
I SAY WE SETTLE THIS THE OLD FASHIONED WAY--WITH OUR FISTS! MANO A MANO!
WHATTA YA SAY?
OKAY!
COOL! I'M GONNA COME OUT NOW--ARE YOU UNARMED?
HOLD ON...
...YEAH!
THEN HERE I COME, SUCKAH!
ARE YOU SERIOUS?
NO.

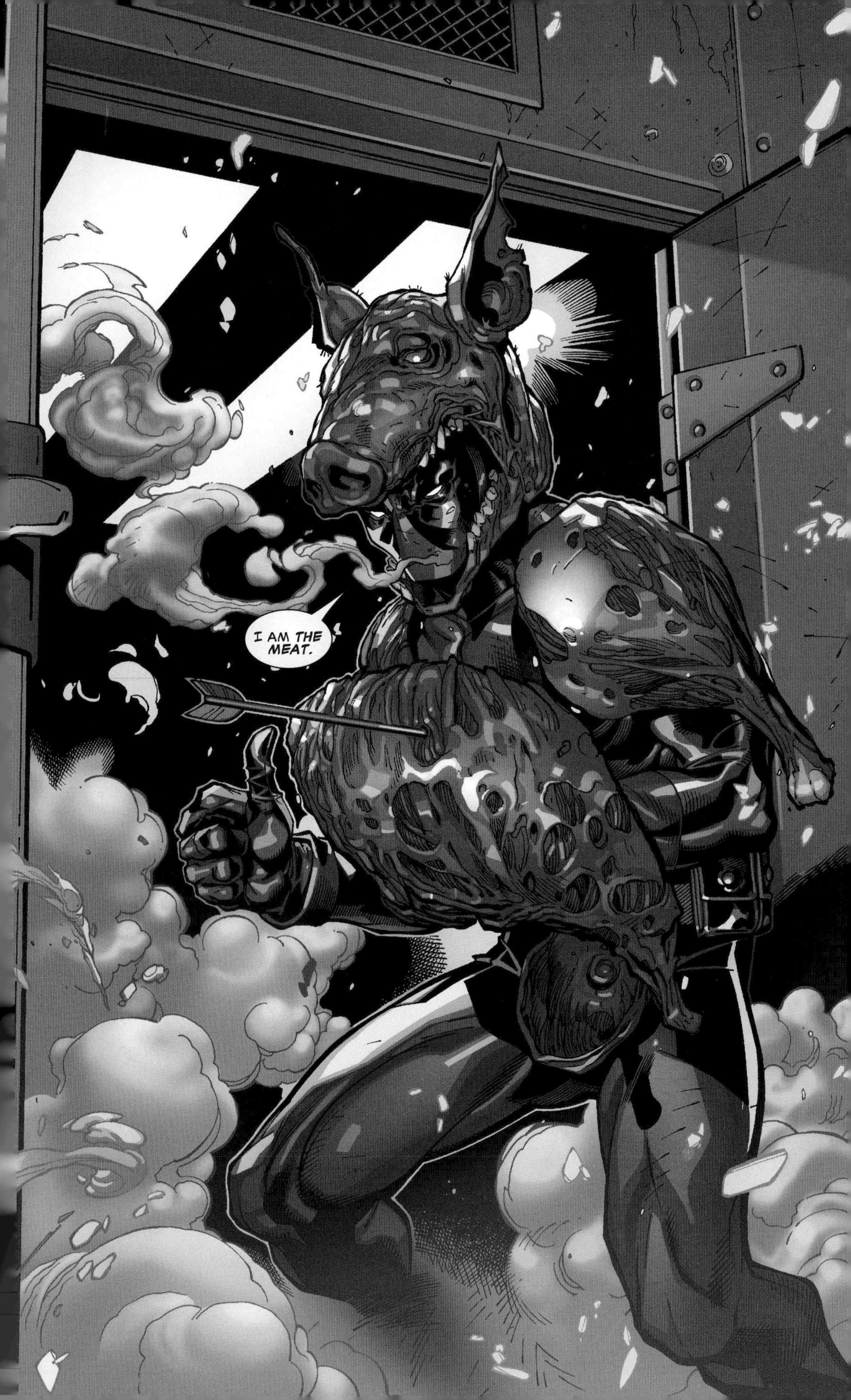
I AM THE MEAT.

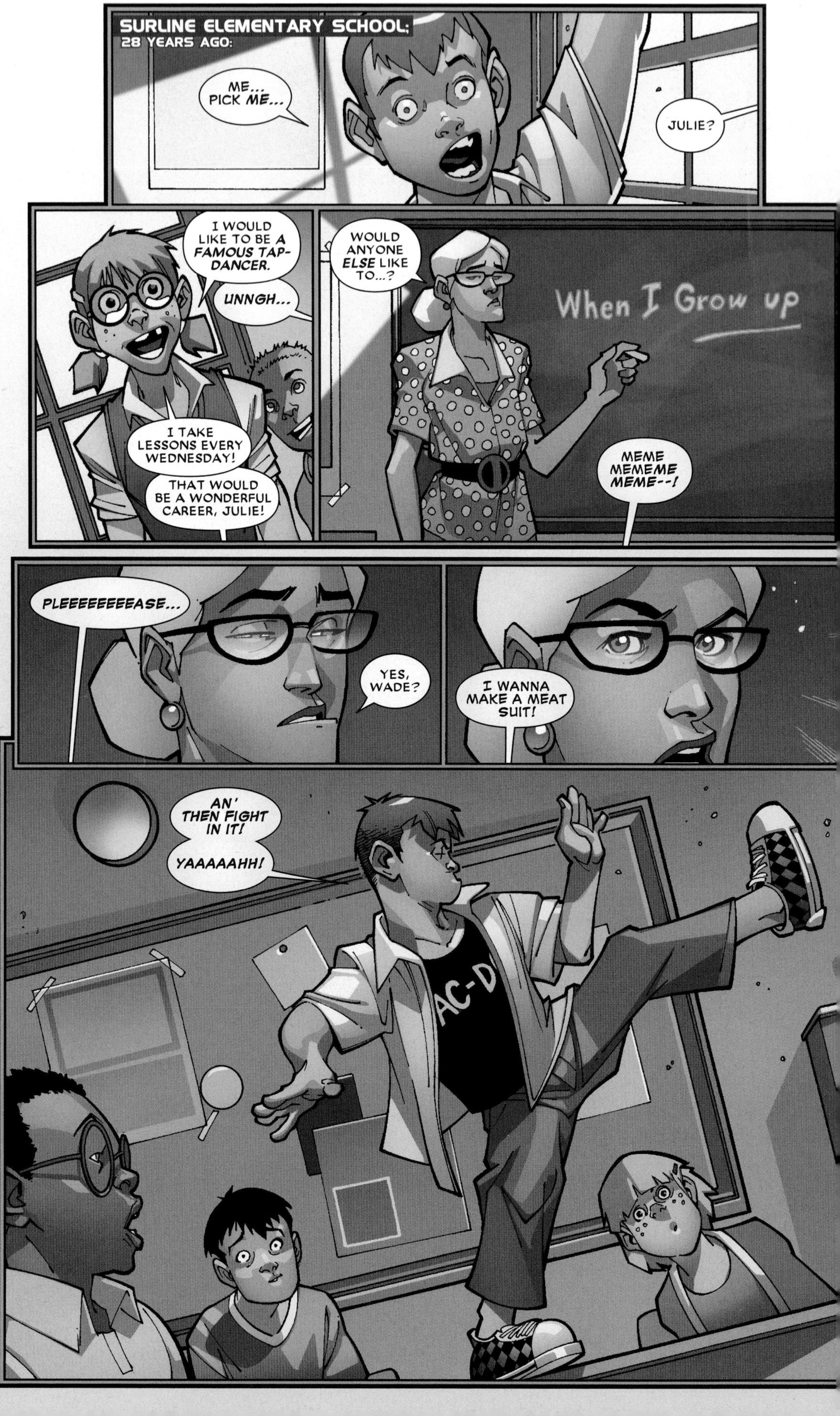

SURLINE ELEMENTARY SCHOOL;
28 YEARS AGO:
ME... PICK ME...
JULIE?
I WOULD LIKE TO BE A FAMOUS TAP-DANCER.
UNNGH...
I TAKE LESSONS EVERY WEDNESDAY!
THAT WOULD BE A WONDERFUL CAREER, JULIE!
WOULD ANYONE ELSE LIKE TO...?
When I Grow up
MEME MEMEME MEME--!
PLEEEEEEEEASE...
YES, WADE?
I WANNA MAKE A MEAT SUIT!
AN' THEN FIGHT IN IT!
YAAAAAHH!
AC-D

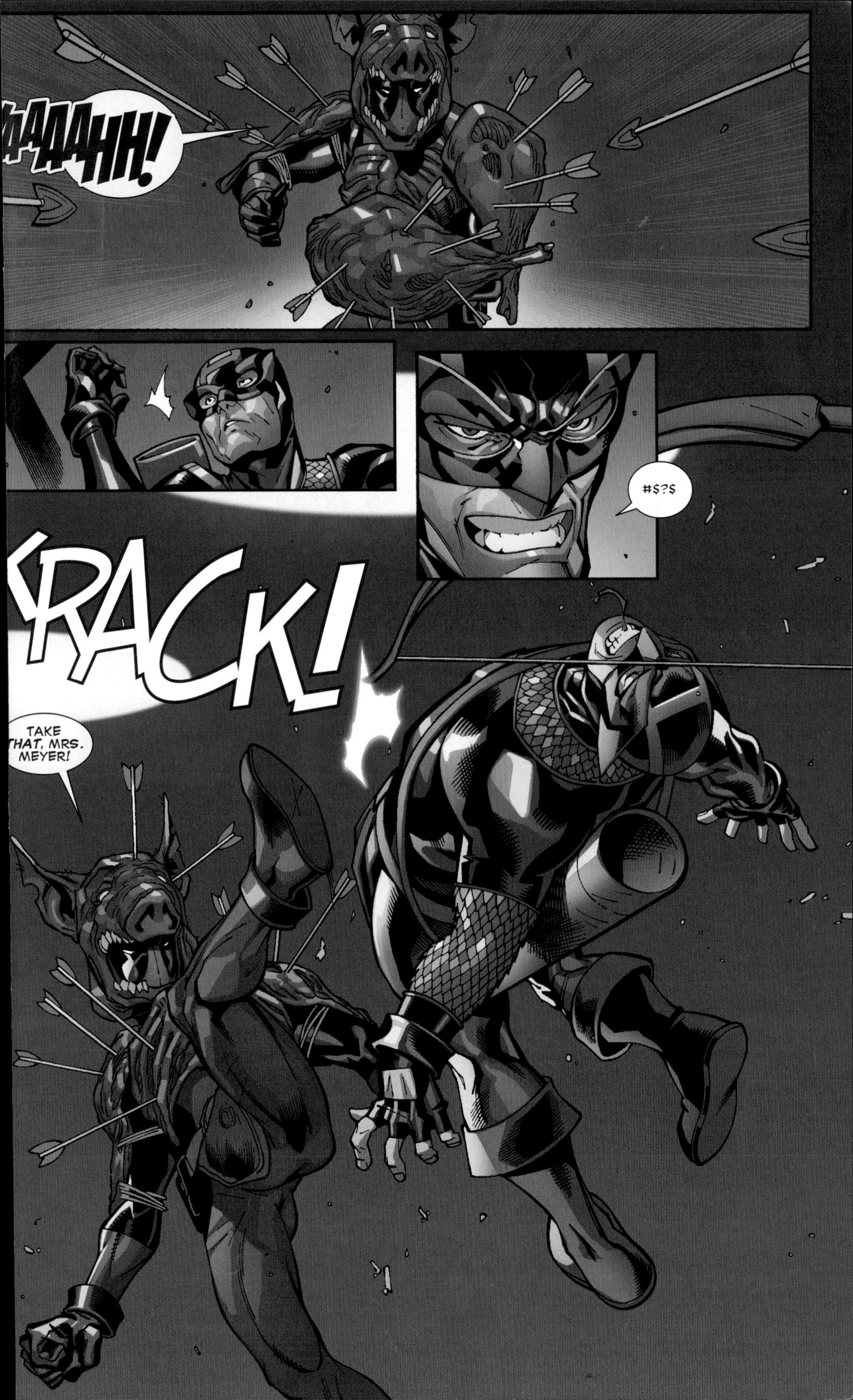
AAAAHH!
#$?$
KRACK!
TAKE THAT, MRS. MEYER!

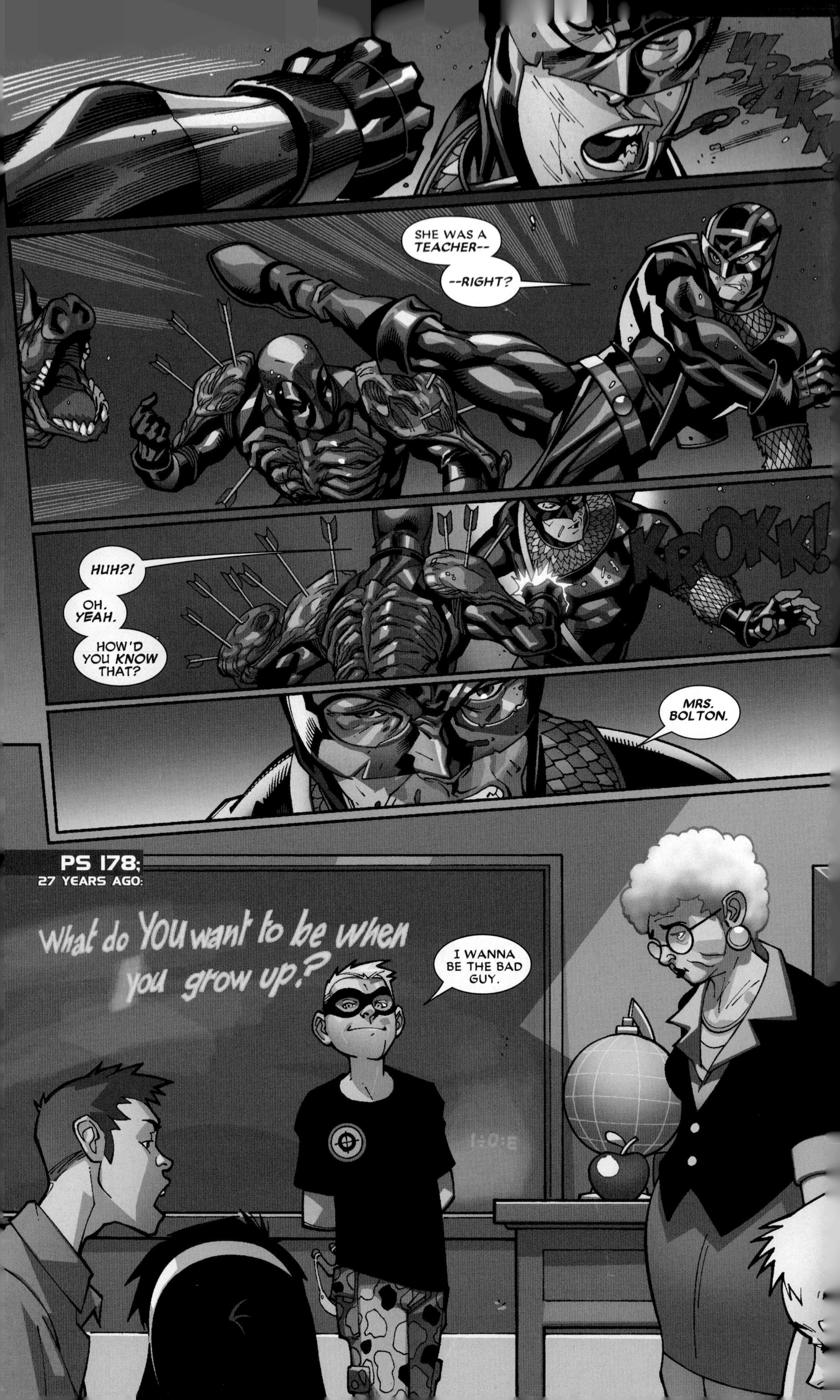

WHAKK
SHE WAS A TEACHER--
--RIGHT?
HUH?!
KROKK!
OH. YEAH.
HOW'D YOU KNOW THAT?
MRS. BOLTON.
PS 178;
27 YEARS AGO:
What do You want to be when you grow up?
I WANNA BE THE BAD GUY.

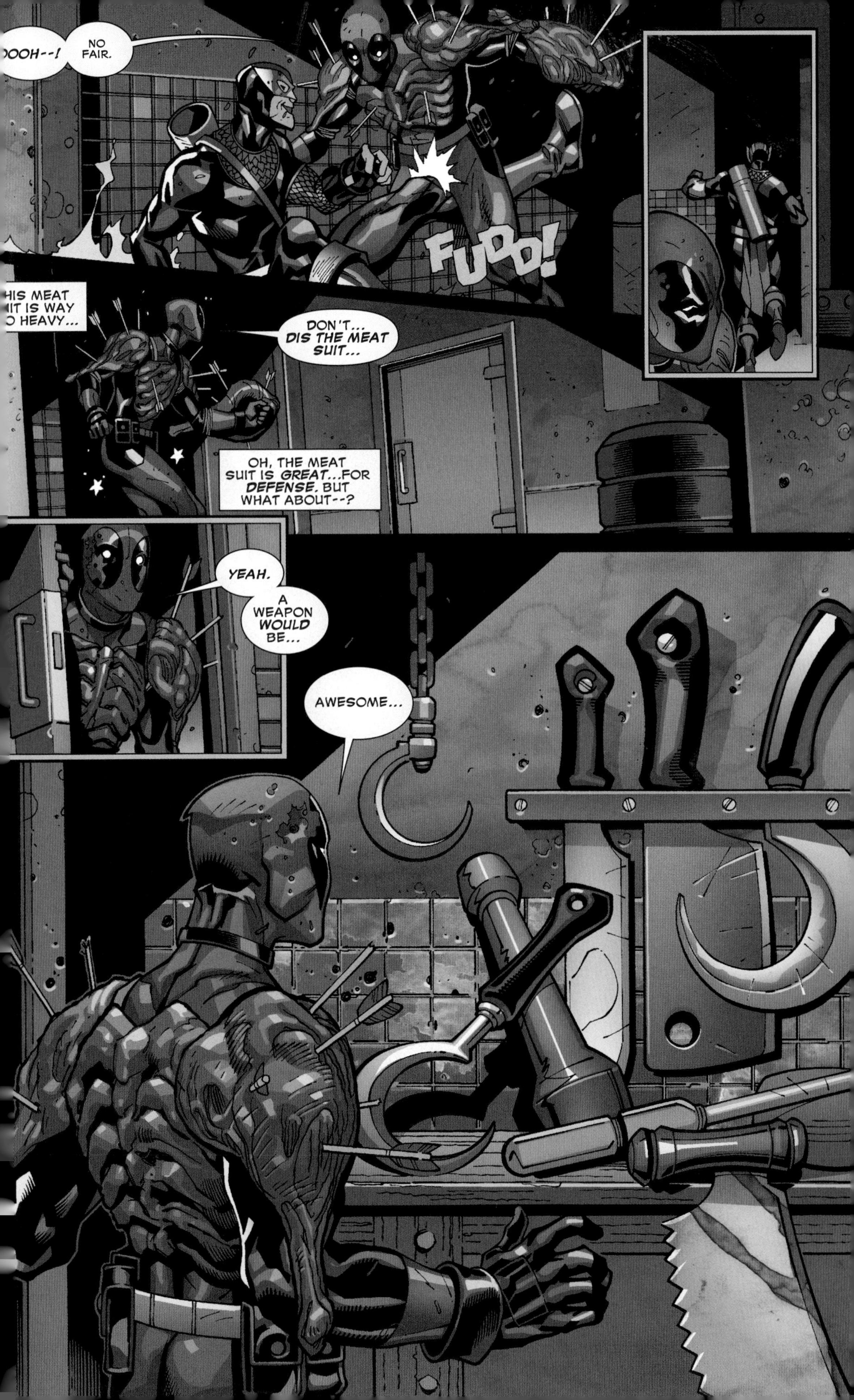
OOOH--!
NO FAIR.
FUDD!
HIS MEAT
IT IS WAY
O HEAVY...
DON'T... DIS THE MEAT SUIT...
OH, THE MEAT SUIT IS GREAT...FOR DEFENSE. BUT WHAT ABOUT--?
YEAH.
A WEAPON WOULD BE...
AWESOME...

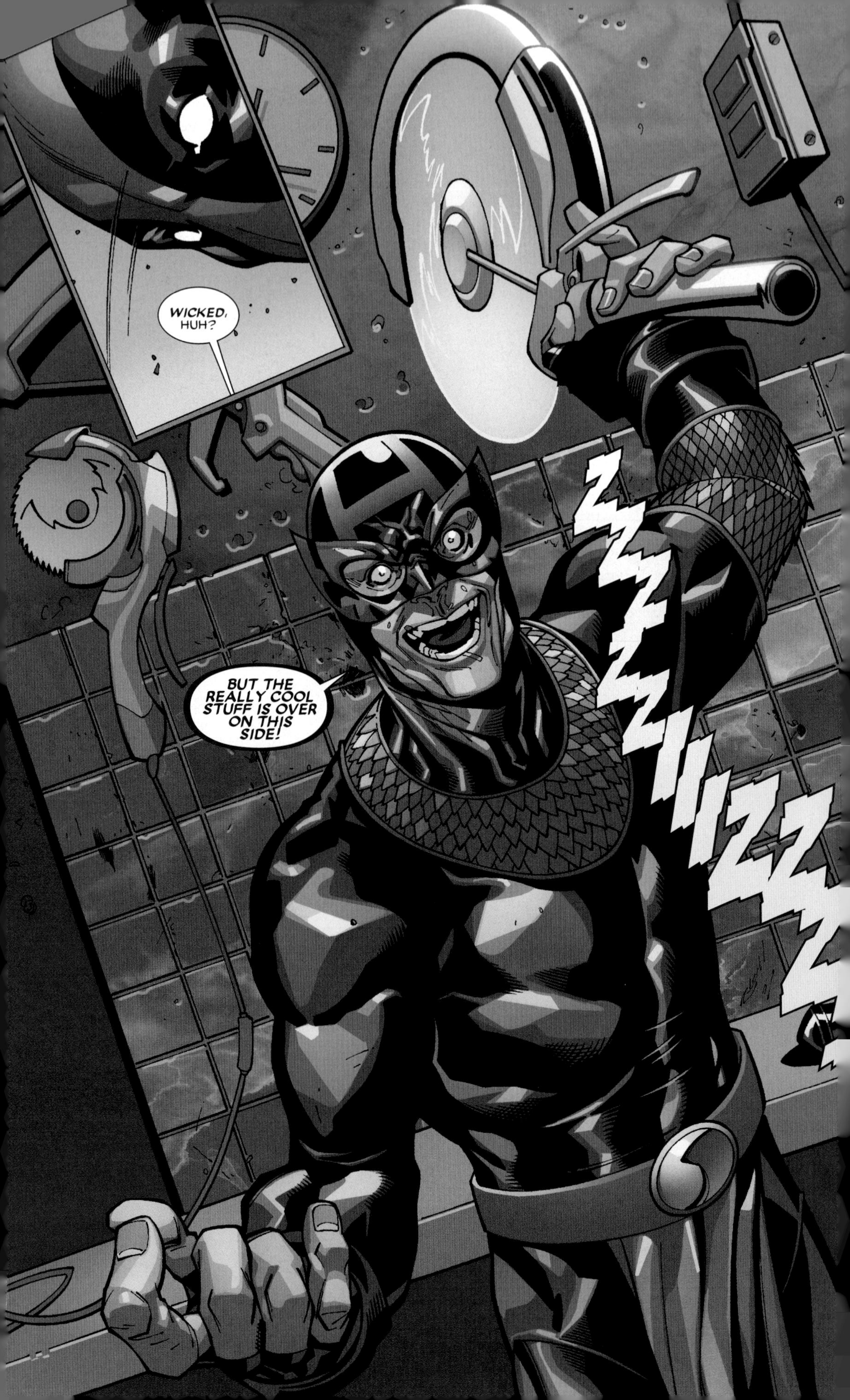
WICKED, HUH?
BUT THE REALLY COOL STUFF IS OVER ON THIS SIDE!
ZZZZZIIIIZZZZ

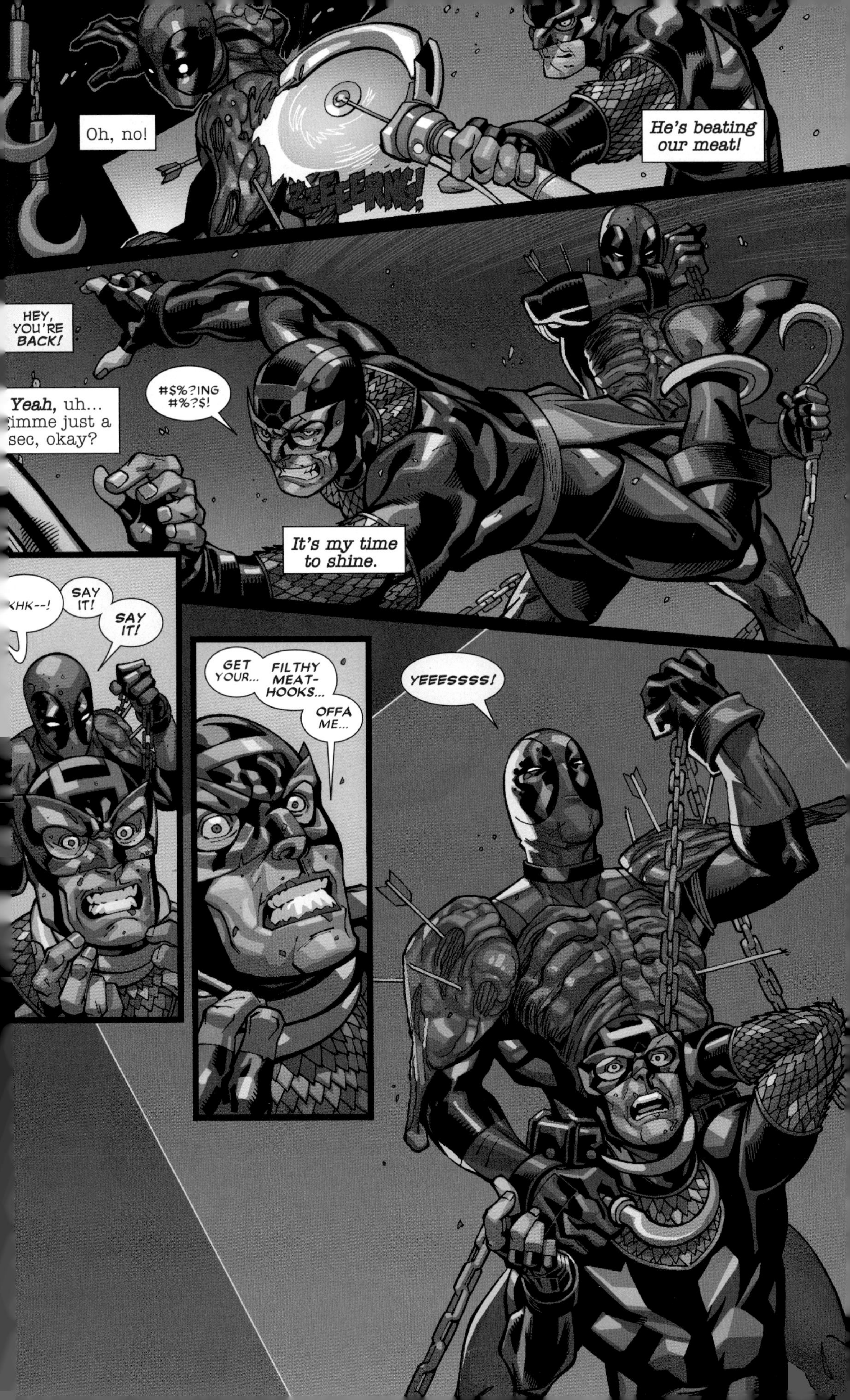
Oh, no!
ZZEEERNG!
He's beating our meat!
HEY, YOU'RE BACK!
Yeah, uh... gimme just a sec, okay?
#$%?ING #%?$!
It's my time to shine.
KHK--!
SAY IT!
SAY IT!
GET YOUR...
FILTHY MEAT-HOOKS...
OFFA ME...
YEEESSSS!

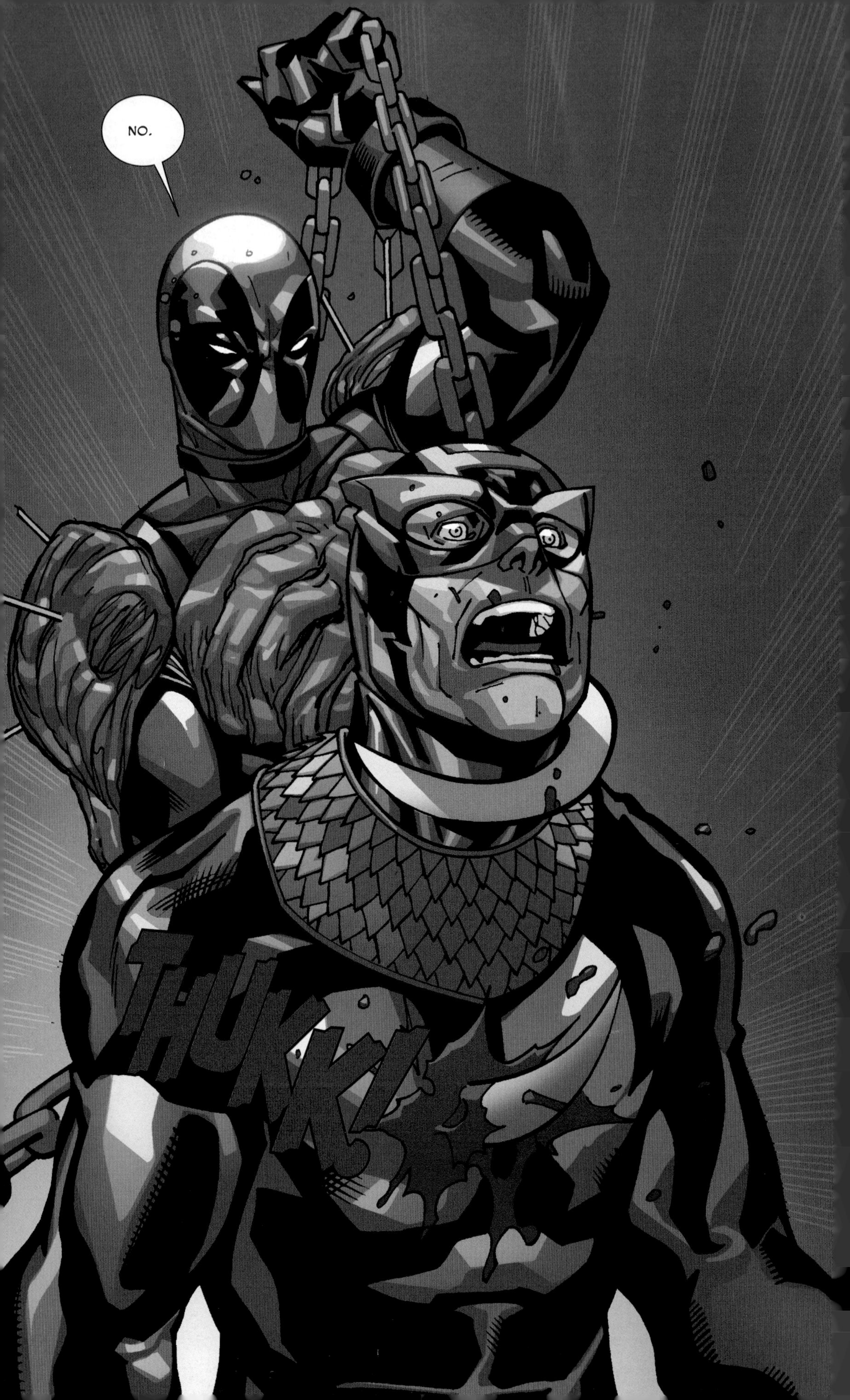
NO.
THUNK!

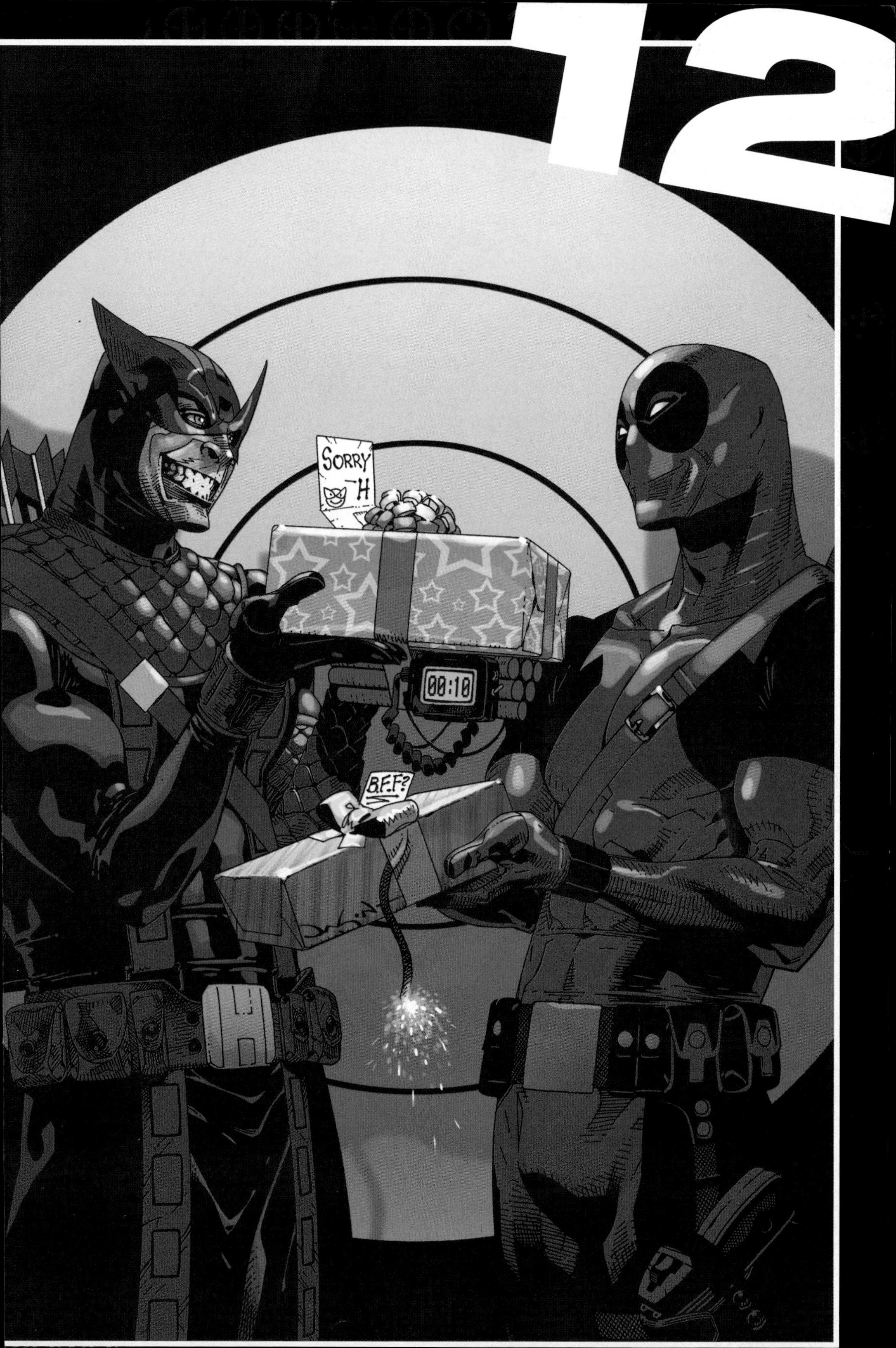
12
SORRY
-H
00:10
B.F.F?

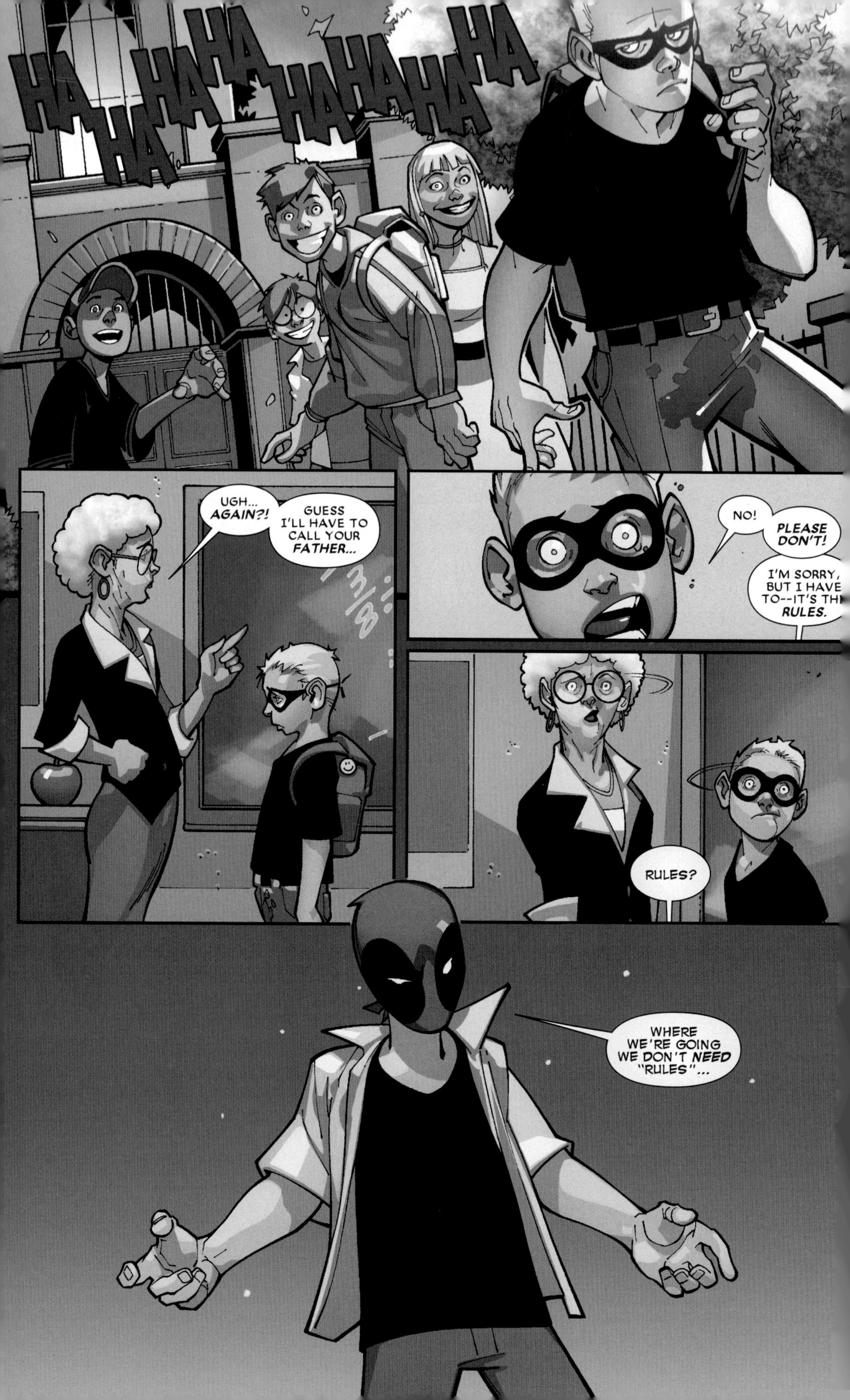
HA HA HA HA HA HA HA HA HA HA
UGH... AGAIN?!
GUESS I'LL HAVE TO CALL YOUR FATHER...
NO!
PLEASE DON'T!
I'M SORRY, BUT I HAVE TO--IT'S TH RULES.
RULES?
WHERE WE'RE GOING WE DON'T NEED "RULES"...

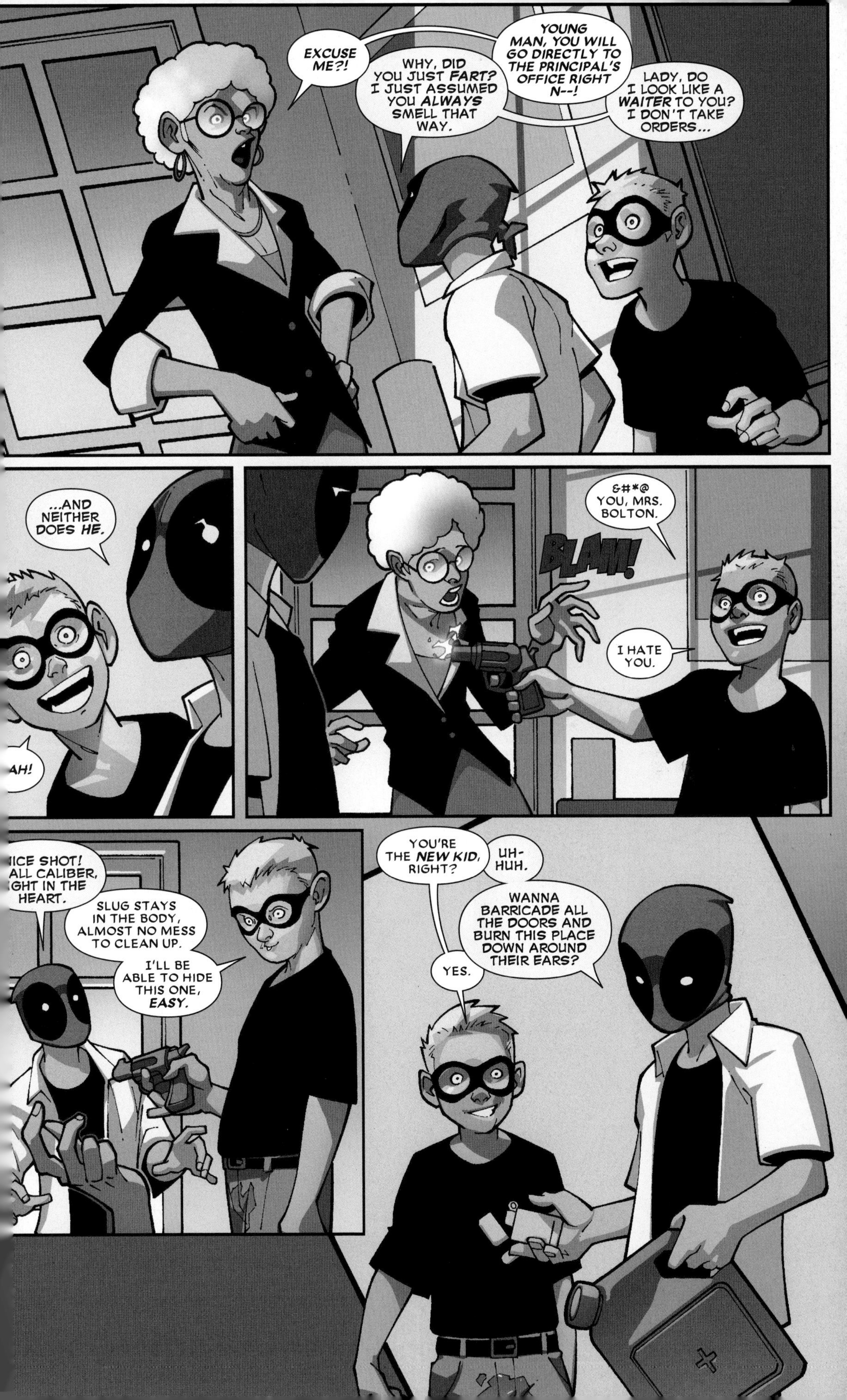
EXCUSE ME?!
WHY, DID YOU JUST FART? I JUST ASSUMED YOU ALWAYS SMELL THAT WAY.
YOUNG MAN, YOU WILL GO DIRECTLY TO THE PRINCIPAL'S OFFICE RIGHT N--!
LADY, DO I LOOK LIKE A WAITER TO YOU? I DON'T TAKE ORDERS...
...AND NEITHER DOES HE.
AH!
&#*@ YOU, MRS. BOLTON.
BLAM!
I HATE YOU.
ICE SHOT! ALL CALIBER, GHT IN THE HEART.
SLUG STAYS IN THE BODY, ALMOST NO MESS TO CLEAN UP.
I'LL BE ABLE TO HIDE THIS ONE, EASY.
YOU'RE THE NEW KID, RIGHT?
UH-HUH.
WANNA BARRICADE ALL THE DOORS AND BURN THIS PLACE DOWN AROUND THEIR EARS?
YES.

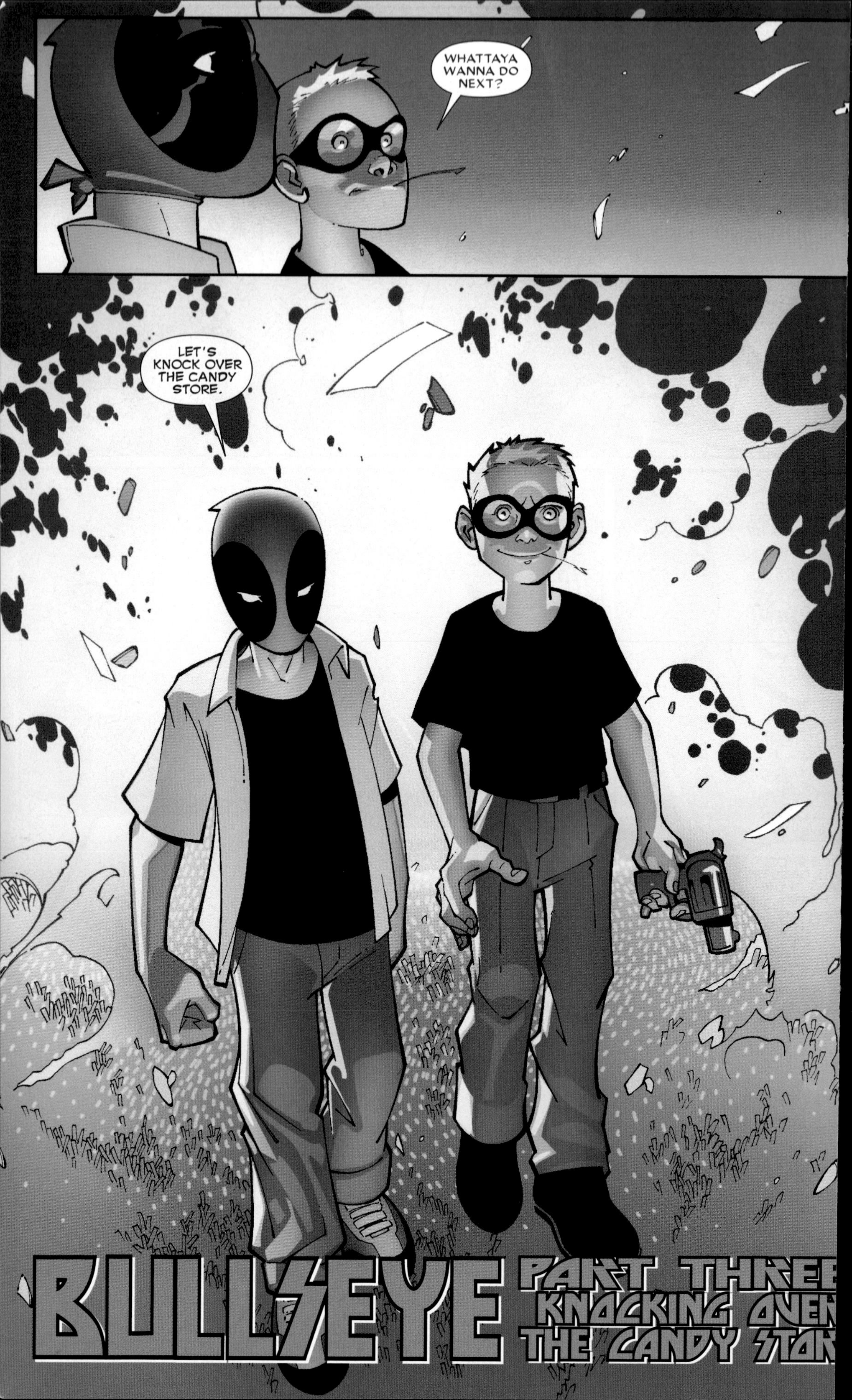
WHATTAYA WANNA DO NEXT?
LET'S KNOCK OVER THE CANDY STORE.
BULLSEYE
PART THREE
KNOCKING OVER
THE CANDY STOR

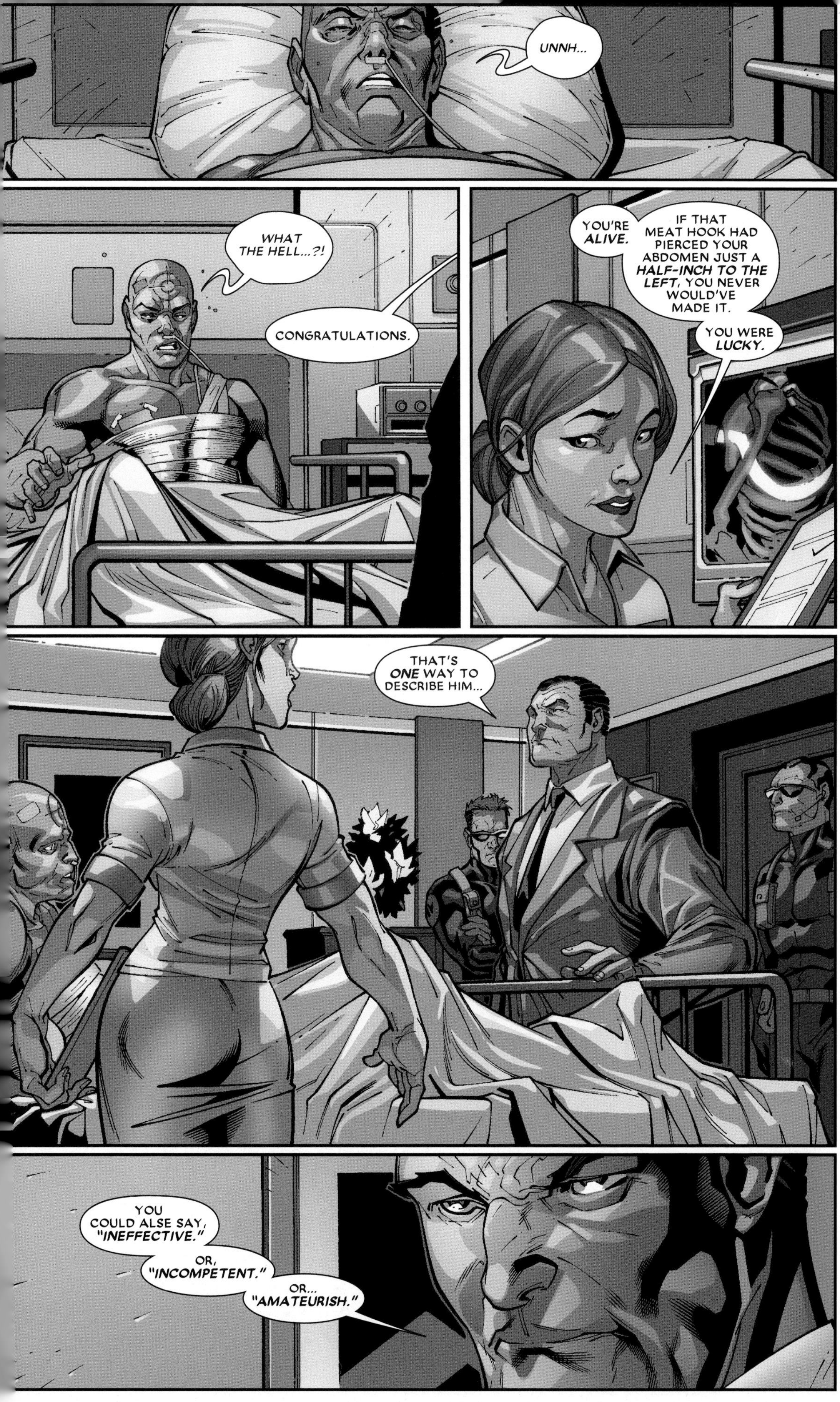
UNNH...
WHAT THE HELL...?!
CONGRATULATIONS.
YOU'RE ALIVE.
IF THAT MEAT HOOK HAD PIERCED YOUR ABDOMEN JUST A HALF-INCH TO THE LEFT, YOU NEVER WOULD'VE MADE IT.
YOU WERE LUCKY.
THAT'S ONE WAY TO DESCRIBE HIM...
YOU COULD ALSE SAY, "INEFFECTIVE."
OR, "INCOMPETENT."
OR... "AMATEURISH."

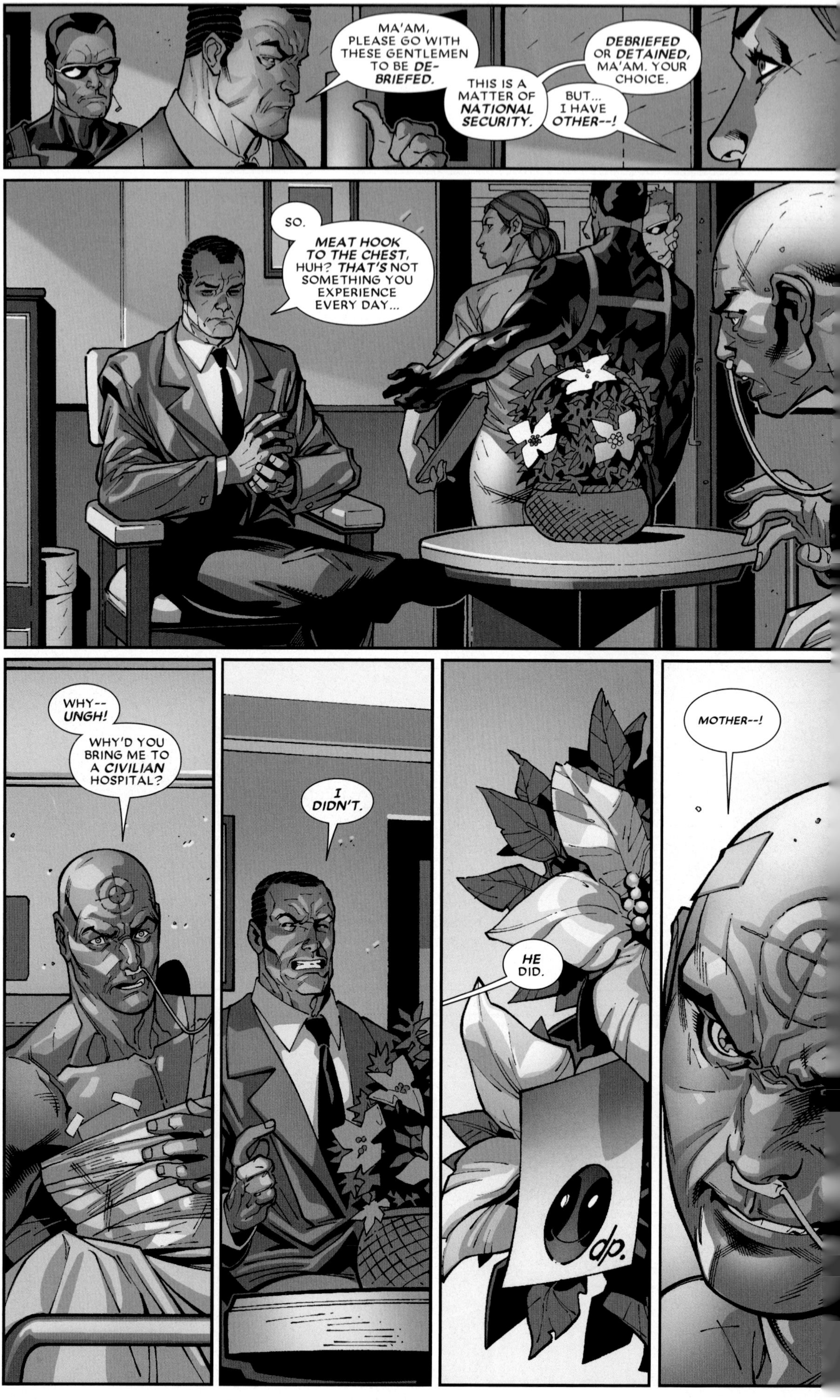
MA'AM, PLEASE GO WITH THESE GENTLEMEN TO BE DE-BRIEFED.
THIS IS A MATTER OF NATIONAL SECURITY.
BUT... I HAVE OTHER--!
DEBRIEFED OR DETAINED, MA'AM. YOUR CHOICE.
SO.
MEAT HOOK TO THE CHEST, HUH? THAT'S NOT SOMETHING YOU EXPERIENCE EVERY DAY...
WHY-- UNGH!
WHY'D YOU BRING ME TO A CIVILIAN HOSPITAL?
I DIDN'T.
HE DID.
dp.
MOTHER--!

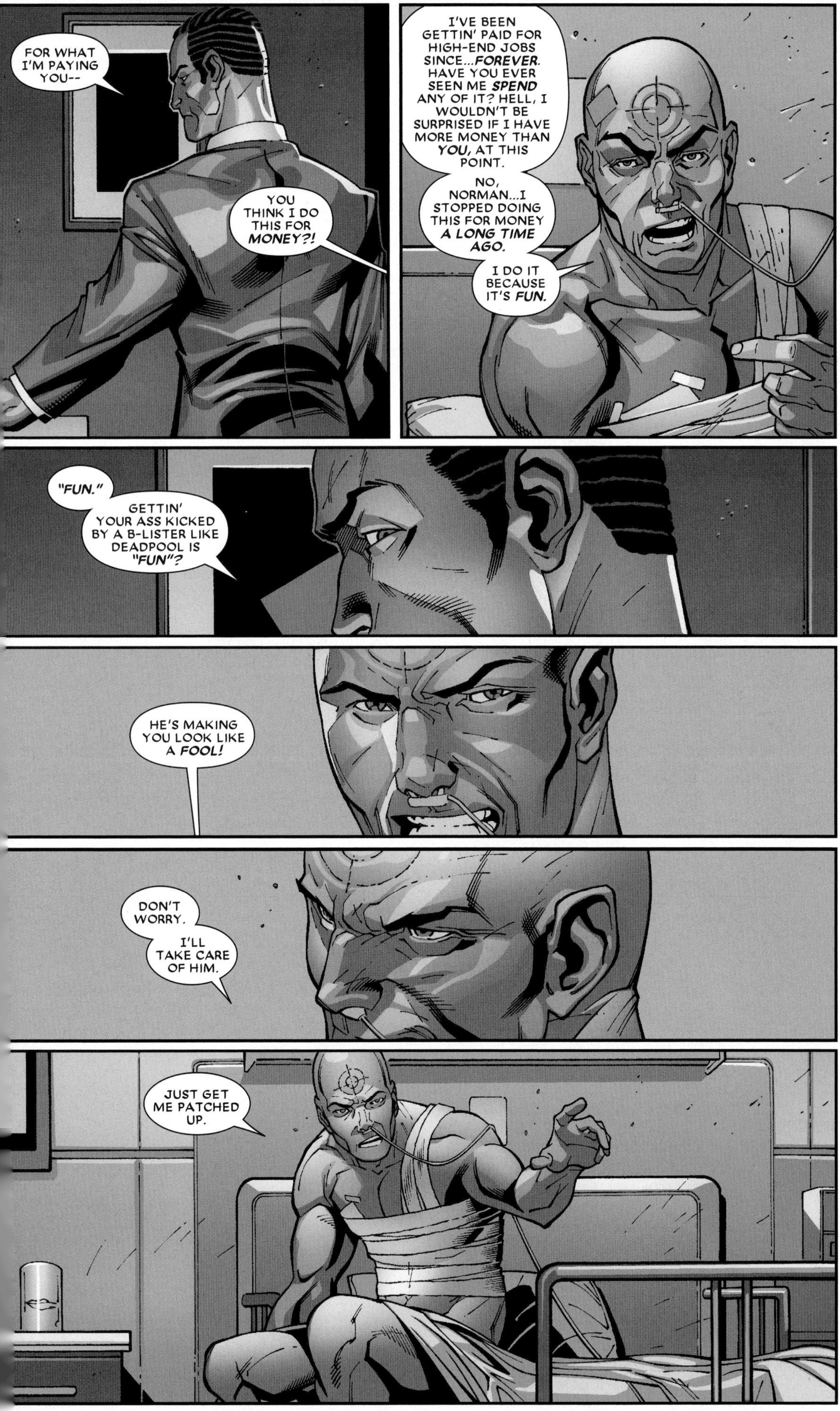
FOR WHAT I'M PAYING YOU--
YOU THINK I DO THIS FOR MONEY?!
I'VE BEEN GETTIN' PAID FOR HIGH-END JOBS SINCE...FOREVER. HAVE YOU EVER SEEN ME SPEND ANY OF IT? HELL, I WOULDN'T BE SURPRISED IF I HAVE MORE MONEY THAN YOU, AT THIS POINT.
NO, NORMAN...I STOPPED DOING THIS FOR MONEY A LONG TIME AGO.
I DO IT BECAUSE IT'S FUN.
"FUN."
GETTIN' YOUR ASS KICKED BY A B-LISTER LIKE DEADPOOL IS "FUN"?
HE'S MAKING YOU LOOK LIKE A FOOL!
DON'T WORRY.
I'LL TAKE CARE OF HIM.
JUST GET ME PATCHED UP.

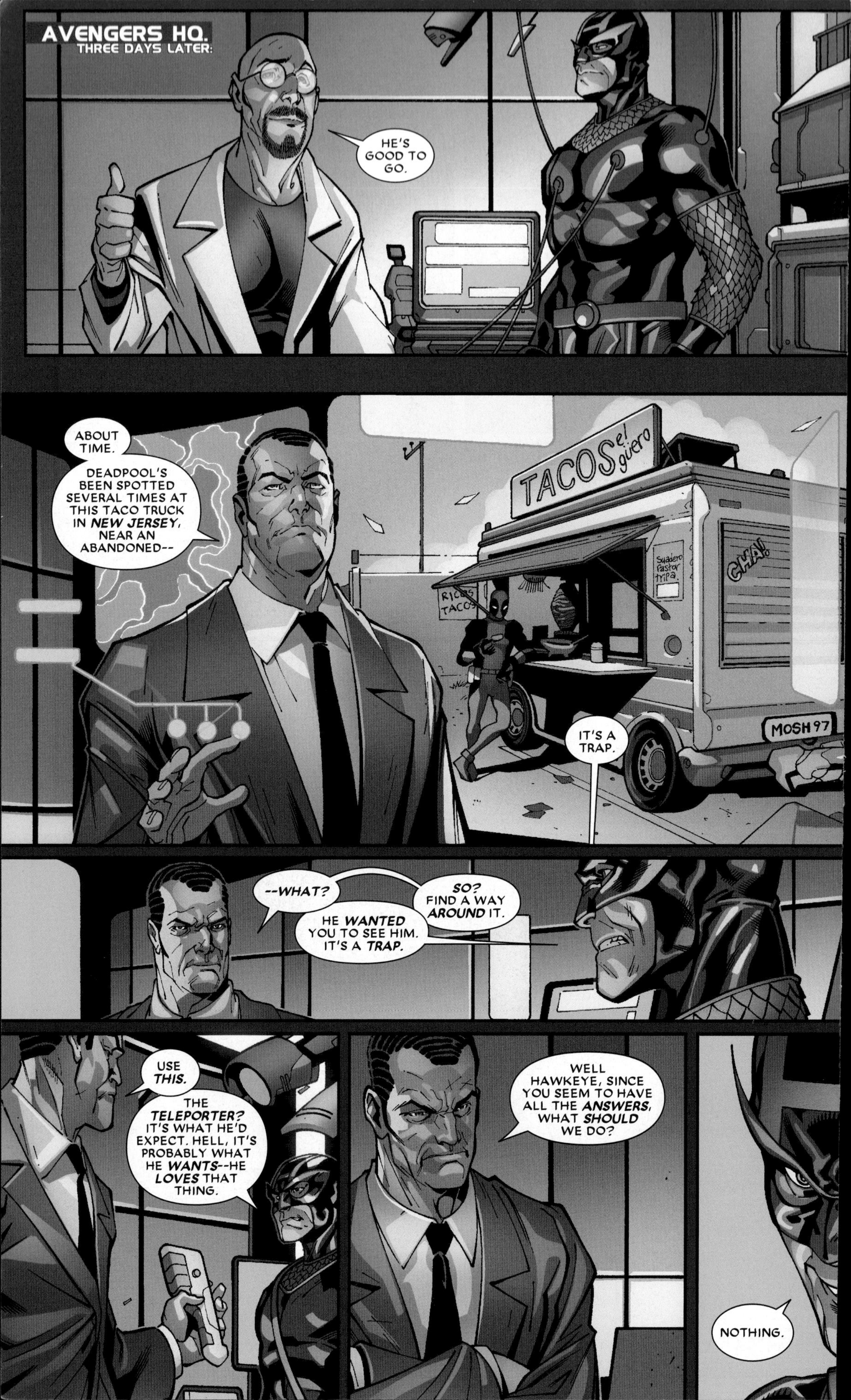
AVENGERS HQ. THREE DAYS LATER:
HE'S GOOD TO GO.
ABOUT TIME.
DEADPOOL'S BEEN SPOTTED SEVERAL TIMES AT THIS TACO TRUCK IN NEW JERSEY, NEAR AN ABANDONED--
TACOS el guero
Suadero pastor tripa
RICOS TACOS
CHA!
MOSH 97
IT'S A TRAP.
--WHAT?
HE WANTED YOU TO SEE HIM. IT'S A TRAP.
SO? FIND A WAY AROUND IT.
USE THIS.
THE TELEPORTER? IT'S WHAT HE'D EXPECT. HELL, IT'S PROBABLY WHAT HE WANTS--HE LOVES THAT THING.
WELL HAWKEYE, SINCE YOU SEEM TO HAVE ALL THE ANSWERS, WHAT SHOULD WE DO?
NOTHING.

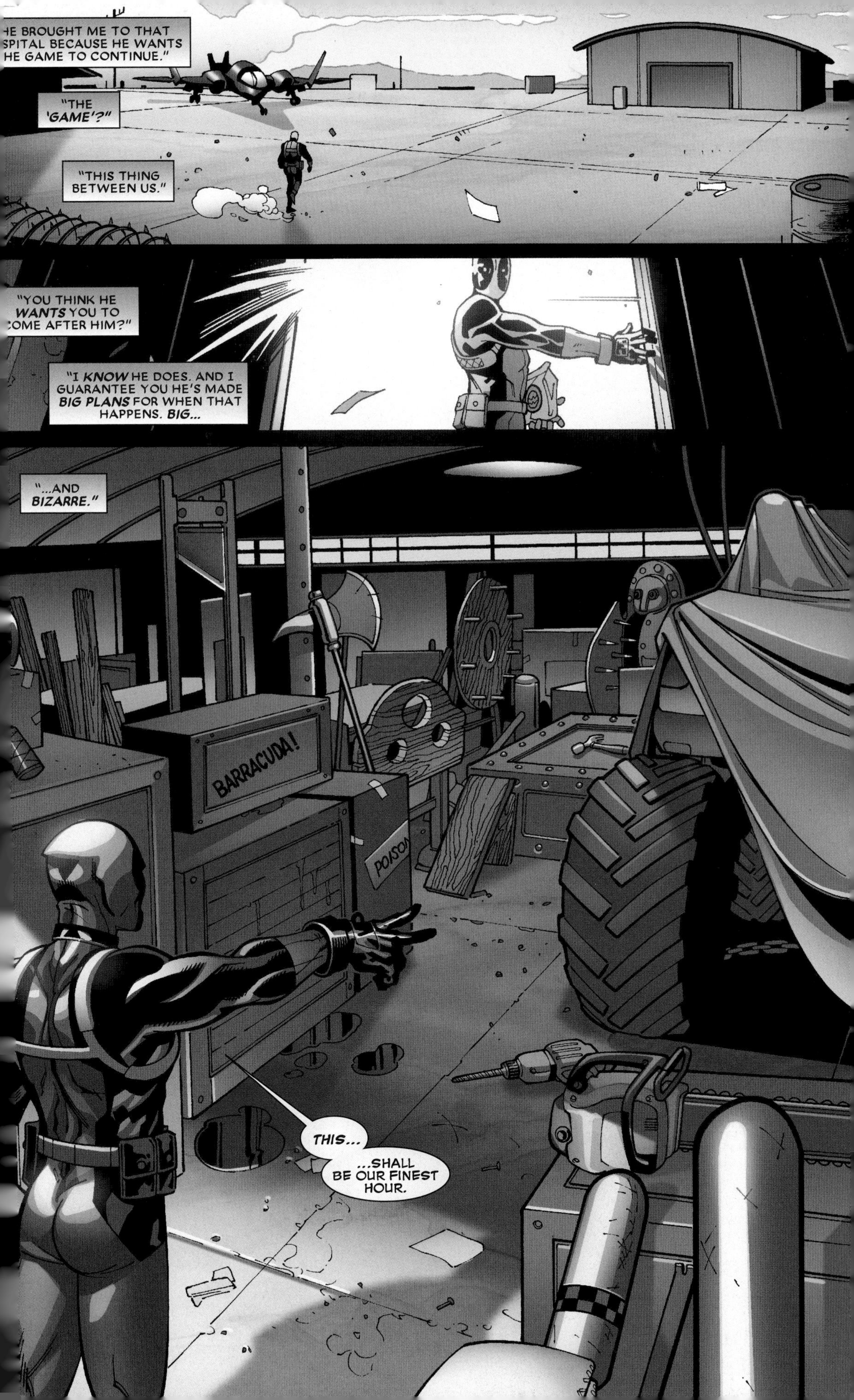

HE BROUGHT ME TO THAT
SPITAL BECAUSE HE WANTS
HE GAME TO CONTINUE."
"THE 'GAME'?"
"THIS THING BETWEEN US."
"YOU THINK HE WANTS YOU TO
OME AFTER HIM?"
"I KNOW HE DOES. AND I GUARANTEE YOU HE'S MADE BIG PLANS FOR WHEN THAT HAPPENS. BIG...
"...AND BIZARRE."
BARRACUDA!
POISON
THIS...
...SHALL BE OUR FINEST HOUR.

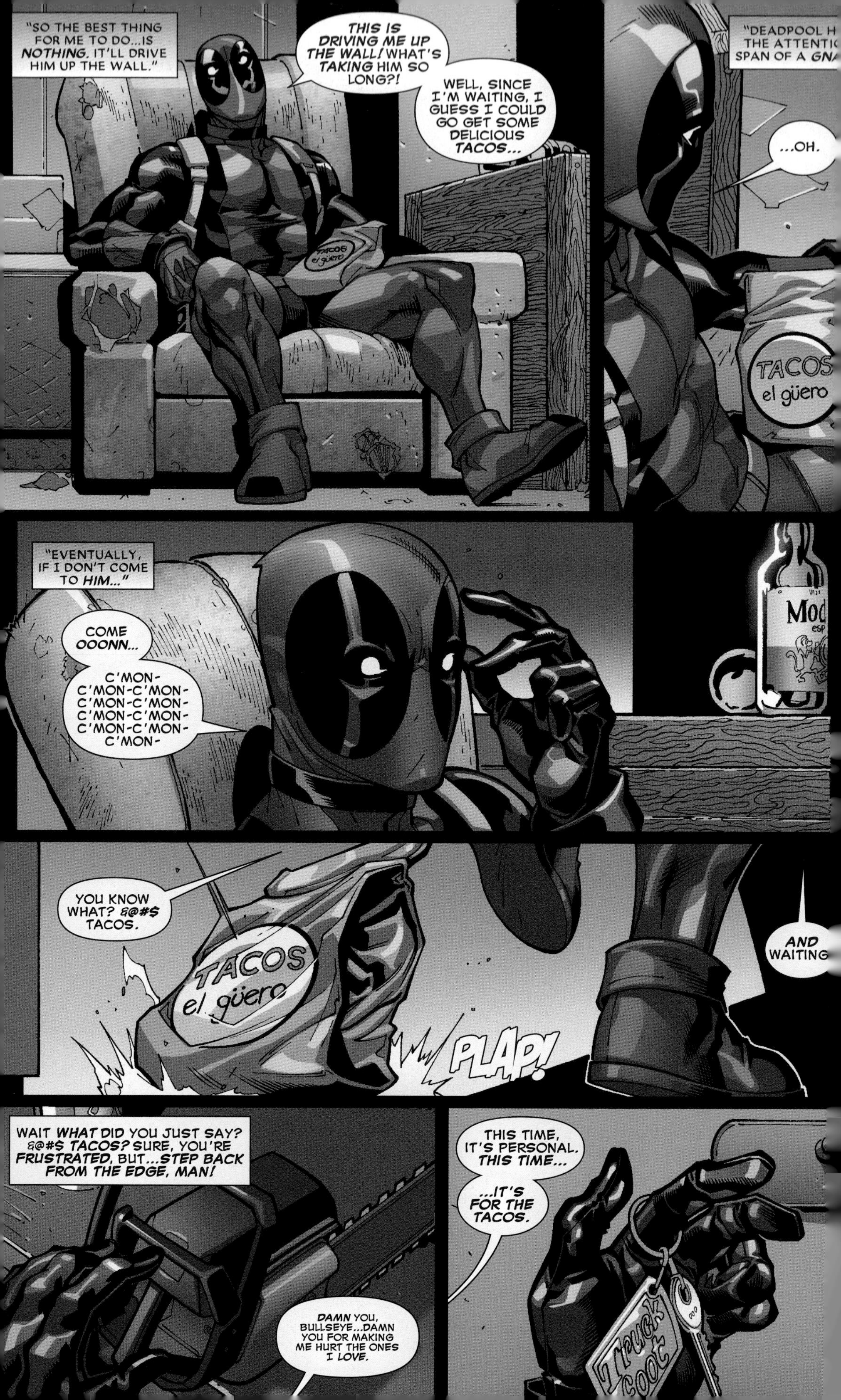
"SO THE BEST THING FOR ME TO DO...IS NOTHING. IT'LL DRIVE HIM UP THE WALL."
THIS IS DRIVING ME UP THE WALL! WHAT'S TAKING HIM SO LONG?!
WELL, SINCE I'M WAITING, I GUESS I COULD GO GET SOME DELICIOUS TACOS...
TACOS el güero
"DEADPOOL H THE ATTENTIC SPAN OF A GNA
...OH.
TACOS el güero
"EVENTUALLY, IF I DON'T COME TO HIM..."
COME OOONN...
C'MON-C'MON-C'MON-C'MON-C'MON-C'MON-C'MON-C'MON-C'MON-C'MON-
YOU KNOW WHAT? &@#$ TACOS.
TACOS el güero
PLAP!
AND WAITING
WAIT WHAT DID YOU JUST SAY? &@#$ TACOS? SURE, YOU'RE FRUSTRATED, BUT...STEP BACK FROM THE EDGE, MAN!
DAMN YOU, BULLSEYE...DAMN YOU FOR MAKING ME HURT THE ONES I LOVE.
THIS TIME, IT'S PERSONAL. THIS TIME...
...IT'S FOR THE TACOS.

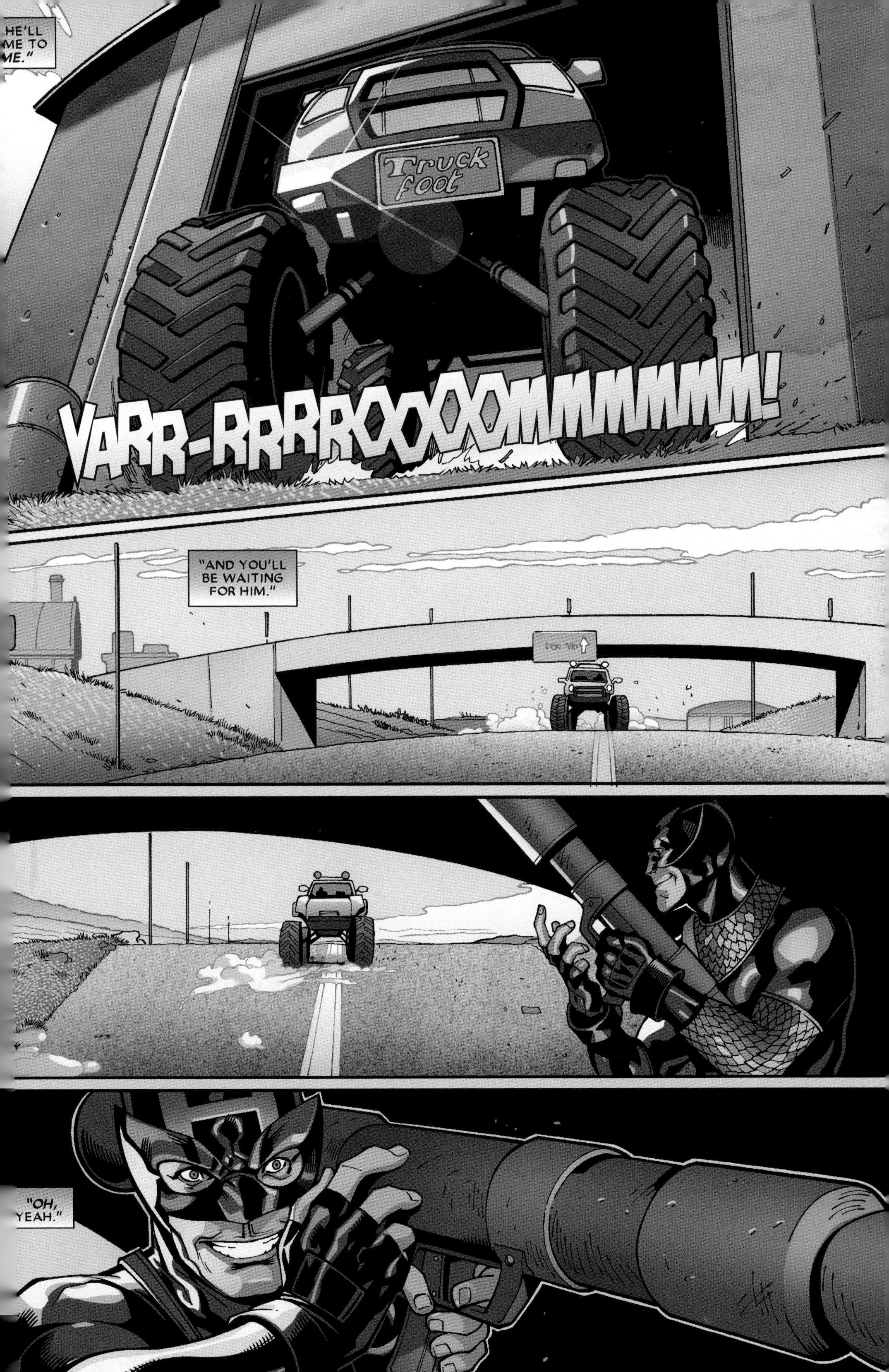

HE'LL
ME TO
ME."
Truck foot
VARR-RRRROOOOMMMMMMMMM!
"AND YOU'LL BE WAITING FOR HIM."
"OH, YEAH."

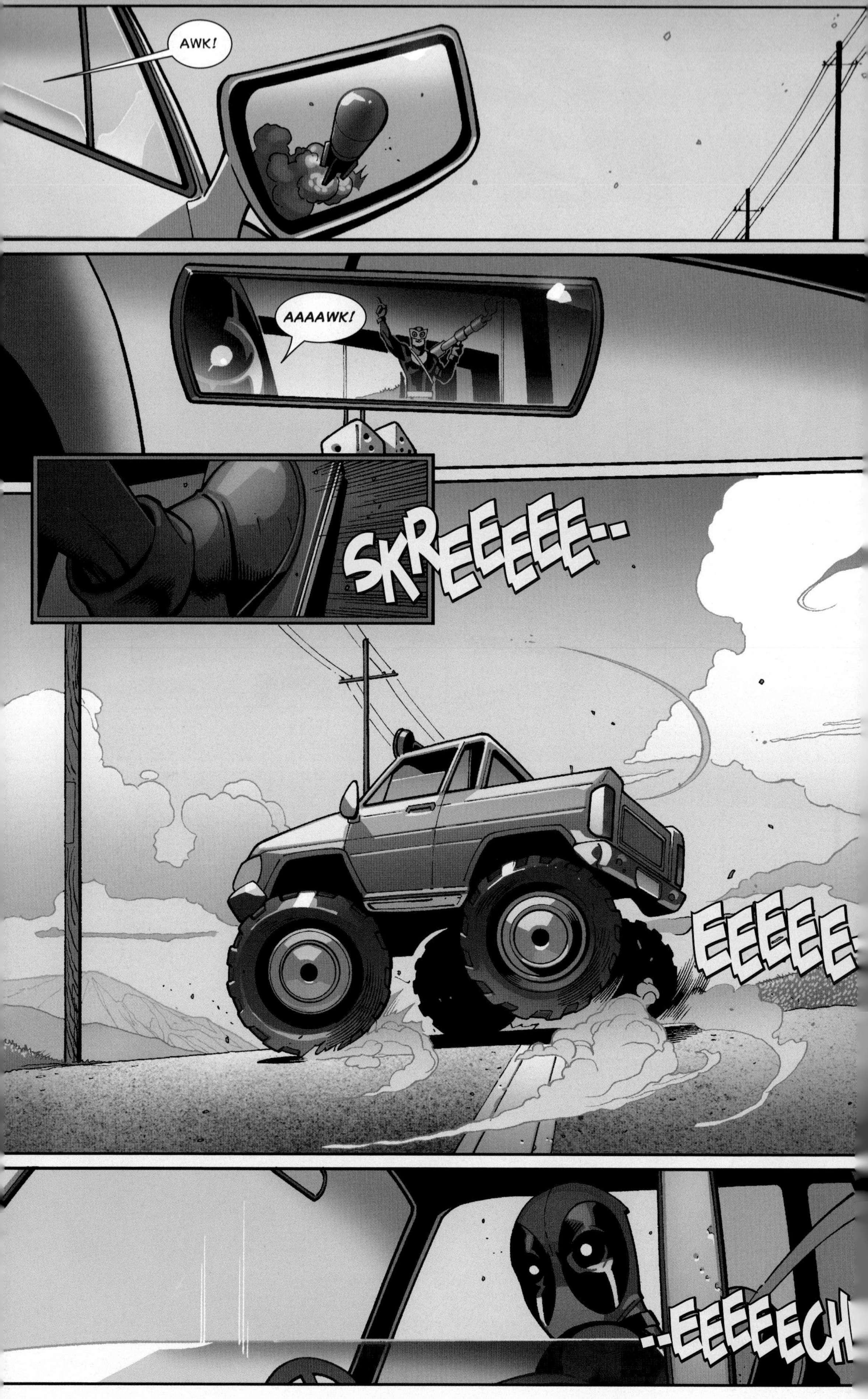
AWK!
AAAAWK!
SKREEEEEE--
EEEEEE
--EEEEEECH

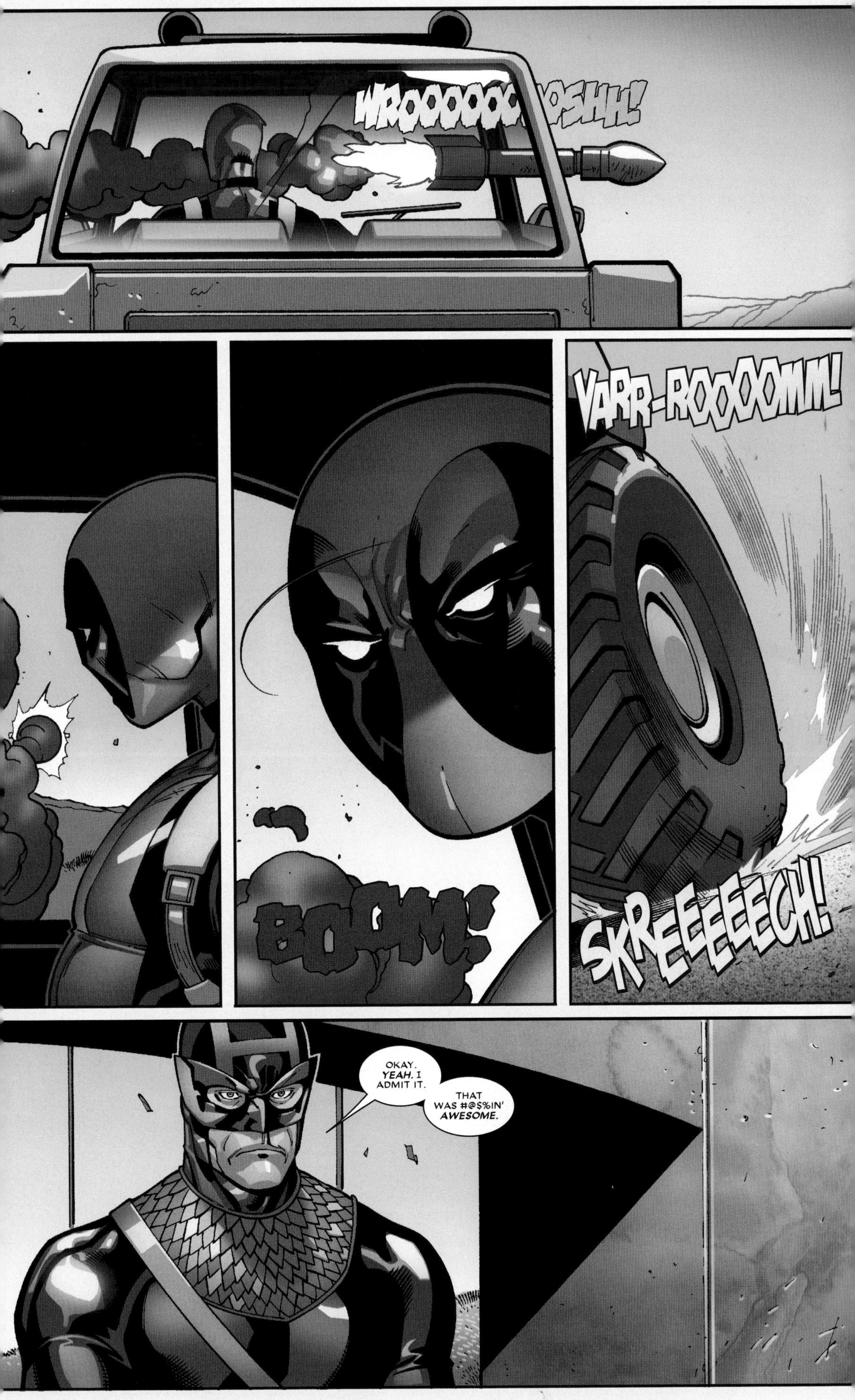
WROOOOOO...OSHH!
VARR-ROOOOMM!
BOOM!
SKREEEEEECH!
OKAY. YEAH, I ADMIT IT.
THAT WAS #@$%IN' AWESOME.

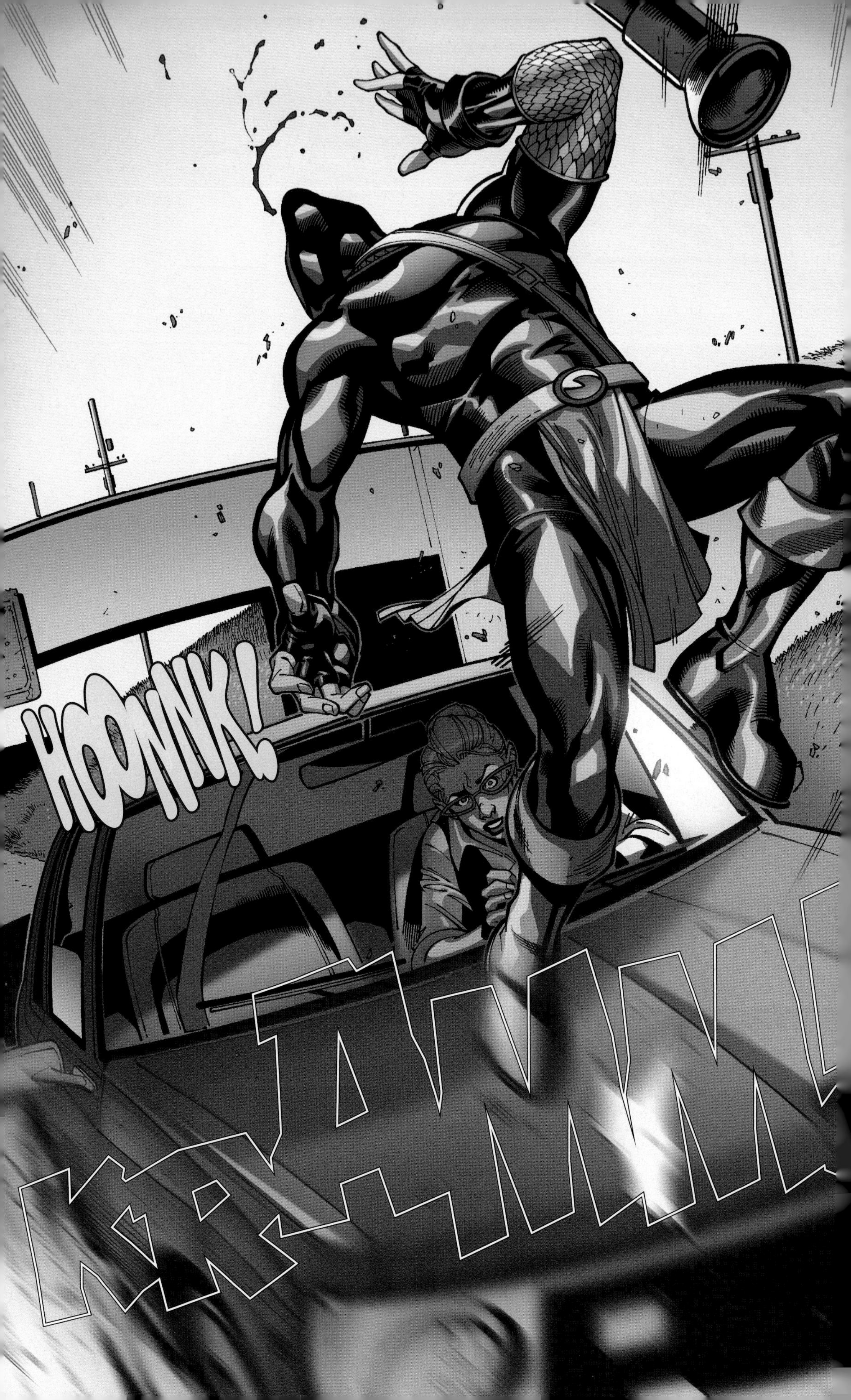
HOONNK!
KRAMM

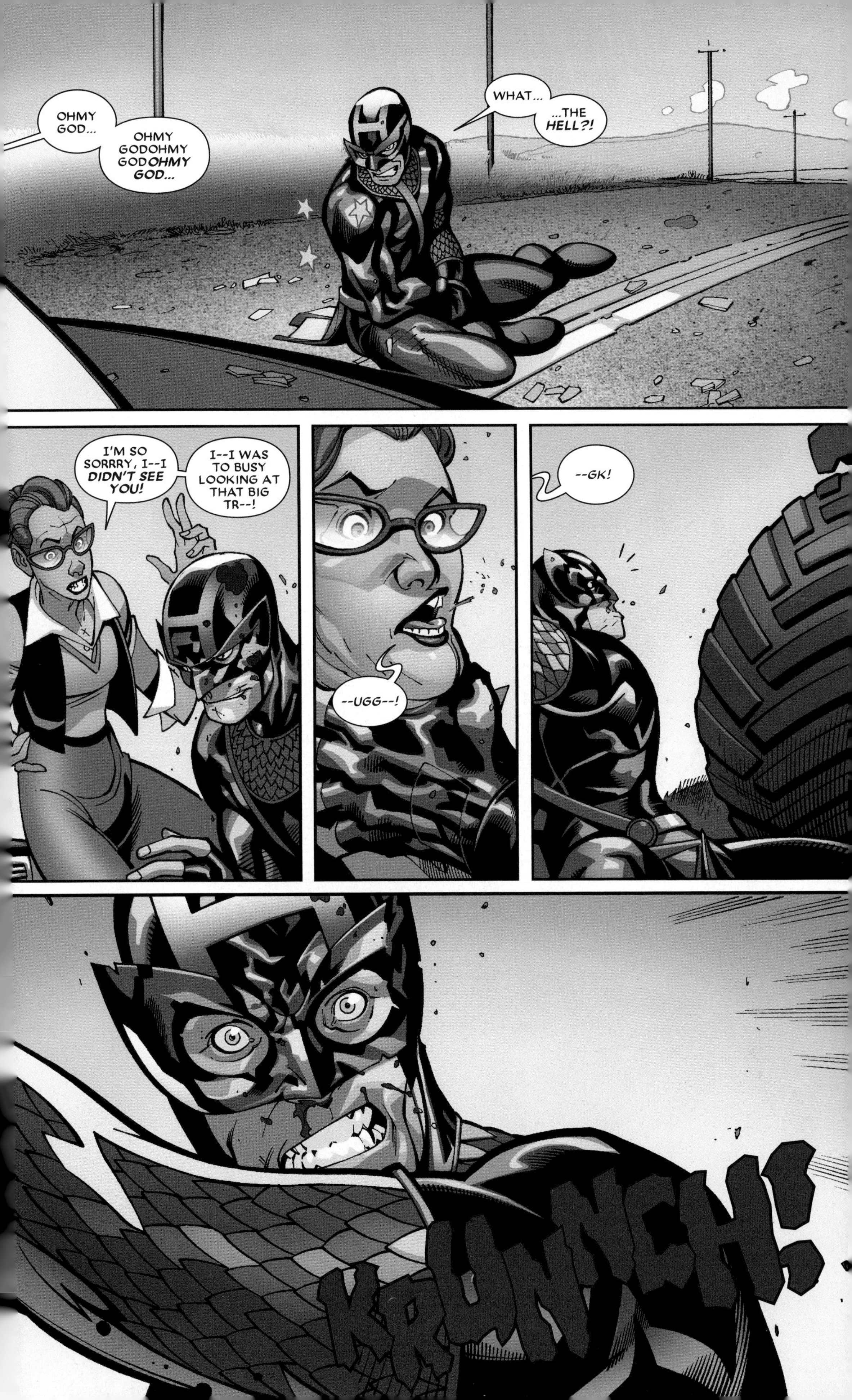
OHMY GOD...
OHMY GODOHMY GOD**OHMY GOD...**
WHAT...
...THE **HELL?!**
I'M SO SORRRY, I--I **DIDN'T SEE YOU!**
I--I WAS TO BUSY LOOKING AT THAT BIG TR--!
--UGG--!
--GK!
KRUNNCH!

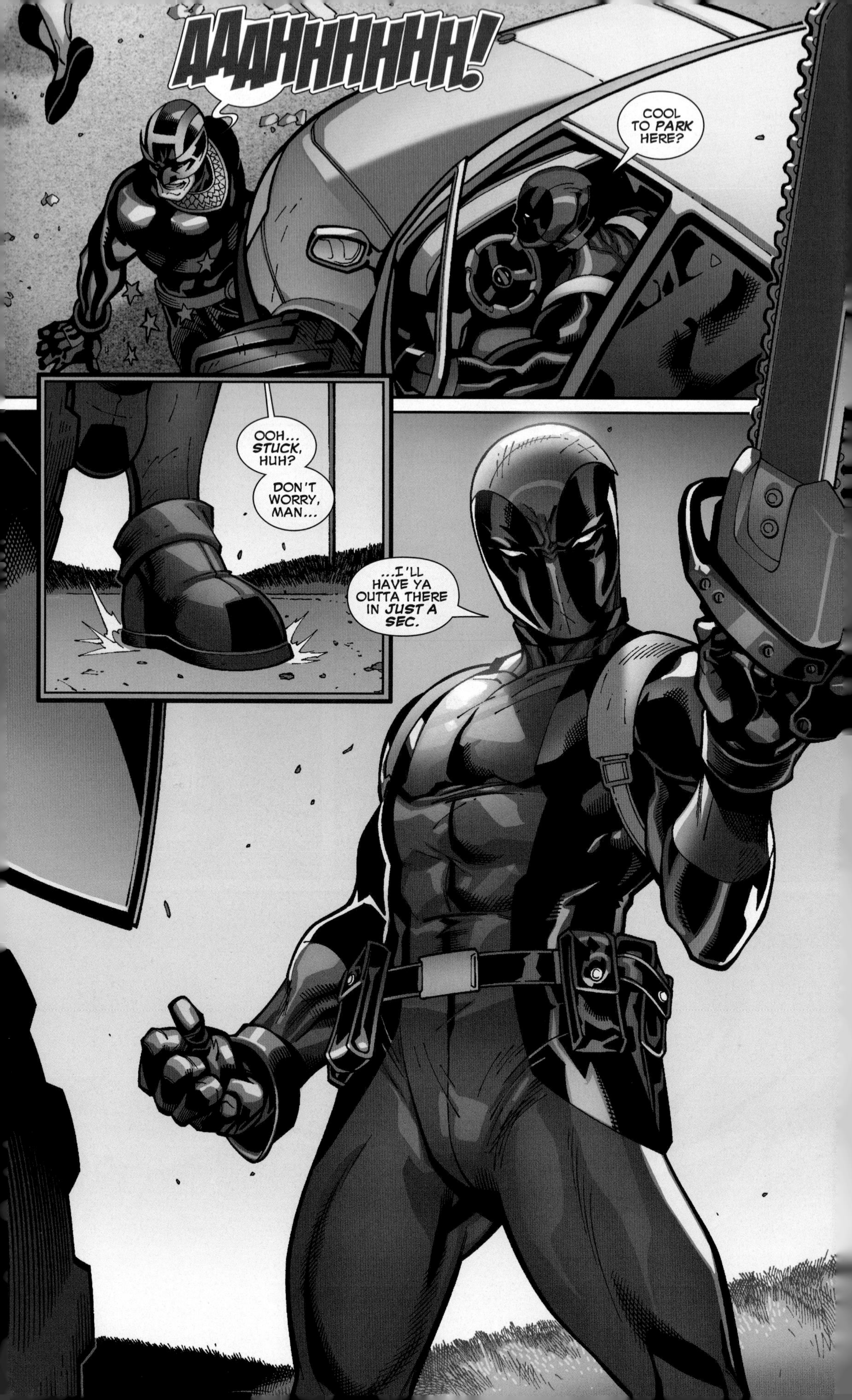

AAAHHHHHH!
COOL TO PARK HERE?
OOH... STUCK, HUH?
DON'T WORRY, MAN...
...I'LL HAVE YA OUTTA THERE IN JUST A SEC.

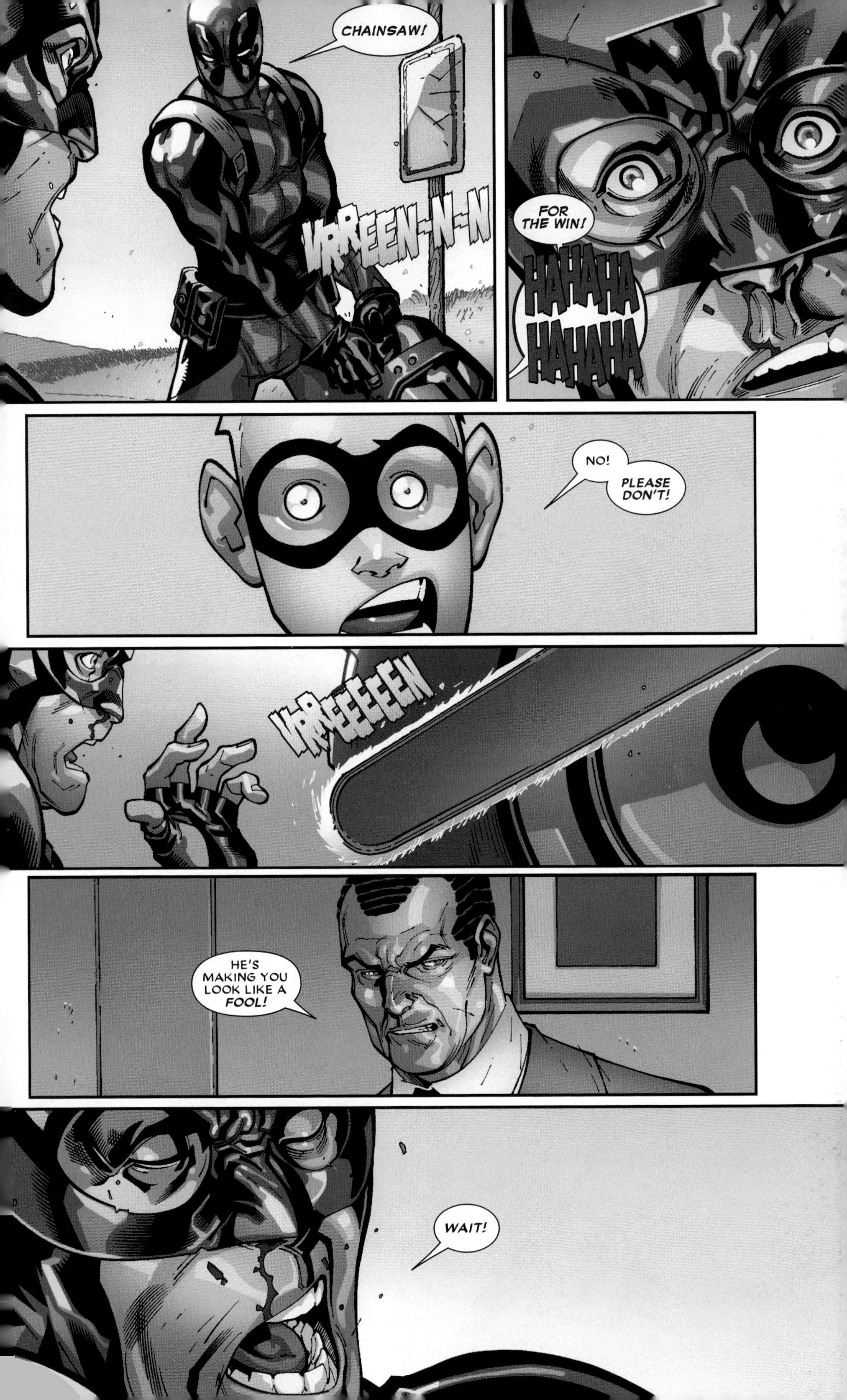
CHAINSAW!
VRREEN-N-N
FOR THE WIN!
HAHAHA HAHAHA
NO!
PLEASE DON'T!
VRREEEEEN
HE'S MAKING YOU LOOK LIKE A FOOL!
WAIT!

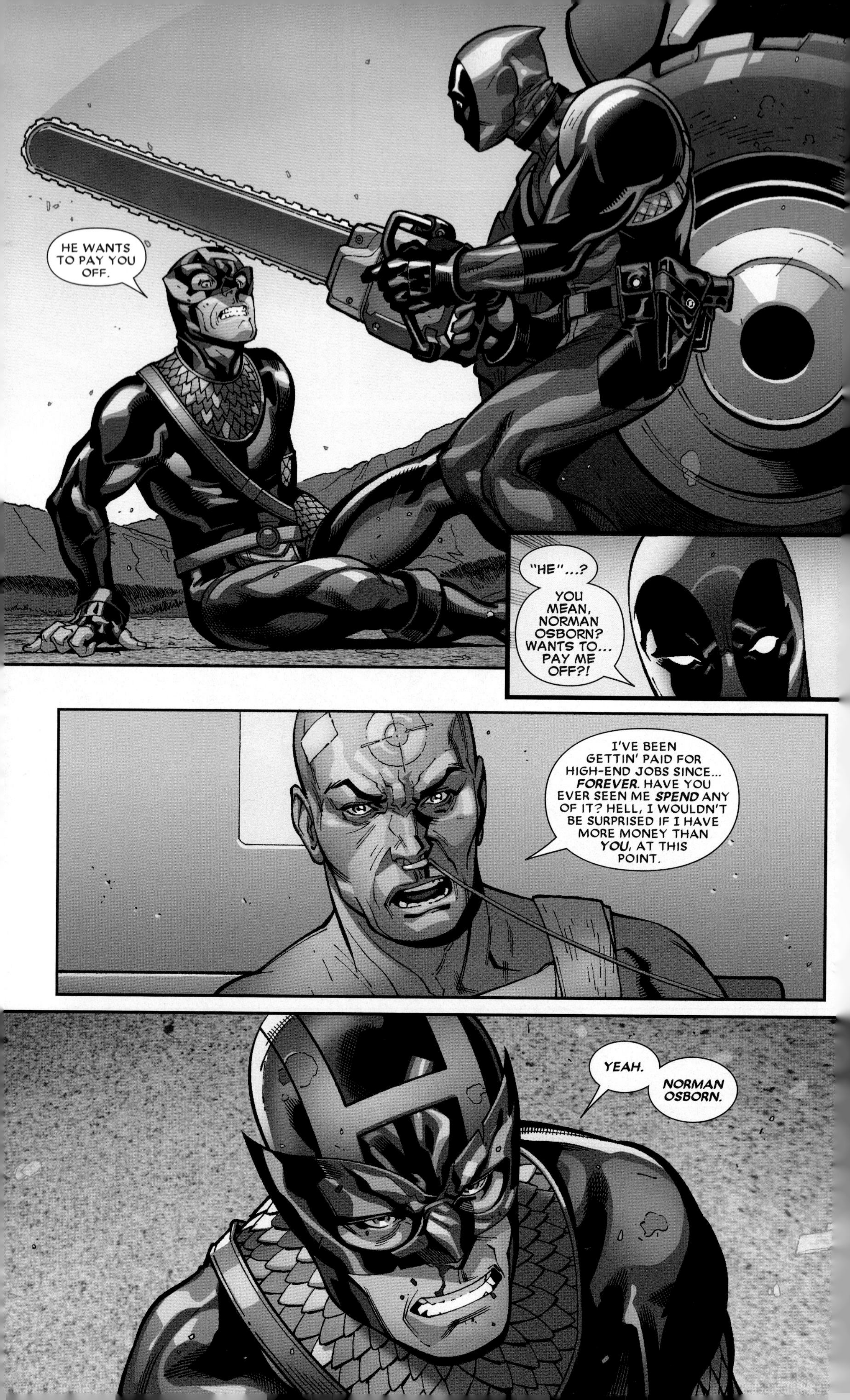
HE WANTS TO PAY YOU OFF.
"HE"...?
YOU MEAN, NORMAN OSBORN? WANTS TO... PAY ME OFF?!
I'VE BEEN GETTIN' PAID FOR HIGH-END JOBS SINCE... FOREVER. HAVE YOU EVER SEEN ME SPEND ANY OF IT? HELL, I WOULDN'T BE SURPRISED IF I HAVE MORE MONEY THAN YOU, AT THIS POINT.
YEAH.
NORMAN OSBORN.

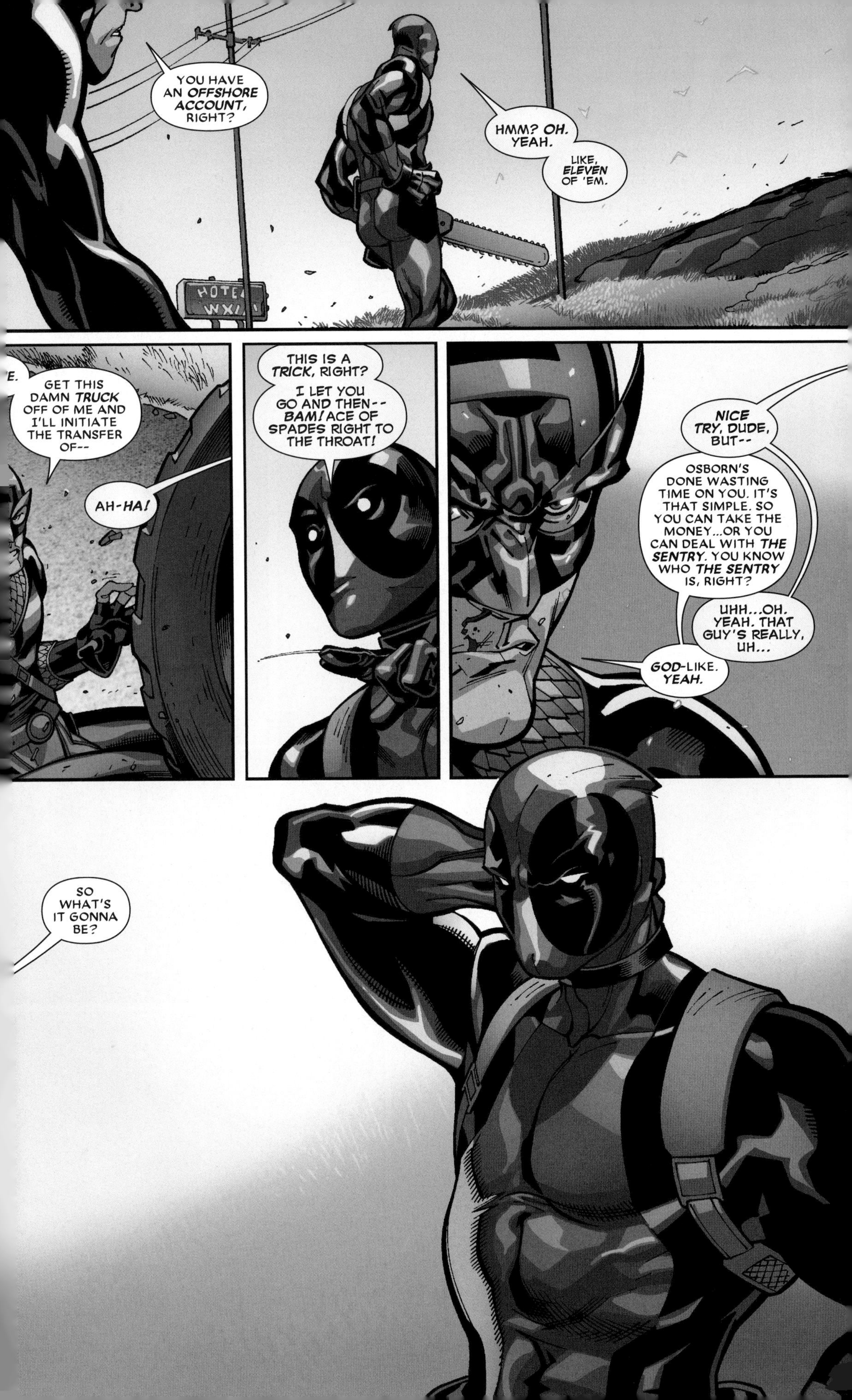

YOU HAVE AN OFFSHORE ACCOUNT, RIGHT?
HMM? OH. YEAH.
LIKE, ELEVEN OF 'EM.
HOTEL WXI
GET THIS DAMN TRUCK OFF OF ME AND I'LL INITIATE THE TRANSFER OF--
AH-HA!
THIS IS A TRICK, RIGHT?
I LET YOU GO AND THEN--BAM! ACE OF SPADES RIGHT TO THE THROAT!
NICE TRY, DUDE, BUT--
OSBORN'S DONE WASTING TIME ON YOU. IT'S THAT SIMPLE. SO YOU CAN TAKE THE MONEY...OR YOU CAN DEAL WITH THE SENTRY. YOU KNOW WHO THE SENTRY IS, RIGHT?
UHH...OH. YEAH. THAT GUY'S REALLY, UH...
GOD-LIKE. YEAH.
SO WHAT'S IT GONNA BE?

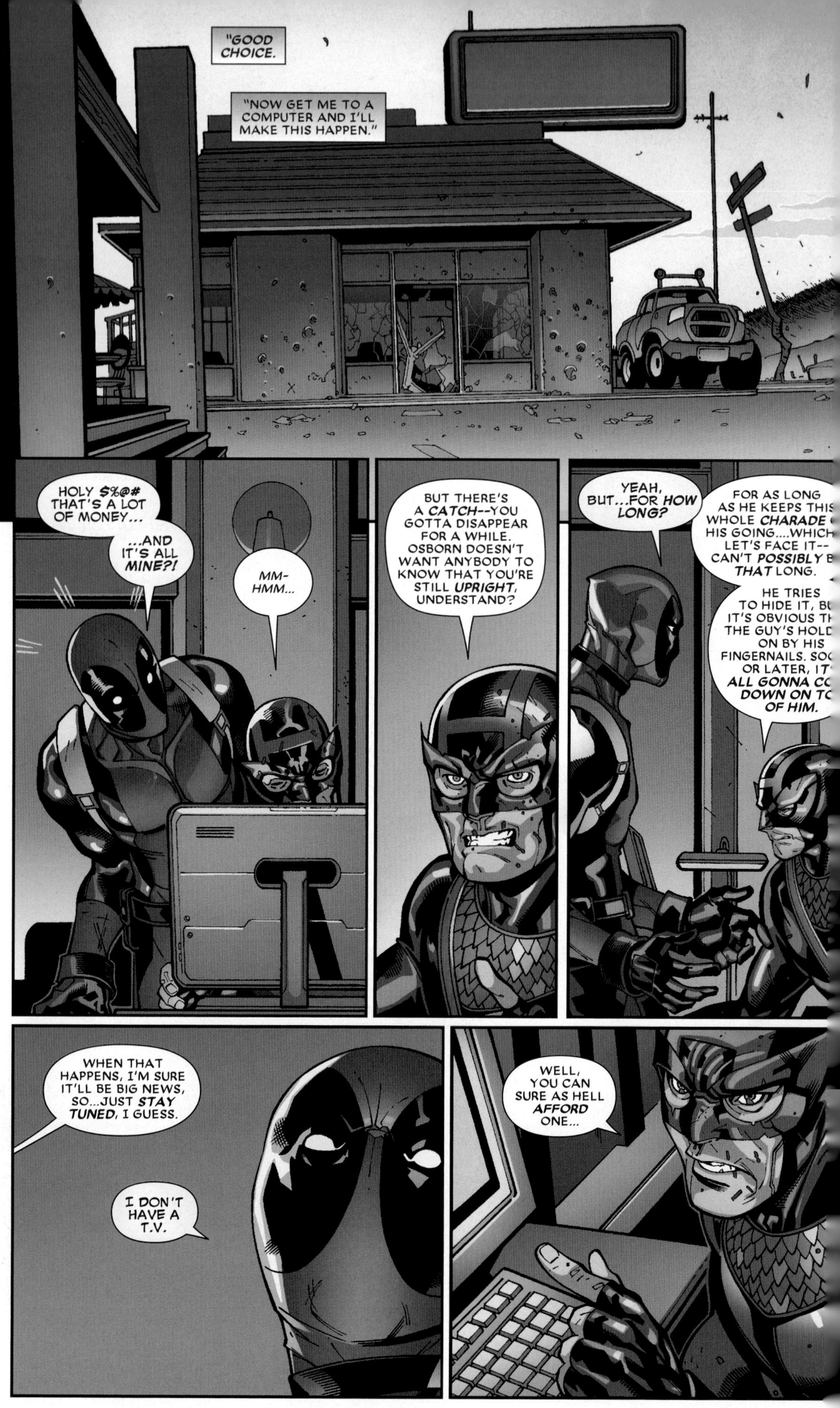
"GOOD CHOICE.
"NOW GET ME TO A COMPUTER AND I'LL MAKE THIS HAPPEN."
HOLY $%@# THAT'S A LOT OF MONEY...
...AND IT'S ALL MINE?!
MM-HMM...
BUT THERE'S A CATCH--YOU GOTTA DISAPPEAR FOR A WHILE. OSBORN DOESN'T WANT ANYBODY TO KNOW THAT YOU'RE STILL UPRIGHT, UNDERSTAND?
YEAH, BUT...FOR HOW LONG?
FOR AS LONG AS HE KEEPS THIS WHOLE CHARADE HIS GOING....WHICH LET'S FACE IT-- CAN'T POSSIBLY THAT LONG.
HE TRIES TO HIDE IT, BU IT'S OBVIOUS TH THE GUY'S HOLD ON BY HIS FINGERNAILS. SOO OR LATER, IT' ALL GONNA CO DOWN ON TO OF HIM.
WHEN THAT HAPPENS, I'M SURE IT'LL BE BIG NEWS, SO...JUST STAY TUNED, I GUESS.
I DON'T HAVE A T.V.
WELL, YOU CAN SURE AS HELL AFFORD ONE...

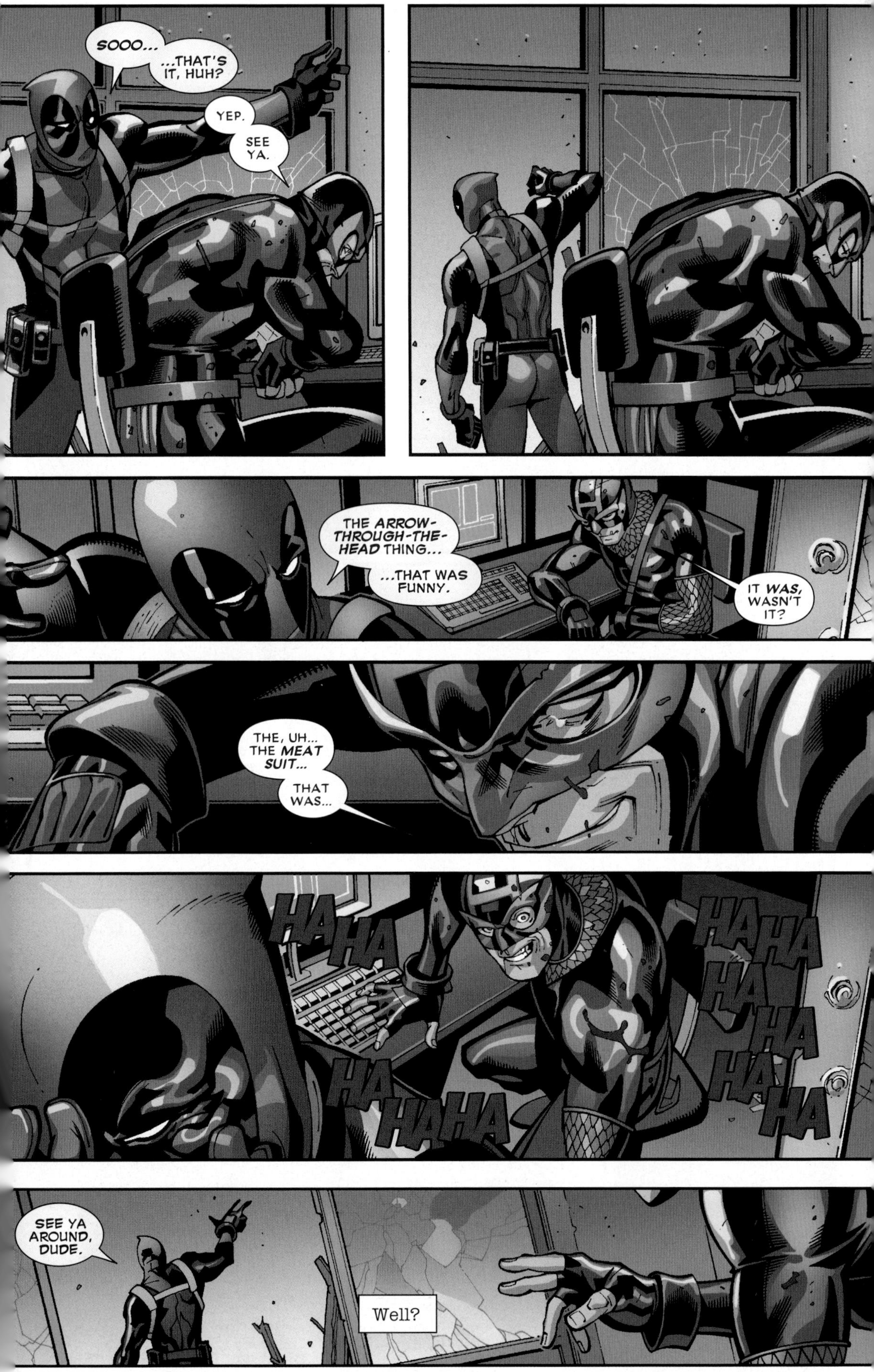
SOOO...
...THAT'S IT, HUH?
YEP.
SEE YA.
THE ARROW-THROUGH-THE-HEAD THING...
...THAT WAS FUNNY.
IT WAS, WASN'T IT?
THE, UH... THE MEAT SUIT...
THAT WAS...
HAHA
HAHA
HAHA
HAHA
HAHAHAHAHAHA
SEE YA AROUND, DUDE.
Well?

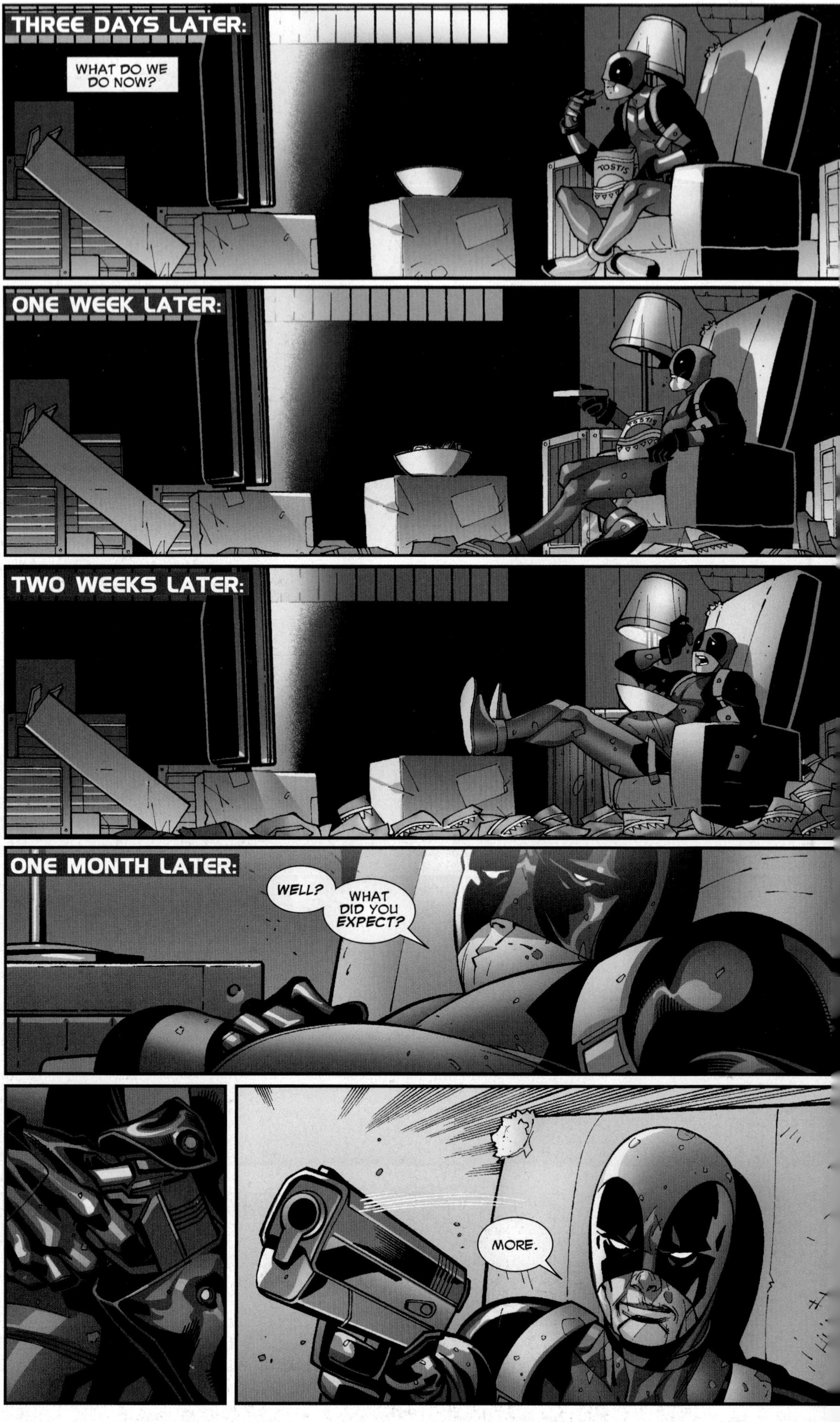
THREE DAYS LATER:
WHAT DO WE DO NOW?
TOSTIS
ONE WEEK LATER:
TWO WEEKS LATER:
ONE MONTH LATER:
WELL?
WHAT DID YOU EXPECT?
MORE.

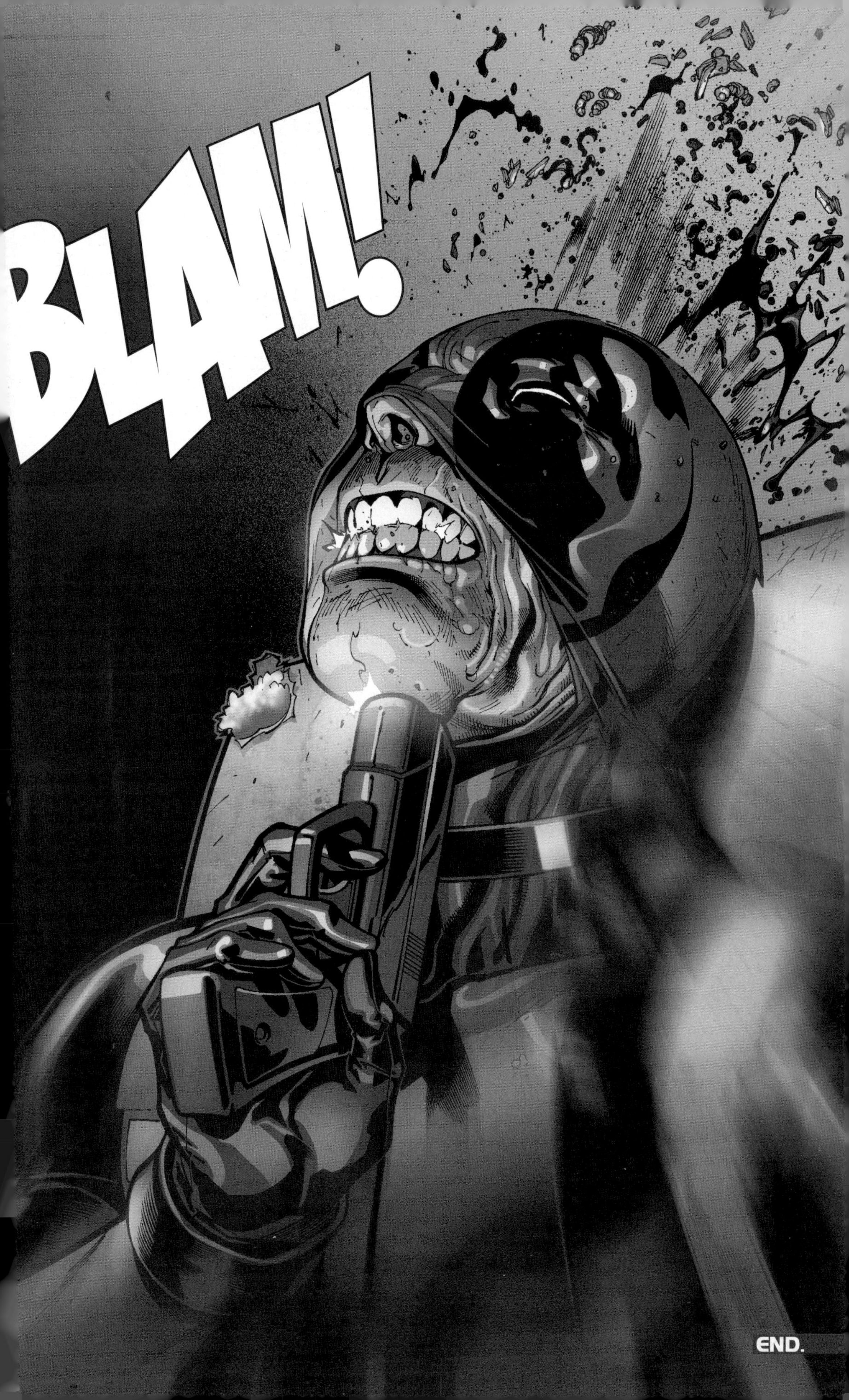
BLAM!
END.

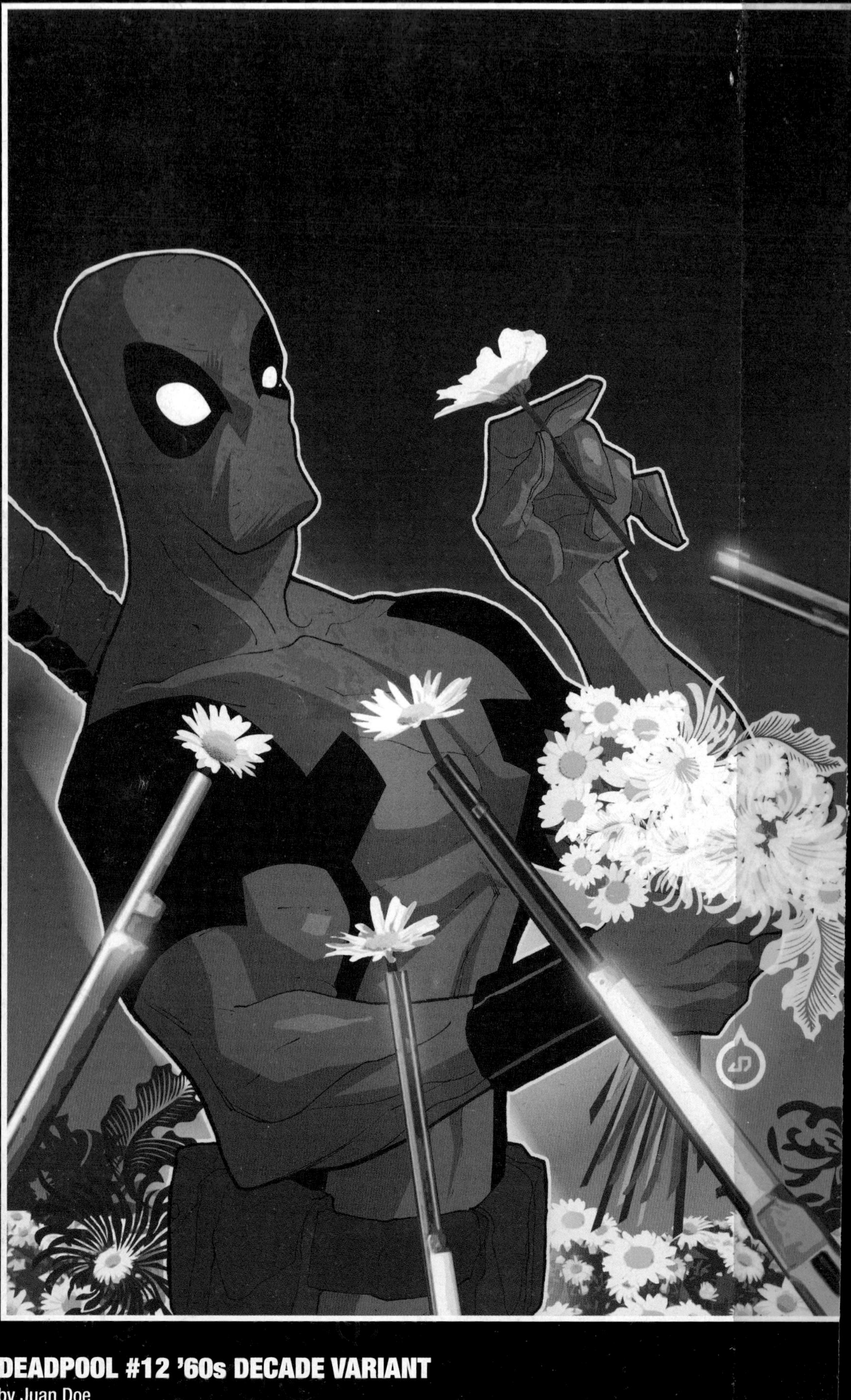

DEADPOOL #12 '60s DECADE VARIANT
by Juan Doe